THE COMIC BOOK IN AMERICA

AN ILLUSTRATED HISTORY

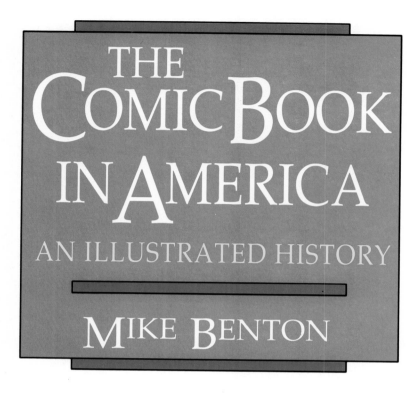

THE COMIC BOOK IN AMERICA

AN ILLUSTRATED HISTORY

MIKE BENTON

Taylor Publishing Company
Dallas, Texas

Published by Taylor Publishing Company
1550 West Mockingbird Lane
Dallas, Texas 75235

Photography by Laura Benton

Design by Dale Crain

Library of Congress Cataloging-in-Publication Data

Benton, Mike.
    The comic book in America: an illustrated history / Mike Benton.
        p.   cm.
    Includes index.
    ISBN 0-87833-659-1
    1. Comic books, strips, etc.—United States—History and criticism.   I. Title
PN6725.B38   1989
741.5′0973—dc20   89-5077
                                                                                                             CIP

Printed in the United States of America

10 9 8 7 6 5 4 3 2

To the Comic Book Makers,
Past, Present, and Future

The author deeply appreciates the help, support, and assistance given by the following people: Laura Benton, Jon Berk, Dale Crain, Michael Dachs, Scott Deschaine, Jim Donovan, Mike Dudley, John Franks, John Gillum, Kurt Goldzung, Howard Harris, Max Lakin, Michael Lerner, Dee Nelson, Bob Overstreet, Vaughn Ritchie, Mike Roy, Michael Sanchez, Steven Sheffler, Ed Sobolak, Ron Tatar, Don Thompson, Maggie Thompson, and Bill Wallace.

CONTENTS

II. The Comic-Book Publishers 89

The eternal dilemma. *Archie Comics #117,*
© March 1961 Archie Comic Publications

III. The Comic-Book Genres   153

Donald Duck Illustration, © Walt Disney Productions

INTRODUCTION

Once upon a time, there were no comic books.
There were no stories of super-powered heroes, talking ducks and cats, or adventures on faraway planets. There was no Superman, no Wonder Woman, no Spider-Man, no Donald Duck nor Mighty Mouse.

And then, less than a lifetime ago, there suddenly was a book full of brightly colored pictures and comical characters. It told stories filled with fantasy, humor, and adventure. And soon millions of such books, thousands of such characters, and hundreds of such titles captured the imaginations of readers on every block in every city in America.

Now there were comic books, and they were good.

In many ways the comic book is America's happiest contribution to world literature and entertainment. It was born of American ingenuity, imagination, and old-fashioned capitalism. It arose out of the dreams of men and women who faced the uncertainties of a depression and an impending war, with optimism and artistic bravado. It took root and flourished by becoming the most democratic of all art forms, appealing to every class of citizen at a price that even its youngest and poorest could afford.

The modern comic book attracted young creators with its freshness and vitality, and it entertained even younger readers with its boldness, simplicity, and ability to tell a story with stunning impact.

In its nearly sixty-year history, the American comic book has touched the lives of nearly everyone alive today. More comic books have been printed, read, and sold than all the Top Ten best-selling books of the last fifty years combined. During their peak years in the 1950s, an average of fifteen comic books was read each month by every other household in the United States.

Today the comic book has grown beyond American shores. To many of the world's citizens American comic-book characters are better known than American presidents. In Japan, almost ninety percent of both children and adults are comic-book readers.

Yet for all their pervasiveness and influence, comic books have had a difficult time being taken seriously. Perhaps precisely because of their simplicity, boldness, and ease of reading, for years comic books were perceived as mere simple-minded fodder for the nursery room. Since the comic book's greatest supporters often were children, adults made the common mistake of dismissing their children's interests as childish and unimportant.

Today those children are grown. And comic books are emerging from the ghetto of children's literature to assume their role as one of the most honest, viable, and uniquely American of all twentieth-century art forms.

This book is their story, told from the perspective of someone whose earliest memories are of comic books and whose own life has been forever altered, shaped, and fashioned by the stories that they tell. The child and the adult live in us all, and where they often come together is in the pages of pictures of the comic book.

In the last six decades over three hundred comic-book publishers have produced more than ten thousand different comic-book titles. Several thousand different comic-artists and writers have created more than one hundred thousand different issues of comic books.

Clearly, no single volume can tell the whole story of a medium so rich in creative output. A brief survey of the major comic-book artists and writers alone has already filled four volumes, and a simple listing of all the comic-book titles published and their collectors' prices takes up most of a five-hundred-page guide to the field.

With such a vast ocean of information and titles, this book can only act like a pebble skipping across its surface. But this historical survey is meant to give you an overview of the vast output of a rich medium. It is a handshake introduction not only to the most significant comic-book titles, but also to typical, average, and mundane comic books that played a part in developing this story.

It's one story, told three different ways: first, the chronological tale of the development and marketing of comic books, then the tale of how individual publishers responded to the market opportunities, and finally the tale told by the various genres. Every major publisher is surveyed; every year is reviewed; and nearly every major comic-book title is mentioned here. With such broad coverage comes also a necessary veneer, and what is missing may be as important as what is included.

For example, space permits little more than brief mention of the major comic-book artists and writers, and then only in connection with the significant books that they have created. The comic-book creators themselves are the real story behind the development of comic books. Fortunately, the recognition that these men and women long deserved is slowly coming forth as they emerge from their early years of anonymity.

Future histories no doubt will place their work in the perspective it so richly warrants. In the meantime, the quotes ascribed to them will, I hope, allow their voices to enrich this tale.

For now, however, this is as good a place as any to begin telling the comic-book story.

> **"We think in pictures; we dream in pictures."**
> **—GEORGE PERRY,**
> author of *The Penguin Book of Comics*

THE
COMIC BOOK
STORY

The Yellow Kid, R.F. Outcault

Comic Monthly #1, © 1921 Newspaper Feature Service, Inc.

1896–1932 B.C.: BEFORE COMIC BOOKS

Before there could be a comic book, there had to be comics. Simple enough, but before the late 1890s, there had not been anything even resembling a newspaper comic strip, much less a comic book.

On February 16, 1896 the New York *World* newspaper tested its new yellow ink by printing it on the nightgown of a kid who appeared in a cartoon drawn by Richard Outcault.

The "yellow kid," as he was christened by an appreciative public, became the first color comic strip to appear in a newspaper. He proved to be such a circulation booster for the newspaper that the future of the comic strip was assured.

Then began a series of "firsts" which led to the modern comic book. In March 1897, the Hearst *New York American* gathered Outcault's "Yellow Kid" newspaper strips into a short-lived publication called the *Yellow Kid Magazine*, thus creating the first published collection of an American comic strip. Then, in 1899, E. P. Dutton & Company published a collection of comic strips by F. M. Howarth, which had originally appeared in *Puck* magazine. Entitled *Funny Folks*, the hardcover book looks nothing at all like the comic book of the later twentieth century.

Over the next ten years, other publishers followed Dutton's lead in issuing hardcover books of comics. Instead of reprinting cartoons from humor magazines such as *Puck* or *Judge*, however, these publishers collected the Sunday newspaper comic strips.

At least seventy such hardcover books of comics appeared between 1900 and 1909, consisting of Sunday-page reprints from such strips as "Buster Brown," "Foxy Grandpa," "Katzenjammer Kids," and "Little Nemo."

The first daily comic strip to be successful was Bud Fisher's "A. Mutt," the precursor to "Mutt and Jeff," which appeared in 1907. In 1910, Fisher's daily strips were collected and published by Ball Publishing Company in a sixty-eight-page hardcover book that retailed for fifty cents.

Ball published four more editions of the *Mutt and Jeff* books in 1911, 1912, 1915, and 1916. Each was promptly reprinted and widely distributed.

In 1919, Cupples and Leon published the sixth *Mutt and Jeff* book, which consisted of fifty-two black-and-white pages with a stiff cover, retailing for twenty-five cents.

Cupples and Leon published seventeen more *Mutt and Jeff* books in the series, along with books reprinting many other daily comic strips including "Barney Google," "Bringing Up Father," "Joe Palooka," and "Little Orphan Annie."

In 1917, the Saalfield Publishing Company came out with the first publication to call itself a "comic book." Saalfield's *Comic Book*, which reprinted newspaper comic strips such as "Clancy the Cop" in black and white, was

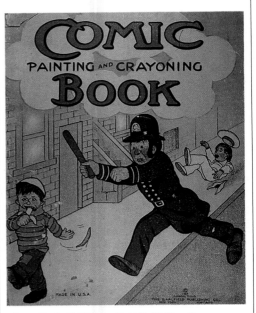

Comic Book, © 1917 Saalfield Publishing Co.

the first publication to use the phrase comic book.

In January 1922, Embee Publishing began the first monthly publication of comics. *Comic Monthly* reprinted daily comic strips from the previous year, retailed for ten cents a copy, and featured one comic strip per issue such as "Barney Google," "Tillie the Toiler," and "Polly & Her Pals." *Comic Monthly* lasted for twelve issues, until December 1922. It became the first regularly published book of comics, although not in the format that we know it.

In 1929, George Delacorte of the Dell Publishing Company began the first full-color newsstand publication of comics, called *The Funnies*. Because of its large size *The Funnies* looked just like a Sunday comic section from the newspaper, but it came out on Saturday and featured *original* comic strips not previously published in newspapers.

For all its originality, *The Funnies* failed by the next year. Its unwieldy size, and the fact that it looked like an incomplete portion of a regular Sunday newspaper, spelled its demise.

Following the collapse of *The Funnies*, Dell tried again with two issues of *Clancy the Cop* in 1930 and 1931, but these books too failed to find a lasting place on the newsstand.

In 1932 Whitman Publishing Company issued the first "Big Little Book," *The Adventures of Dick Tracy*. The "Big Little Books" continued throughout the 1930s and 1940s, reprinting a panel from a comic strip on one page and a page of narrative on the facing page. Since they measured 3 1/2 by 4 1/2 inches and ran between three hundred and four hundred pages, the "Big Little Books" were even further removed from the modern comic book than the earlier comic-strip reprints.

Between 1897 and 1932, over five hundred books of comics were published. It would not be until 1933, however, that the first "comic book" as we know it appeared.

Funnies on Parade #1, © 1933 Eastern Color Printing Co.

1933: THE FIRST COMIC BOOK

It was 1933. Four years earlier, the Eastern Color Printing Company of Waterbury, Connecticut, had printed the thirteen issues of the *The Funnies* for Dell Publishing. The four-color, tabloid-sized "comic magazine" had come and gone, but it evidently had not been forgotten by several men connected with Eastern Color.

These gentlemen, among them Harry Wildenberg, George Janosik, and a salesman named Max C. Gaines, considered the possibility of producing a book of comics in a format smaller than the tabloid size of *The Funnies*. This so-called "comic book" would then be sold to manufacturers who could use it as a premium, or inducement, for their customers.

This idea no doubt was inspired by the previous success of the *Mutt and Jeff* comic-strip books, which newspapers had been using as promotional items since 1911.

At the time Eastern Color was considering the idea of publishing a comic book as a premium, the company's printing plant had just printed some broadsides for the Philadelphia *Ledger*. These broadsides were actually full-color reductions of the *Ledger*'s Sunday comic pages. The reduced comic pages had been printed with seven-by-nine-inch printing plates, which were just about half the size of a regular newspaper tabloid page.

This new way of reducing and printing tabloid-size Sunday strips sparked an idea among the Eastern employees. Why not reduce and print two Sunday comic pages side by side on one tabloid page? Then, by folding the pages in half and binding them together, they could use their existing color presses to produce an economical, eight-by-eleven-inch, full-color book of comics—a comic book.

Anxious to try this new printing experiment, Harry Wildenberg of Eastern Color struck a deal with the newspaper syndicates to reprint such Sunday strips as "Mutt & Jeff," "Joe Pa-

looka," "Hairbreadth Harry," "Skippy," and others for ten dollars a page.

Next, Max C. Gaines, a premium salesman, convinced Procter & Gamble to purchase ten thousand copies of this new comic book. The book would be made available to those Procter & Gamble customers who clipped and sent in coupons from their soap products.

With an order and presses in place, Eastern Color Printing Company produced America's first modern comic book, *Funnies on Parade*, in the spring of 1933. Within weeks, the entire print run of ten thousand copies was exhausted, and Gaines knew he was on to a good thing.

After the success of this first modern comic book, Gaines quickly approached other advertisers—including Milk-O-Malt, Canada Dry, Wheatena and Kinney Shoes—to sponsor publication of another giveaway, or premium, comic book.

Their response resulted in Eastern Color printing *Famous Funnies: A Carnival of Comics*, the second modern American comic book. Released in 1933, the thirty-six-page *Carnival of Comics* had an initial print run of one hundred thousand books—ten times greater than *Funnies on Parade*.

Gaines wondered if there might be an even greater market for his new comic book, beyond that as a premium giveaway. As an experiment, he pasted a ten-cent-price sticker on the front cover of several dozen copies of *Famous Funnies: A Carnival of Comics* and dropped the priced comic books off at several newsstands at the start of a weekend. He returned on Monday to discover that every one had sold! The seed planted in Gaines's mind would bear fruit a few months later.

Meanwhile, with the success of *A Carnival of Comics*, Gaines's clients quickly demanded another comic-book premium. Instead of a

Century of Comics #1, © 1933 Eastern Color Printing Co.

Famous Funnies, © 1933 Eastern Color Printing Co.

Famous Funnies #1, © 1934 Eastern Color Printing Co.

Skippy's Comics #1, © 1934 Percy Crosby

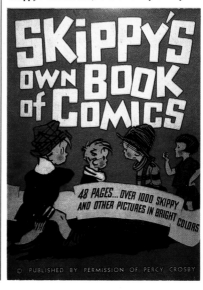

thirty-six-page comic book, however, Gaines and Eastern Color packaged a one-hundred-page comic book called *Century of Comics*. Eventually, between one hundred thousand and two hundred and fifty thousand copies of both *Carnival of Comics* and *Century of Comics* would be given away that year, and the modern comic book was still very much an infant.

1934: BUT WILL ANYONE BUY IT?

In early 1934, Gaines and Eastern Color Printing Company published the fourth modern American comic book, *Skippy's Own Book of Comics*, as a premium giveaway for Phillip's Tooth Paste. The 52-page book was advertised on the "Skippy Radio Show." It also

was the first modern comic book to feature a single character, instead of the previous collections of several different comic strips in one book. This time Gaines printed half a million copies of the comic book—and again the supplies were exhausted!

By this time Eastern Color had become interested in getting a share of the profits that Gaines was enjoying from his new publishing venture. The men at Eastern Color were aware of the Gaines experiment of selling *Famous Funnies: A Carnival of Comics* on the newsstand and felt that the public would buy such a product from magazine dealers. But Eastern Color was a printing company with no editorial experience.

However, the men remembered printing *The Funnies* for Dell Publishing Company five years earlier, so they approached Dell's

George Delacorte to produce a new comic book, also to be called *Famous Funnies*.

Delacorte was sufficiently interested to take a chance on publishing thirty-five thousand copies through Eastern Color. Perhaps because he remembered the newsstand failure of his earlier 1929 tabloid-size publication, *The Funnies*, Delacorte bypassed regular magazine distribution and instead released all thirty-five thousand copies of *Famous Funnies* through big chain department stores.

Famous Funnies (more exactly referred to as *Famous Funnies: Series 1*) was noteworthy because it contained sixty-eight pages and retailed for ten cents. This set the standard size and price for all newsstand comic books during the next several years.

Famous Funnies: Series 1 was released around February 1934. Half of its pages were reprinted from the first comic book, *Funnies on Parade*, while sixteen pages were reprinted from the second comic book, *Carnival of Comics*. The remaining sixteen pages were "new" reprints of Sunday strips.

Famous Funnies: Series 1 was as popular as its predecessors and sold out its initial print run of thirty-five thousand copies. Dell Publishing Company, however, perhaps remembering its failure with *The Funnies*, was still cautious about proceeding with this venture. The company surveyed a group of advertisers for their reaction to this new type of publication, the comic book.

The advertisers responded that (1) comic books were printed on bad paper and were too different from their regular magazine accounts, and (2) since the books were reprints, the public wouldn't pay to read something it had already seen for free in the Sunday papers. The pessimistic report gave George Delacorte little confidence in proceeding with additional issues.

Still, he approached the American News Company in New York, which controlled newsstand sales, with the idea that perhaps they could sell the comic book to newsstands. But they, too, turned the project down.

Delacorte then released his option to the name and concept of *Famous Funnies* back to Eastern Color.

Shortly thereafter, Harold A. Moore of Eastern Color saw a full-page advertisement in the New York *Daily News* that attributed the success of its Sunday edition to its color "funny pages." Moore went directly to the president of American News, Harry Gould, and waved the advertisement in his face.

Gould read the ad carefully, waited a few days, and then called Moore with an order for 250,000 copies of a comic magazine.

In May 1934, Eastern Color, through the American News Company, released the first monthly newsstand comic book (cover-dated July 1934), which was called *Famous Funnies: Series 2*. The first issue of the second series of *Famous Funnies* was not a sensational success—it actually lost $4,150.60. Within six months, however, it would show a

$2,664.25 profit and remain in the black for the rest of its long publication life.

The critical question had been answered: Yes, people will pay money for a newsstand magazine of comic-strip reprints.

The editor of America's first newsstand comic book was Stephen A. Douglas, who began his comic-book career at the ripe age of twenty-seven. He followed Max Gaines's lead with *Funnies on Parade*, and structured *Famous Funnies* along the same lines. He selected a wide mixture of humor and adventure Sunday strips and reprinted exactly four Sunday pages, or one month's worth, of each strip.

Famous Funnies was to be the only regularly published comic book for the rest of 1934. After that first issue was published in May with its July cover date, the second issue followed eight weeks later, in July, with a September cover date. The third through seventh issues came out on a regular monthly basis, with cover dates of October 1934 (#3), November 1934 (#4), December 1934 (#5), January 1935 (#6), and February 1935 (#7).

Notice that although *Famous Funnies #7* has a cover date of February 1935, it actually was published and put on sale in December 1934. From the very beginning, comic books have been cover-dated two to three months after the date they actually are put on the market. This publishing practice means that the comic book does not go out of date within a few weeks, but instead enjoys a newsstand life of two to three months.

Throughout this book, the cover date of a comic book is used as its official publication date.

1935: COMIC BOOK NUMBER TWO

In the late fall of 1934, Major Malcolm Wheeler-Nicholson, a former U.S. Cavalry of-

Famous Comics, © 1934 United Features Syndicate

Famous Funnies #2, © 1934 Eastern Color Printing Co.

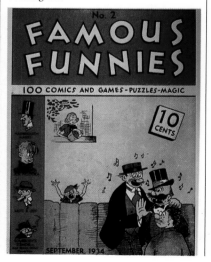

New Comics #1, © 1935 DC Comics, Inc.

"Hello! Here we are with the first number of *New Comics*—the International Picture Story Magazine. Here's something you have always wanted—eighty pages packed and jammed with new comic features, written and drawn especially for *New Comics*—never printed before anywhere. Here is a magazine of picturized stories chock full of laughter and thrills, comic characters of every hue, knights and Vikings of ancient days, adventuring heroes, detectives, aviator daredevils of today and hero supermen of the days to come!"
—Editorial message,
New Comics #1
(December 1935)

ficer and pulp magazine writer, was carefully charting the appearances and sales of *Famous Funnies* on the newsstands of Manhattan.

Noting the new comic book's success, Wheeler-Nicholson reasoned that a comic book featuring original material would sell even better than one reprinted from the Sunday pages.

In February 1935, Wheeler-Nicholson's *New Fun Comics* appeared from his company, National Allied Publications. Thirty-six pages long, the book had a full-color cover but black-and-white interior pages. It measured ten by fifteen inches—similar in size to a Sunday-comic tabloid section, and one and a half times larger than *Famous Funnies*. Only one strip was longer than a page. Most of the strips looked like rejected Sunday-newspaper pages, although one did feature the first appearance of Oswald the Rabbit.

New Fun Comics also was the first modern comic book to feature advertising, including a Charles Atlas body-building ad which would become a ubiquitous feature of comic books for forty years to come.

For most of the rest of 1935, the tabloid-size *New Fun* and the magazine-size *Famous Funnies* were the only comic books on the newsstands. (In the summer of 1935, the first issue of *Mickey Mouse Magazine* appeared. Although not a comic book, it did feature Disney-strip reprints and eventually would become *Walt Disney's Comics and Stories* five years later.)

Neither *New Fun* nor *Famous Funnies* was selling fantastically well, and Wheeler-Nicholson was struggling to keep his new publishing enterprise afloat. In 1935, few distributors would take on the "new" comic magazines. Newsstands had no regular display space allocated for comic books, so news dealers often stuck the comic books in with newspapers or pulp magazines or, even more frequently, returned them unsold without ever having displayed them.

Toward the end of 1935 *Famous Funnies* was selling modestly well, but Wheeler-Nicholson's *New Fun* with its awkward size and unheard-of comic characters was floundering. Started as a monthly, *New Fun* was struggling along on sort of a bimonthly basis with its fifth issue dated August 1935.

For the sixth issue in October 1936, Wheeler-Nicholson gambled and increased the page count of *New Fun* from thirty-six to sixty-eight pages. *New Fun #6* also featured the first comic-book work of Jerry Siegel and Joe Shuster, two teenagers from Cleveland who eventually would become known as the creators of Superman. Their one-page strip, "Dr. Occult," featured a supernatural detective who fought the forces of evil. Their new character stood out from *New Fun*'s other strips, which often seemed to be second-rate imitations of Sunday humor and adventure strips.

In December 1935, Wheeler-Nicholson and National came out with their second title and

New Fun #6, © 1935 DC Comics, Inc.

the third newsstand comic book, *New Comics*. Like *New Funnies*, *New Comics* also featured original material. Walt Kelly, the artist and creator of "Pogo," had his first work published in *New Comics #1*, as did Sheldon Mayer, who would later play a major role in the development of the modern comic book.

New Comics, unlike *New Funnies*, was published as a regular-size comic book and contained eighty pages—sixteen more than its competitor, *Famous Funnies*. Unlike *Famous Funnies*, however, *New Comics* still printed many of its pages in black and white, not in full color.

By the end of 1935, there were two comic-book publishers and three comic-book titles. The nineteen comic books published that year compared to a total of seven comic books published the previous year and only three in 1933. Within the next year, however, the number of comic books published would nearly quadruple.

1936: THE BOOM BEGINS

With the publication of *New Comics* in December 1935, Wheeler-Nicholson decided that perhaps he should rename his other title, *New Fun Comics*, to avoid confusion. With issue #7 (January 1936), *New Fun Comics* became *More Fun Comics*. With issue #9, he changed *More Fun Comics* from its large tabloid-size comic pages to the same (magazine) size as *New Comics* and *Famous Funnies*.

A few months later, Wheeler-Nicholson also issued the *Big Book of Fun Comics* (Spring 1936), a fifty-six-page collection of strips reprinted from his *New Fun Comics*. That was soon followed by another collection, called the *New Book of Comics* (July 1936) which was one hundred pages long and reprinted strips from both *New Comics* and *More Fun Comics*.

Eastern Color, under George Janosik, continued to publish only *Famous Funnies*. Although *Famous Funnies* was now showing a healthy profit as it entered its eighteenth issue, Janosik could not be persuaded to publish any other new comic-book titles.

It would be up to George Delacorte of Dell Publishing Company to give the growing comic-book industry a strong push. Delacorte arranged through the McClure newspaper syndicate to publish a new comic book called *Popular Comics*.

Packaging *Popular Comics* for Delacorte was M. C. Gaines, who seemed to have his hand in the birthing of all the new comic books. As he did with *Famous Funnies*, Gaines made *Popular Comics* an anthology of reprinted Sunday strips. The comic book featured "Dick Tracy," "Little Orphan Annie," "Terry & the Pirates," "Moon Mullins," and "Gasoline Alley."

Gaines hired Sheldon Mayer, a teenaged cartoonist, to edit and paste up the book. Gaines then rigged up a pair of two-color presses to print the four-color *Popular Comics*, and actually produced a product that was brighter and better colored than *Famous Funnies*.

Popular Comics #1, © 1936 Dell Publishing Co., Inc.

With *Popular Comics #1* (February 1936), Dell became the third publishing company to enter the newsstand comic-book field. But it would soon have plenty of company.

The McKay Company of Philadelphia had just made a handsome deal with the Hearst syndicate to reprint King Features's comics. Entitled *King Comics* (April 1936), the first issue featured some of the most popular and widely circulated strips in the world, such as

Tip Top Comics #2, © 1936 United Features Syndicate

Alex Raymond's "Flash Gordon" and E. C. Segar's "Popeye."

Not to be outdone, United Features, another major syndicate, came out with a new comic book called *Tip Top Comics* (April 1936) which featured Hal Foster's "Tarzan" and Al Capp's "Li'l Abner" Sunday strips.

Tip Top Comics was edited by Lev Gleason, who had worked with Harry Wildenberg at Eastern Color. (Gleason would later go on to become a publisher in his own right in the 1940s.) *King Comics* was edited by Ruth Plumly Thompson, L. Frank Baum's successor as the author of the *Oz* books.

By the spring of 1936, there were now five comic-book publishers and six titles. In May 1936, the sixth comic-book publisher, Comic Magazine Company, Inc., entered the field with *The Comics Magazine #1*.

Unlike *Popular*, *King*, and *Tip Top*, this new comic book contained only original comic material, similar to Wheeler-Nicholson's *More Fun* and *New Comics*. The striking similarities of *The Comics Magazine* to Wheeler-Nicholson's comic books was more than coincidental. The publishers were the ex-editor and the former business manager of Wheeler-Nicholson's company, National Comics, and they used many of the cartoonists who had worked for *More Fun* and *New Fun*.

Among these cartoonists were Jerry Siegel and Joe Shuster, who took their "Dr. Occult" strip from *New Fun Comics #6* and *More Fun Comics #9* and renamed the character "Dr. Mystic" to run in *The Comics Magazine*. In the process they also gave him super powers and thus created the world's first comic-book superhero.

The Comics Magazine changed its name to *The Comic Magazine Funny Pages* for the second issue, and then simply to *Funny Pages* by issue #6 (November 1936). This same company also published *Funny Picture Stories* (November 1936) and *Detective Picture Stories*

"I went to work for M.C. Gaines in January of 1936. I had been up to see him the previous summer, and a half a year later he gave me a call and offered me a few days of paste-up work. I started pasting up newspaper strips in the comic book format. It was agony cutting up beautiful original newspaper strip art. Nobody would dream of wasting money on photostats in those days."
—SHELDON MAYER,
early comic-book editor, writer and artist

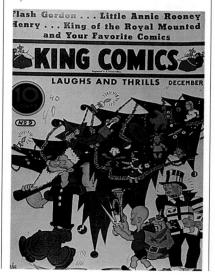

King Comics #9, © 1936 King Features Syndicate

(November 1936). The last title is noteworthy because it was the first anthology comic book devoted to one subject: detectives.

McKay Publishers brought out its second title, *Wow Comics* (July 1936), three months after *King Comics*. Magazine-sized and fifty-two pages long, *Wow Comics* featured both original and reprint material. It lasted but four issues, with its demise perhaps caused by its unusual size as the format of comics was becoming standardized.

Finally, near the end of 1936, Dell Publishing Company and George Delacorte issued *The Funnies #1* (October 1936). They borrowed the name from their failed 1929 experiment, but this time they showcased such popular Sunday reprints as "Alley Oop," "Mutt and Jeff," and "Captain Easy."

In 1936, at least seventy-six comic books and ten titles were being produced by the six publishers who made up the comic-book industry. The next year would see a doubling of both the number of comic books and the number of titles published.

Detective Comics #1, © 1937 DC Comics, Inc.

1937: DETECTIVE COMICS, INC.

In late 1936 and early 1937, the groundwork was being laid for the transformation and growth of perhaps the largest and most successful comic-book publishing company of all time.

Major Malcolm Wheeler-Nicholson's fledgling comic book empire still consisted of only two titles, *More Fun Comics* and *New Comics* (which he renamed *New Adventure Comics* with issue #12, January 1937).

Wheeler-Nicholson originally had advertised a third new title, *Detective Comics*, in his December 1936 issues of *More Fun* and *New Comics*. But because of his growing financial problems (he was now living, uninvited, with one of his cartoonists), Wheeler-Nicholson was unable to publish any new comic titles.

To get *Detective Comics* out, Wheeler-Nicholson approached Harry Donenfield with a partnership offer. Donenfield owned the printing plant that printed the Major's comic-book covers, and he had an interest in the Independent News Company, which distributed Wheeler-Nicholson's comic books, as well. Not surprisingly, Wheeler-Nicholson also owed Donenfield money.

In exchange for financial support in getting the first issue of *Detective Comics* out, the Major formed an enterprise with Donenfield called Detective Comics, Inc. This company would later become known as National Periodicals, and eventually even more widely known as DC Comics—the publisher of Superman, Batman, Wonder Woman, and other superheroes.

Detective Comics #1 (March 1937) began life as an anthology of "private eye" stories. It eventually would become the longest running comic-book title in history and the cornerstone of one of the world's largest comic-book publishers.

Unfortunately, Wheeler-Nicholson would not enjoy this success. Unable to continue beyond three titles in 1937, by the next year he had sold his interest in Detective Comics, Inc. to Harry Donenfield.

About the same time that *Detective Comics* was under way, Harry "A" Chesler, an early packager of comic-strip materials, was planning his entry into the new field. Under his watchful gaze his Manhattan studio, often referred to with little affection as the "sweat shop," turned out comic pages with assembly-line rapidity.

Chesler packaged and published two new comic titles in February 1937, *Star Comics* and *Star Ranger*. Both were large-size books that featured original material. Chesler's other 1937 title was *Feature Funnies* (October 1937), which consisted of reprinted newspaper strips—most notably Joe Palooka and Mickey Finn.

Comics Magazine Company, Inc., fresh from the success of *Detective Picture Stories*, tried its hand at a western comic-book anthology, *Western Picture Stories* (February 1937). The title shares credit with Chesler's

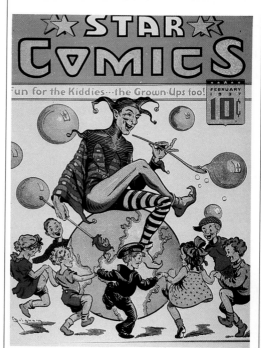

Star Comics #1, © 1937 Ultem Publications

Star Ranger as the first continuously published "Westerns" in the comic books.

Impressed with the sales of *King Comics*, McKay Publishing Company brought out its second title, *Ace Comics* (April 1937). Another reprint title, in its first year of publication, *Ace Comics* featured "Jungle Jim," "Krazy Kat," and "The Phantom" newspaper strips.

The following month (May 1937) McKay also launched the *Feature Book* series, which spotlighted a single newspaper-strip character each issue—such as Popeye, Dick Tracy, or

Western Picture Stories #1, © 1937 Comics Magazine

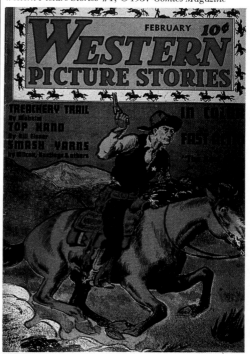

Little Orphan Annie. The *Feature Book* series, originally in black and white (and only later in color), would last eleven years.

Dell Publishing Company, pleased with the reception given to its two 1936 titles, *Popular Comics* and *The Funnies*, released *The Comics #1* (March 1937), another reprinted collection of newspaper strips. Dell also released two other hundred-page anthologies that year, *Western Action Thrillers* (April 1937) and *100 Pages of Comics*.

Although more than one hundred and seventy comic books and twenty titles were published in 1937 (over twice as many as the previous year), it would not be until the middle of 1938 that the future of the comic book would be assured.

The Comics #5, © 1937 Dell Publishing Co., Inc.

1938: SUPERMAN AND THE GOLDEN AGE OF COMICS

The first five months of 1938 gave no indication of the monumental event in comic-book history that was to occur this year.

For the most part, the early comic-book publishers were content to continue raiding the Sunday comic pages for their material. By early 1938 reprint comic books had become the norm. After five years, no major original character or concept had come out of the pages of the American comic book.

Exactly two years after publishing *Tip Top Comics*, United Features Syndicate brought out its second title, *Comics on Parade* (April 1938). This comic book was pretty much a collection of the same Sunday strips that appeared in *Tip Top*. United Features' other 1938 title, *Single Series*, devoted each issue to a single popular character, such as Tarzan, Li'l Abner, or Fritzi Ritz).

Dell Publishing Company added *Super Comics* (May 1938) as its fourth reprint title. But Dell was beginning to run out of popular

> "All of a sudden, it hits me—I conceive a character like Samson, Hercules, and all the strong men I ever heard of rolled into one. Only more so."
> —JERRY SIEGEL,
> co-creator of Superman

Action Comics #1, © 1938 DC Comics, Inc.

newspaper strips to reprint. Indeed, many of the features in *Super Comics*, such as "Dick Tracy" and "Terry & the Pirates," were taken from *Popular Comics'* original line-up.

In early 1938 Comics Magazine Company, Inc. and Harry "A" Chesler, two of the three comic-book publishers from 1937, turned their titles over to a new publisher called Centaur Publications. In March Centaur came out with three titles: *Funny Pages* and *Star Comics* (both continued from Chesler), and *Funny Picture Stories* (picked up from *Comic Magazine*). Centaur and National Periodical Publications (later known as Detective Comics, Inc.) were the only 1938 publishers that concentrated on original material.

And what about National Periodical Publications? Its originality came about almost by accident. By 1938 the founder of the comic-book line, Major Wheeler-Nicholson, was gone. Harry A. Donenfield, the new owner of National Periodical, was allowing Vincent Sullivan, the editor of *More Fun*, *New Adventure*, and *Detective Comics*, to fill up the books with whatever original features he could find.

Action Comics #4, © 1938 DC Comics, Inc.

Jumbo Comics #1, © 1938 Fiction House, Inc.

Before Wheeler-Nicholson left National, however, he and Sullivan had been working on a fourth title that was to be called *Action Funnies*, to complement *Detective Comics*.

About this same time, Sheldon Mayer, the teenage editor of *Popular Comics*, was back working at McClure Syndicate with M. C. Gaines, the gentleman who got this whole "funny book" business underway in the first place.

Mayer was at McClure when Jerry Siegel and Joe Shuster brought the syndicate the idea of using their newly created character, Superman, as a newspaper strip. The two boys from Cleveland had been peddling their superhero from Krypton, to dozens of publishers and syndicates, but to no avail.

Mayer recognized the potential of the strip at once, but he couldn't get the McClure syndicate to buy it. He kept telling Gaines that Siegel and Shuster's Superman was just the thing for the newspapers.

Gaines eventually was convinced of the character's potential, but decided to take him to a comic-book publisher instead of a newspaper-strip syndicate. Since Harry Donen-field's *Detective Comics* was one of the few books publishing original material, Gaines showed the "Superman" strip to the comic book's editor, Vincent Sullivan. To Sullivan's credit, he recognized the appeal of the cos-tumed superhero immediately. Besides which, he also was desperately seeking a lead feature for his new comic book, which was now called *Action Comics*.

Cover-dated June 1938, *Action Comics #1* hit the newsstands in early spring. *Action* really stood out from the other dozen or so comic-book titles on the stands that month. Its cover pictured a muscular man wearing a brightly colored red-and-blue costume with a cape, lifting a car over his head as criminals flee in terror.

When Donenfield saw the cover of *Action Comics*, he worried that the character was too fantastic and ridiculous, and ordered Sullivan to take Superman off the covers of future books. For the next five issues, Superman was not to be seen on the outside of *Action Comics*, even though he remained the lead feature inside.

Obviously, no one was aware that a new publishing phenomenon had occurred. And for good reason. The sales of the first three issues of *Action Comics* were not that im-pressive—about the same as its companion title, *Detective Comics*. No public outcry nor hurrah greeted the coming of Superman.

With the fourth issue of *Action Comics*, however, sales sailed "up, up, and away!" Whereas in 1938 most comic titles might sell two hundred thousand copies per issue, *Ac-tion Comics* was now rising quickly toward the half-million mark.

Donenfield still was unsure of why the comic book was doing so well. So he ordered a newsstand survey and found out that the kids were not asking for *Action Comics*—they were

Detective Comics #13, © 1938 DC Comics, Inc.

asking for the comic book "with Superman!"

Donenfield then told Sullivan to put Super-man back on the cover of the book and watched in fascination as each succeeding issue sold out.

So unexpected and rapid was the success of Superman, it would be almost another year before he was joined by any serious imitators.

If the Golden Age of Comic Books began in June 1938 with *Action Comics #1*, you could hardly tell it by looking at the other comic books published during the rest of the year.

The same month that *Action #1* came out, Dell offered a new title called *Crackerjack Funnies*. This actually was a replacement for the now-defunct title, *The Comics*, and fea-tured pretty much the same strip reprints.

Also in the same month as Superman Globe Syndicate came out with *Circus Comics*. It lasted for three issues and was the first and last comic book from this publisher.

Later that year Centaur Publications be-came the real powerhouse. In addition to its three titles published earlier that year, Cen-taur produced seven more titles in 1938: *Cow-boy Comics* (July), *Keen Detective Funnies* (July), *Little Giant Comics* (July), *Amazing Mystery Funnies* (August), *Little Giant Movie Funnies* (August), *Little Giant Detective Funnies* (October) and *Star Ranger Funnies* (October).

Like many other early comic-book pub-lishers, Centaur did not have a regular staff of artists and writers. All of its books were pack-aged by comic-book studio shops which had sprung up in the Manhattan area during the past year.

These studio shops had arisen to meet the growing demand for original comic-book ma-terial. Early comic-book publishers would en-gage a comic-book studio to develop not only comic-book pages, but also original charac-ters, titles, and story lines for them, as well.

The comic-book studios run by Harry "A"

Super Comics #5, © 1938 Dell Publishing Co., Inc.

Funny Pages, © 1938 Centaur Publications

"I wrote my first story, 'Steve Malone, District Attorney,' for *Detective Comics*. I got paid in early January 1938, and then I went on to write four thousand two hundred comic books."
—GARDNER FOX,
comic-book writer for such publishers as DC Comics, Marvel Comics, EC Comics, Warren Publishing, Magazine Enterprises, and Columbia Comics

Chesler, Bill Everett (best known as creator of the Sub-Mariner), and Will Eisner (creator of the Spirit) would supply strips for Centaur titles over the next few years.

Another studio active in the late 1930s was run by S. M. Iger, who had some of the brightest (and youngest) of the new comic-book artists.

In September 1938 the Iger shop created and packaged a comic for a new publisher, Fiction House. Actually, Fiction House already was well-known as a publisher of garish science-fiction, adventure, and "jungle pulp" fiction magazines. Its first comic book, *Jumbo Comics* (September), is noteworthy for introducing Sheena, "Queen of the Jungle." Originally created for a newspaper strip in England, the Jungle Queen strip was reprinted in comic-book form in *Jumbo*.

Although the early issues were black and white, Sheena's "jungle magnetism" still enticed a generation of developing males to plunk down their monthly dimes for *Jumbo Comics*.

A few single-issue comic-book titles also came out in 1938, such as Whitman's *Donald Duck*. The book contained black-and-white reprints of 1936 and 1937 Sunday comic pages and qualifies as the first Disney comic book.

Three months after the first appearance of Superman, Centaur Publishing featured a costumed hero, the Arrow, in its *Funny Pages*. The next month, *Detective Comics* (October) would feature a third hero in costume, the Crimson Avenger. These characters reflected more an emerging trend than a response to Superman, whose impact on the comic-book field had not yet been fully recognized when these other books appeared.

It would not be until the next year that the comic-book industry would slowly awaken to the overpowering newsstand appeal of the comic-book superhero.

1939: THE COMING OF THE SUPERHEROES

During the first four months of 1939, Superman's impact was being carefully measured and weighed by both National (DC Comics) and the other comic-book publishers.

Remarkably enough, during early 1939 no new continuing titles appeared at all. This five months would be the quietest time ever in the midst of comic-book publishing history.

Finally, in Spring 1939, National published a comic book to be a commercial tie-in with the 1939 World's Fair. Called *New York World's Fair Comics*, the book featured Superman and other National characters. Originally published at twenty-five cents, the experimental book didn't sell well until it was re-stickered with a fifteen-cent price tag.

National also was experimenting with other titles in early 1939. The company entered into an agreement with M. C. Gaines, the "mid-

Detective Comics #27, © 1939 DC Comics, Inc.

wife of American comic books," to produce a series of comics under its "All-American" imprint.

Harkening back to his roots, Gaines came up with the first reprint anthology comic for National. It was called *All-American Comics* (April 1939) and featured such newspaper stars as Mutt and Jeff, and Skippy.

That same month, Gaines also came out with *Movie Comics* (April 1939), which consisted of re-colored movie stills presented as a comic book. Although this certainly was an innovative attempt to capture the movie-going audience, *Movie Comics* failed within the year.

National's next innovation fared much better. Cover-dated May 1939, the twenty-seventh issue of *Detective Comics* featured the debut of Batman, a superhero who would become second only to Superman in recognition and popularity. Writer Bill Finger and artist Bob Kane created a super detective: a Sherlock Holmes in cape, possessing the athletic prowess of Tarzan and the dramatic flair of the successful "pulp" character, the Shadow.

Batman was the perfect complement to the almost bright and cheery Superman. As an ordinary mortal with no super powers, Batman was known as the "dark avenger," a mysterious hero who adopted the ways of the bat in the night.

The same month that Batman debuted, another new costumed hero appeared who was strikingly similar to Superman in appearance and powers. Wonder Man began in *Wonder Comics* (May 1939), which was the first book from a new publisher: Victor Fox.

Fox's Wonder Man was no accidental imitation of National's Superman. Fox, a former accountant at Detective Comics, Inc. (National), was all too familiar with the now-rocketing sales of *Action Comics*.

Wonder Comics #1, © 1939 Fox Features Syndicate

"Criminals are a cowardly, superstitious lot, so my disguise must be able to strike terror into their hearts! I must be a creature of the night. Black, terrible . . . a . . . a bat!"
—BATMAN,
Detective Comics #33

So Fox decided to start his own comic-book business and set up office in the same building as National, under the name of Fox Feature Syndicates. He contracted with Will Eisner and Jerry Iger of the Eisner-Iger studio to create his very own "super man" comic book.

When Harry Donenfield of National saw *Wonder Comics*, he slapped a lawsuit against Fox for copyright infringement. Fox quickly buried Wonder Man after only one appearance, but the entrepreneur would return later with other superheroes.

Another new publisher that year was Quality Comics. Its first title, *Feature Comics* (#21, June 1939), was a continuation of the title started by its original publisher, Harry

"A" Chesler.

By July, four more costumed heroes joined the ranks of National's Superman and Batman. National added the Sandman to *Adventure Comics* (#40, July 1939). Centaur introduced the Fantom of the Fair in *Amazing Mystery Funnies* (July 1939) and the Masked Marvel in *Keen Detective Funnies* (July 1939). Fox rebounded with the Flame, a hero in *Wonderworld Comics #3* (July 1939).

McKay Publishing, ignoring all the costume-hero brouhaha, issued its third newspaper-strip-reprint anthology, *Magic Comics* (August 1939), which featured Mandrake the Magician from the Sunday pages.

The big news that summer, however, was the first issue of *Superman Comics* (Summer

1939). This marked the first time an original comic-book character rated the title of a comic book on his own.

Superman Comics #1 also marked the beginning of the end of recycling newspaper strips and syndicated characters in comic books. Instead, it demonstrated that original material, original characters, and original concepts would be the future of the comic-book industry. Moreover, Superman proved that superheroes were indeed the wave of the future.

Later that summer, Victor Fox came out with a trio of costumed heroes (the Flame mentioned before, the Blue Beetle, and the Green Mask) in the first issue of his *Mysterymen Comics* (August 1939). Four months later, he published *Fantastic Comics* (December 1939), which featured two other superheroes, Stardust and Samson. By the end of the year, Fox's *Blue Beetle* (Winter 1939) became the second costumed hero to rate his own book.

During the summer, Centaur Publishing premiered its hero, Amazing Man, in *Amazing Man Comics #5* (August 1939). That same

Fantastic Comics #1, © 1939 Fox Features Syndicate

month, Quality Comics came out with *Smash Comics* (August 1939). Although *Smash* was devoid of costumed heroes for the first few issues, Quality did present its first superhero, Doll Man, to readers in *Feature Comics* (#27, December 1939).

In the fall of 1939, five more new comic-book publishers rushed titles to the newsstands. Harvey Comics, headed by brothers Alfred and Leon Harvey, came out with *Speed Comics* (October 1939) and *Champion Comics* (December 1939). Both were original anthology adventure titles, which would later feature superhero characters.

MLJ Comics (later known as Archie Comics) began its career with two anthology titles: *Blue Ribbon Comics* (November 1939) and *Top-Notch Comics* (December 1939). *Top-Notch* featured the first appearance of the Wizard, a quasi-magician superhero. These and other early MLJ titles became homes to many costumed heroes.

Better Publications started its new line of comic books with *Best Comics* (November 1939). This comic book featured the Red Mask, but it was published in an experimental large-size format that had to be read *sideways*. The sideways comic book failed, but Better Publications would be back the next year with comic books in what had become the "regular" format.

The next month Lev Gleason entered the comic-book-publishing business with *Silver Streak Comics* (December 1939). This comic book featured both superheroes as well as one of the first super villains: the Claw.

Another publisher who jumped wholeheartedly into the superhero fray was Martin Goodman, a publisher of popular-fiction "pulp" magazines, such as *Marvel Science Stories*. Goodman was first approached with the idea of publishing comic books by Frank Torpey, sales manager for Funnies, Inc., a

Mysterymen Comics #8, © 1939 Fox Features Syndicate

Amazing Man #5, © 1939 Centaur Publications

comic-book packaging studio that catered to the needs of the new comic-book publishers.

Goodman agreed to let Funnies, Inc. package a line of comic books for him. The studio was run by Lloyd Jacquet, a Frenchman who had just resigned as the comic-book editor at Centaur Publications. When Jacquet left Centaur, he took along some of the artists who had worked for him. Chief among these was Bill Everett, the artist of Centaur's Amazing Man.

Everett and his staff of cartoonists (some as young as age sixteen) labored mightily and brought forth several new super-powered characters for *Marvel Comics* (November 1939). Two of these characters—the Human

Amazing Mystery Funnies, © 1939 Centaur Publications

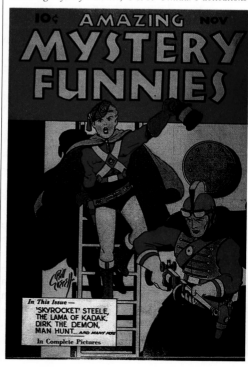

Torch and the Sub-Mariner—would launch an entire line of superhero comics and assure the success of Marvel Comics for years to come.

By the end of 1939, the seven new publishers and over fifty comic-book titles nearly doubled the number of the previous year. Impressive as that sounds, it would take until 1940 for the young comic-book industry to experience its greatest growth.

1940: THE GOLDEN YEAR

If 1938 marked the beginning of "The Golden Age of Comics," then 1940 must be called "The Golden Year." Never before or since would so many significant comic books be published in a single year.

Fueled by the success of Superman, Batman, and the other costumed heroes, 1940 was the year that the superhero comic books passed the newspaper-strip-reprint comics for dominance on the newsstand. It also was the year that publishers ventured squarely into other genres, such as science-fiction, war, and funny-animal comic books.

As the publisher that started it all with Superman and Batman, DC Comics quickly consolidated its position by introducing an entire contingent of superheroes in this one year. *Flash Comics* (January 1940) premiered "the fastest man alive," the Flash, as well as the high-flying Hawkman. *More Fun* (February 1940) featured DC's omnipotent astral hero: the Spectre. The very next month Hourman, a superhero who was super for only one hour at a time, clocked in at *Adventure Comics* (March 1940).

Spring also saw the first issue of *Batman* (Spring 1940) complete with a cover appearance by his new teenaged sidekick: Robin, the Wonder Boy.

Two other major DC heroes that year both

Whiz Comics #3, © 1940 Fawcett Publications, Inc.

"Bill [Parker] and I could feel that any time we tried to do something good, or better than Superman, it was nixed. Finally Bill Parker [Fawcett staff editor] said, 'Dammit, all they want is a carbon copy of Superman, and I'm not going to give it to them. . . .' So we proceeded to give them a character that looked something like Superman, but in character was completely different. . . . They put it out and the public grabbed it right away, because it was different. And it was good."
—C.C. BECK,
Captain Marvel artist and co-creator

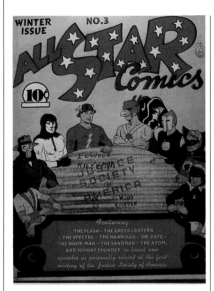

All Star Comics #3, © 1940 DC Comics, Inc.

"Charlie [W.C.] Gaines called us, Shelly [Sheldon Mayer] and me, together and said he wanted to do something as a companion to the Superman and Batman stories that were coming out in books of their own. We decided to take all of the super heroes that we had and form them together into a society."
—GARDNER FOX,
writer and co-creator of the Justice Society of America

Captain Marvel, © 1940 DC Comics, Inc.

appeared in DC's *All American Comics*. The Green Lantern, a hero who had a super-powered ring and magic lantern, debuted in July. DC's smallest superhero, the Atom, joined the Green Lantern in *All American* in October.

DC had introduced so many new super-heroes in the past two years that the publisher started a new title to showcase them all, called *All-Star Comics* (Summer 1940). By the third issue, *All-Star* featured the DC super-heroes working and fighting together as a team, called the Justice Society of America—the first organized group of superheroes, and the model for hundreds to come.

Although by now DC was established as the leading superhero comic-book publisher, a new company called Fawcett Publications began to offer serious competition.

Fawcett's first comic book, *Whiz Comics* (February 1940), featured the origin of Captain Marvel—a new superhero created by artist C. C. Beck and editor/writer Bill Parker. Captain Marvel was a kinder, gentler superhero whose alter-identity was Billy Batson, a boy radio broadcaster. Part of Captain Marvel's appeal to young readers was the fact that Billy could become the world's mightiest mortal simply by saying a magic word: "SHAZAM!"

Fawcett tried another super character, Master Man, in its next comic book: *Master Comics* (March 1940). DC Comics, already upset about the competition from Captain Marvel, managed to get Master Man axed after six issues with an allegation that he infringed on the Superman copyright.

Fawcett's third superhero, Bulletman, debuted in *Nickel Comics* (May 1940).

Both *Master* and *Nickel* were experiments

in marketing. *Master*, priced at fifteen cents, was magazine size, while *Nickel*, priced at five cents, had half the number of pages as a regular ten-cent comic book.

Fawcett's last title that year was *Wow Comics* (Winter 1940), a regular-size comic-book format with a line of minor superheroes, which met with only moderate success.

After trying out several different characters and titles, Fawcett realized that its strongest asset was still Captain Marvel. The company tested the waters for an entire comic book about Captain Marvel by publishing a collection of Captain Marvel stories in a single-issue comic book called *Special Edition* (August 1940).

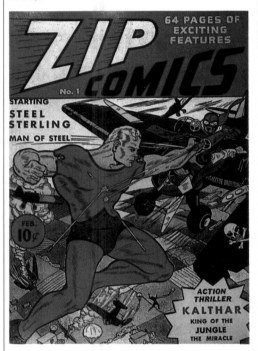

Zip Comics #1, © 1940 Archie Comic Publications, Inc.

Meanwhile, Marvel Comics was busy introducing over a dozen new superhero characters in *Daring Mystery* (January 1940), *Mystic* (March 1940), and *Red Raven* (August 1940). One of the best-selling characters from Marvel Mystery Comics was given his own comic book called *The Human Torch* (Fall 1940).

MLJ (or Archie) Publications introduced its most significant and longest running title with *Pep Comics* (January 1940), which featured the first flag-draped patriotic superhero: the Shield. The company's other new titles that year—*Zip Comics* (February 1940), *Shield Wizard Comics* (Summer 1940), and *Top-Notch Comics* (October 1940)—also featured superheroes aplenty.

This same year Better Publications launched a triumvirate of superhero titles with *Thrilling Comics* (February 1940), *Exciting Comics* (April 1940), and *Startling Comics* (June 1940). The books would be home to Doc Strange, the Black Terror, Pyroman, the Fighting Yank, Miss Masque, and other heroes and heroines.

Prize Publications's first title, *Prize Comics* (March 1940), contained the adventures of the

Exciting Comics #1, © 1940 Better Publications, Inc.
Prize Comics #2, © 1940 Prize Publications

Heroic Comics #1, © 1940 Eastern Color Printing Co.

POWER NELSON—The FUTUREMAN

Target Comics (February 1940) and the Blue Bolt in *Blue Bolt Comics* (June 1940).

Then Holyoke Publishing Company entered the comic-book superhero business with *Crash Comics* (May 1940), which featured the Blue Streak (not to be confused with the aforementioned White Streak or Blue Bolt); the Catman, a popular hero who would eventually get his own title and a young sidekick named Kitten.

Columbia Comics Group, a subsidiary of Eastern Color, featured such superheroes as the Skyman, the Face, and the Cloak in its first comic book, *Big Shot Comics* (May 1940). The group's next title, *Heroic Comics* (August 1940), added Hydroman by Bill Everett (who had previously created the Sub-Mariner for Timely) and Tarpe Mill's Purple Zombie to its growing stable of superhero characters.

Crack Comics #1, © 1940 Everett M. Arnold

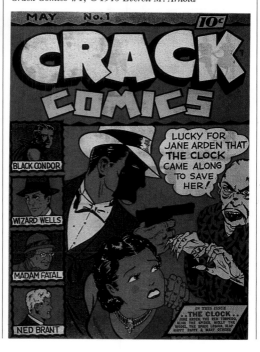

Black Owl, the Green Lama, and later, Yank and Doodle. This comic book also introduced Frankenstein by Dick Briefer, a character played both for laughs and horror during its schizophrenic fourteen-year existence.

Another new publisher, Ace Magazines, tied its success to the superheroes by introducing Flash Lightning in *Sure-Fire Comics* (June 1940) and Magno the Magnetic Man in *Super Mystery Comics* (July 1940). Both titles would eventually become homes for a half-dozen minor superheroes.

The success of the superhero comics also lured Novelty Publications into the burgeoning comic-book industry. Its early efforts, produced by the Bill Everett shop, featured such colorful heroes as the White Streak in

"When you see a comics rack, even at a distance of ten to fifteen feet, you're overwhelmed by the energy and the grossness and the vulgarity and the pure vitality that's spilling off that material."
—GIL KANE,
artist for DC Comics, Marvel, Tower, Eastern Color, Hillman, Fawcett, Street and Smith, Archie/MLJ, Prize, Quality, Fox, Avon, Dell, and Harvey

Centaur Publications had introduced costumed characters in its comic books even before Superman became popular. By 1940, these characters rated their own titles: *Fantoman* (August 1940), *Masked Marvel* (September 1940), and *The Arrow* (October 1940). The publisher's new *Super Spy Comics* (October 1940) and *Wham Comics* (November 1940) were anthology titles featuring both original and reprinted superhero strips.

Victor Fox, the first publisher to imitate Superman's success, came out with *The Green Mask* (Summer 1940), *The Flame* (Summer 1940), and *Samson* (Fall 1940). The latter two heroes then joined up with Fox's *Blue Beetle* to star in a superhero anthology entitled *Big 3* (Fall 1940).

Fox also featured an anthology of minor superheroes, like the Birdman and Voodoo Man, in *Weird Comics* (April 1940). Fox's other 1940 title, *Science Comics* (February 1940), was one of the first science-fiction comic books.

Quality Comics had introduced its first superhero, Doll Man, the previous year. For its new titles, *Crack Comics* (May 1940), *Hit*

Comics (July 1940), and *National Comics* (July 1940), Quality engaged the talents of Lou Fine, Bob Powell, Will Eisner and others to produce such superheroes as the Black Condor, Uncle Sam, and Madame Fatal—the first (and perhaps only) transvestite superhero.

Despite not having published a new title since 1938, United Features Syndicate suddenly released four new comic books. *OK Comics* (July 1940) was an attempt at a superhero anthology, but it lasted only two issues. *Sparkler Comics* (July 1940) featured a superhero called the Sparkman, along with the usual reprinted Sunday pages. Both *OKAY Comics* (July 1940, not the previously mentioned *OK Comics*) and *United Comics* (August 1940) also featured newspaper-strip reprints of famous United Syndicate characters, like Fritzi Ritz and the Captain and the Kids.

Street and Smith, a long time pulp-magazine publisher, entered the comic-book market with versions of its two most famous pulp heroes, the *Shadow* (March 1940) and *Doc Savage* (May 1940). Both the Shadow and Doc Savage had appeared in pulps since the early 1930s, becoming the inspiration and literary prototypes for many of the early comic-book superheroes. Their transition from the pulp magazines to the comic books did not fare well, however, despite the fact that the creator of the original Shadow, Walter Gibson, also wrote the early comic-book stories as well.

Harvey Comics adapted the *Green Hornet* (December 1940), another radio and movie pulp-style hero, into a comic-book superhero. This comic book lasted for nine years, due in large part to the popularity of the radio show.

Another radio and movie character who made it into the comic books was the Ralston-Purina Company's Tom Mix. *Tom Mix Comics* (September 1940) was offered as a premium to the Tom Mix radio audience. *Tom Mix*, along with Hawley Publications's *Red Ryder Comics* cover-dated the same month, became the first two books to be devoted to a single "western" character.

Besides "the western," other comic-book genres were being born in the full bloom of the superhero explosion. Street and Smith published the first comic book devoted entirely to sports and sports heroes with *Sport Comics* (October 1940).

Dell Publishing Company was making comic book anthology history with the first all funny animal title, *Walt Disney's Comics and Stories* (October 1940), and—a sign of the times—the first comic book devoted to war stories: *War Comics* (May 1940).

Fiction House clinched the honor as publisher of the first science-fiction comic, *Planet Comics #1* (January 1940), as well as the premier jungle comic, *Jungle Comics* (January 1940). Fiction House, however, resisted the temptation to publish any superhero characters this year—or in fact at any time during its sixteen-year history. Instead, it specialized in adventure-genre titles like *Fight Comics* (January 1940), a war comic, and *Wings* (Sep-

Marvel Mystery Comics #9, © 1940 Marvel Entertainment Group, Inc.

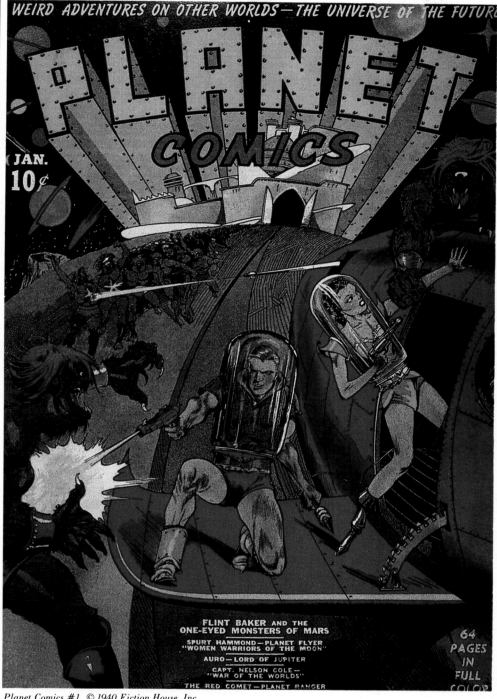

WEIRD ADVENTURES ON OTHER WORLDS—THE UNIVERSE OF THE FUTURE

Planet Comics #1, © 1940 Fiction House, Inc.

> "The Golden Age comics are crude and simplistic by today's standards but with a raw immediacy which gives them a hard-hitting power that is hard for contemporary comics to replicate. Early creators were energized by the visceral thrill of creating a new art form. They looked everywhere for inspiration to shape their newborn medium."
> —**JENETTE KAHN**,
> president and editor-in-chief
> of DC Comics

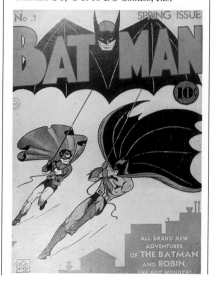

Batman #1, © 1940 DC Comics, Inc.

tember 1940), an aviation title.

Hillman Periodicals entered the comic-book field with two anthology titles, *Miracle Comics* (February 1940) and *Rocket Comics* (March 1940), neither of which lasted through the year.

Many smaller comic-book publishers tried their luck, too, in the rapidly growing comic-book industry. Sun Publications came out with only one issue each of *Colossus Comics* (March 1940) and *Sun Fun Komicks* (March 1940). Nita Publications produced *Whirlwind Comics* (June 1940) the same month that Bilbara Publishing Company issued *Cyclone Comics*, but both titles were blown away before the year ended.

Other one-title comic-book publishers included Hyper Publications's *Hyper Mystery*

(May 1940), Hugo Gernsback's *Superworld* (April 1940), and Pelican Publications's *Green Giant Comics*, named after a supermarket-product character.

One of the more interesting of 1940's comic-book characters was the Spirit. Created by Will Eisner exclusively for a newspaper syndicate that wanted a superhero for its Sunday comic pages, the Spirit had a mask and a dual identity, but no super powers.

The Spirit (June 1940) made its debut as a weekly (Sunday) comic book that was distributed through the newspapers for twelve years. Perhaps one of the best written and illustrated comic books, Eisner's *Spirit* is remembered for its atmospheric stories, grotesque characters, and gentle sense of humor.

During "The Golden Year" of 1940—per-

"You, who are to have this power, must use it to end evil! The light of the Green Lantern must be shed over the dark, evil things . . . for the dark evil things cannot stand light! Power shall be yours, if you have faith in yourself. Lose that faith and you lose the energetic power of the Green Lantern, for *will power* is the flame of the Green Lantern!"
—THE GREEN LANTERN,
All American Comics #16 (July 1940)

Wonder Woman, © 1941 DC Comics, Inc.

haps the most productive year in comic book history—there were approximately one hundred fifty comic-book titles published. Enough comic books were sold to generate an annual revenue of over twenty million dollars. And the sixteen new publishers that entered the field more than doubled the number of new comic-book publishers from the previous year.

Adventure Comics #66, © 1941 DC Comics, Inc.

1941: THE SUPERHERO SUCCESSION

In 1941, two things happened.

First, many of the superheroes introduced in the previous two years were given their own titles or even a second book. Publishers brought out more and more superhero comics as sales figures continued to climb.

Second, World War II was on the horizon for the United States, and the big push was on for patriotic superheroes. By summer, Nazi-bashing in the comics began in earnest, with both superheroes and military men fighting the villainy of the Third Reich. Dell Comics even created the first propaganda comic book for the war effort, called *USA Is Ready* (1941).

The reality of the approaching war also introduced an element of realism into the comic books. Several publishers came out with "real life comics," which adapted historical events or biographies of war heroes into a comic-book story.

Fantasy, however, was still very much the order of the day. In 1941 the comic-book-reading public wanted one thing more than anything else: more superheroes. The publishers obliged them.

DC Comics gave the Green Lantern his own comic, *Green Lantern* (Fall 1941), as well as a continuing starring role in *All American Comics*. Similarly, the Flash, already appearing in *Flash Comics*, got a second title about his ad-

ventures called *All Flash Comics* (Summer 1941).

Although DC already was showcasing its major superheroes in *All-Star Comics*, it now had enough minor superheroes to warrant a second team title. *Leading Comics* (Winter 1941) became a home away from home for characters like the Green Arrow, the Star Spangled Kid, the Crimson Avenger, and the Shining Knight.

By this time Superman had spread to radio, movies, and the newspapers. His comic strip was running in two hundred thirty papers, and the comic book was selling nearly a million copies a month. Batman was a close second, with his comic book selling eight hundred thousand copies a month. And, even though Superman and Batman were already appearing in two comics each (*Action*, *Superman*, *Detective*, and *Batman*), they rated joint exposure in a third title called *World's Finest* (Summer 1941).

DC also introduced two new heroes this year. The Starman joined the Sandman and the Hourman in *Adventure Comics #61* (April 1941) for a four-year run. Perhaps DC's most significant character of the year, however, was Wonder Woman. She first appeared in the eighth issue of *All-Star Comics* (November 1941). Wonder Woman and her adventures continued the following year in *Sensation Comics*.

Marvel Comics also was busy developing its superheroes and titles from the previous year. The *Sub-Mariner* (Spring 1941), following the lead of the Human Torch, was granted his own title.

Marvel also introduced its most popular superhero of the 1940s, *Captain America* (March 1941), in a series of patriotic Nazi-smashing adventures that were initially produced by Joe Simon and Jack Kirby. Simon

USA Comics #1, © 1941 Marvel Entertainment Group, Inc.

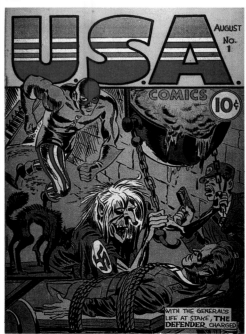

Victory Comics #1, © 1941 Hillman Publications

always in cheek, Plastic Man provided a fresh alternative to the sometimes heavy heroics of his super colleagues. *Police* also served as a home for reprints of Will Eisner's comic-strip newspaper supplement, "The Spirit."

Although *Military Comics* was a war-theme comic, it featured a super team of aviators: the Blackhawks. These were six men from different countries who clubbed together to fight the Nazis. Dressed like a quasi-military group, the Blackhawks had jolly adventures in their airplanes as they lambasted Nazis, the Japanese, or anyone else who threatened the American way of life.

The appeal of the multi-ethnic characters, coupled with consistently good writing and art, guaranteed the Blackhawks an appreciative audience for the next forty years.

Columbia Comics had its own aviator hero as well. The *Skyman* (Fall 1941) received his own title after starring in *Big Shot Comics* with *The Face*, another Columbia hero who also got his own book this year.

Holyoke Publishing quickly gave *Catman*

and Kirby's Captain America captured the essence of the World War II patriotic fighting hero.

Captain America, Sub-Mariner, and the Human Torch were also teamed up in a new title called *All-Winners* (Summer 1941). Bucky and Toro, the sidekicks of Captain America and the Human Torch respectively, got their own team-up title in *Young Allies* (Summer 1941). More Marvel superheroes with a patriotic bent, such as Major Liberty, the American Avenger, and Jap Buster Johnson, were introduced in *USA Comics* (August 1941).

Fawcett Publications also expanded upon the superheroes it had previously introduced in *Whiz Comics*, *Nickel Comics*, and *Master Comics*.

The first Fawcett character to warrant his own book was Captain Marvel, whose *Captain Marvel Adventures* (January 1941) would become one of the most successful comic books of all time. Other heroes who got their own books were *Bulletman* (July 1941), *Minuteman* (July 1941), and the *Spysmasher* (Fall 1941). All four of these heroes also got together in Fawcett's new anthology title, *America's Greatest* (May 1941).

By the end of the year, Fawcett would create perhaps its second most significant superhero, Captain Marvel Jr., who first appeared in *Whiz Comics #25* (December 1941). Captain Marvel Jr. was the first juvenile version of a superhero, anticipating Superboy by almost four years.

After two years in *Feature Comics*, Quality Comics gave *Doll Man* (Fall 1941) his own book. The most significant Quality books that year, however, were *Police Comics* (August 1941) and *Military Comics* (August 1941).

Police Comics featured the origin of Jack Cole's Plastic Man, a crook turned good guy who gains the super power to stretch and ply his body into any shape or form. With tongue

Police Comics #1, © 1941 Everett M. Arnold

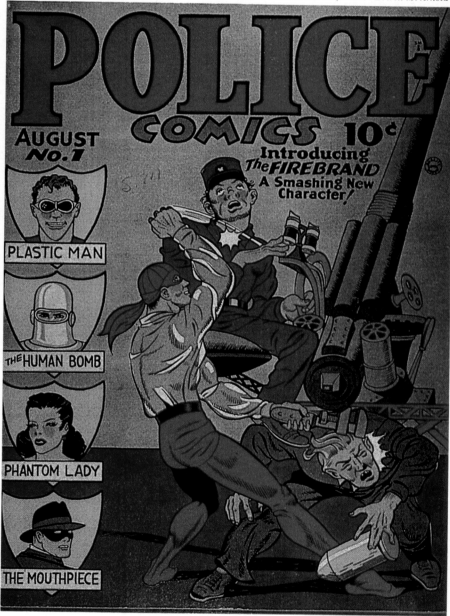

*Captain America #2, © 1941 Marvel
Entertainment Group, Inc.*

"Captain America was
very much a reflection
of his time. He was
patriotic when the
country was patriotic.
He was willing to fight
for his country when his
country was getting
ready to get into a
horrible war. We saw
him as a political
statement fleshed out to
be an active force."
—JOE SIMON,
co-creator of Captain America

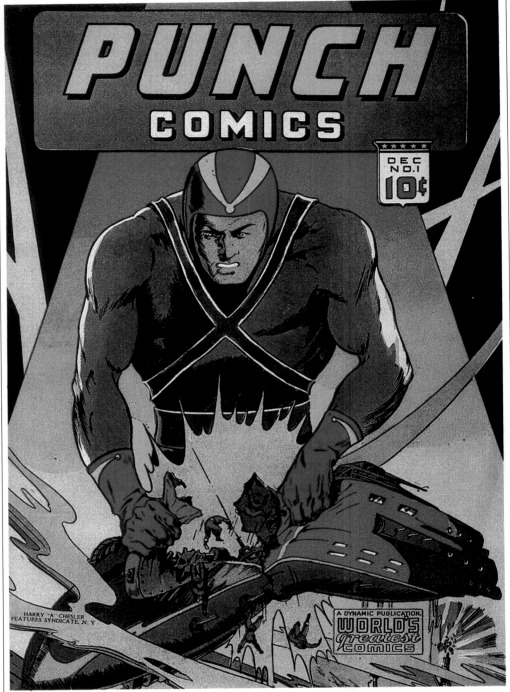

Punch Comics #1, © 1941 Harry A. Chesler

(May 1941), its most popular superhero from *Crash Comics*, his own book title. Lev Gleason, who had a super-speeding hero in *Silver Streak Comics*, now introduced other costumed heroes in *Daredevil* (July 1941), a comic book that featured Hitler as the ultimate super villain.

Ace Magazines, too, put patriotic superheroes into fisticuffs with Nazis in both *Our Flag* (August 1941) and *Banner Comics* (September 1941). Its other new title, *Four Favorites* (September 1941), became a showcase for its four most popular superheroes.

Hillman Periodicals was certainly not lacking in patriotic fervor either. Its *Victory Comics* (August 1941) featured superheroes and war heroes fighting side by side, then *Air*

Fighters (November 1941) took the battle to the skies.

Fiction House sent in its troops as well, with *Rangers Comics* (October 1941), which featured the Rangers of Freedom and Ranger Girl—a woman who proudly displayed both patriotic and physical fervor.

Harry Chesler, who had been packaging comic books for other publishers since 1936, came out with a line of his own comics: *Yankee Comics* (September 1941), *Dynamic Comics* (October 1941), *Scoop Comics* (November 1941), and *Punch Comics* (December 1941). All these books featured superheroes of every ilk and description, but none ever captured a wide following.

MLJ Publications used *Jackpot Comics*

(Spring 1941) to showcase its top superheroes. These superheroes, however, would eventually be replaced by an invasion of teenagers—led by the first appearance of Bob Montana's Archie Andrews in *Pep Comics #22* (December 1941). The eventual success of Archie and his gang would transform MLJ Publications into Archie Publications, while beginning another major trend—comic books about teenagers.

Other publishers also were exploring alternatives to the superhero comic. Dell Publishing Company had seen the market for funny-animal comics after the success of its *Walt Disney's Comics and Stories.* The company next bought the rights to publish Warner Brothers cartoon characters, which it did in *Looney Tunes* (Fall 1941)—but that wasn't all, folks. Dell also came out with perhaps the ultimate funny-animal title, *Animal Comics* (December 1941), which featured the first appearance of Walt Kelly's Pogo Possum.

Pogo, © Walt Kelly Estate

Meanwhile, the Parents Magazine Institute, publisher of *Parents Magazine*, had become dismayed by the proliferation of comic books which only offered children escapist fantasy. To upgrade the reading habits of the youth of America, the Institute published the first educational comic book, *True Comics* (April 1941). This comic book featured stories of famous historical events, scientific discoveries, and heroic individuals. These stories about real-life heroes proved so popular with an audience already obsessed with superheroes, that the Institute next published *Real Heroes* (September 1941). It also issued another true fact and biographical comic-book anthology especially for girls, called *Calling All Girls* (September 1941).

Better Publications took notice of *True Comics,* and immediately came out with *Real Life Comics* (September 1941), another factual and historical comic-book anthology.

Gilberton Publications, however, outmaneuvered both *True Comics* and *Real Life Comics* in the educational field. It began a line of comic-book literary adaptations called *Classic Comics* (October 1941), which became enor-

Crackajack Funnies #36, © 1941 K.K. Publications

mously popular with school children (who sometimes read the comics for class assignments in lieu of the original books).

By the end of the year, about one hundred sixty different comic-book titles had come on the market. Interestingly enough, however, the great flood of new comic-book publishers entering the field had subsided. Only four new publishers had started up in 1941, and two of them disappeared almost immediately. The rest of the publishers, however, were enjoying a boom that seemed to be going nowhere else but up, up, and away.

1942: TEENAGERS, SUPER MICE, AND WONDROUS WOMEN

At the beginning of 1942, there were 143 comic-book titles on the newsstands being read by over fifty million people each month. The comic book was no longer a passing publishing fad. It had become an established part of Americana, finding its way into the bedrooms and bivouacs of children and servicemen everywhere.

During this year the American Institute of Graphic Arts mounted a history of "narrative illustration." This exhibit traced the comic book's family tree through early wood-block prints and illuminated manuscripts to ancient hieroglyphics and cave paintings. Some educators praised the comic book as a boon for young readers, but others dismissed it as "sadistic drivel." It would be many years before the comic book would be acknowledged as an American literary art form in its own right, and even then, not without condescension and trepidation.

For DC Comics, this was "the year of the woman"—Wonder Woman, that is. After a several-month run in *Sensation Comics* (January 1942), the Amazon from Paradise Island got her own book: *Wonder Woman* (Summer

Miss Fury #1, © 1942 Marvel Entertainment Group, Inc.

1942). Dr. William Marston, a psychologist writing under the name Charles Moulton, created Wonder Woman along with artist Harry Peter.

Wonder Woman was explicitly designed by the doctor as an expression of the values he held as a pioneer theorist of the women's liberation movement in the 1940s. Whether or not Dr. Marston's psychological doctrine got through to his young readers, Wonder Woman was immensely popular among girl readers.

A few months later, Wonder Woman appeared in a third title, *Comic Cavalcade* (Winter 1942), along with the Flash and the Green Lantern. DC's other new title of the year was another Simon/Kirby creation, *Boy Commandos* (Winter 1942), about a gang of fighting kids who did their part to win World War II. This was the first kid-gang comic, and it soon was followed by a host of imitators.

Marvel Comics' *Tough Kid Squad* (March 1942), which also featured pint-sized heroes in action, was a suitable follow-up to its *Young Allies* title. For most of this year, however, Marvel concentrated on its new line of

All Flash #5, © 1942 DC Comics, Inc.

Archie #1, © 1942 Archie Comic Publications, Inc.

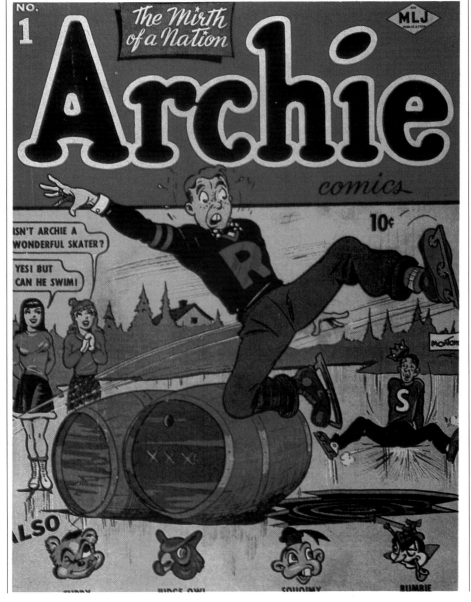

humor comics, like *Comedy* (April 1942), *Joker* (April 1942), *Krazy* (July 1942), and *Terry-Toons* (October 1942)—the future home of Mighty Mouse.

Meanwhile, Fawcett Publications was busy raising its Marvel Family of superheroes. *Captain Marvel Jr.* (November 1942) received his own comic book, and then Mary Marvel, his teenage female counterpart, made her superheroic debut in *Captain Marvel #18* (December 1942). *Captain Midnight* (September 1942) also joined the Marvel Family in the air, while *Fawcett's Funny Animals* (December 1942) introduced the Marvel Family "pet," Hoppy the Marvel Bunny.

Better Publications got its line of superheroes off the ground quickly. The *Fighting Yank* (September 1942) and the *Black Terror* (Winter 1942) each was given its own book, then joined together to star in Better's superhero anthology: *America's Best* (February 1942).

Better also made a nod to the growing funny-animal market with *Coo Coo Comics* (October 1942). Even here, though, Better could not escape the lure of the costumed hero. *Coo Coo Comics* featured the origin of Super Mouse, perhaps the first funny-animal parody of the superhero.

Lev Gleason, on the other hand, was doing very well without superheroes or funny animals. He introduced two titles in 1942 that would form the basis of his comic-book empire.

Boy Comics #3 (April 1942) featured the Crimebuster as well as a series of realistic adventure stories. It would survive, and often thrive, for the next fourteen years.

However, Gleason's other new book that year was a real industry trendsetter. *Crime Does Not Pay* (June 1942) was the first all-crime comic book. It was so unusual for its time that newsstand dealers were uncertain what to do with it. But over the next five years sales of the book climbed rapidly. This comic would eventually launch an industry-wide boom in crime comics and be read by nearly four million people every month.

Another trend-setting book also was published this year, but in another area. *Archie Comics* (Winter 1942) formalized the introduction of "America's favorite teenager" into the comic-book ranks. The popularity of Archie and his friends would be responsible for dozens and dozens of teen titles all through the 1940s and 1950s.

Dell Publishing added *New Funnies #65* (July 1942) and the Walter Lantz cartoon characters to its funny animal zoo. Dell's first issue of *Donald Duck* (August 1942) featured the first comic-book artwork by Carl Barks, while *Our Gang Comics* (September 1942) was graced by the presence of Walt Kelly.

Dell Comics took notice of the war, as well. Its *War Heroes* (July 1942) and *War Stories* were among the first comics to deal with World War II.

Catechetical Guild was the only new comic-book publisher this year. It produced the first continuous comic book with a religious theme, called *Topix Comics* (November 1942). *Topix* featured stories of saints and Catholic heroes, along with Bible tales and wholesome morality lessons. It was distributed almost entirely through Catholic schools and eventually was popular enough to appear on a weekly basis near the end of its ten-year span.

The number of titles published this year fell from over one hundred forty in January to a little more than one hundred by autumn. The decline was probably due more to war-time paper allocations than to any real industry slump.

But total circulation remained about the same, so the comic-book industry enjoyed one of its best years ever. The twelve to fifteen million comic books sold each month produced an annual industry revenue of fifteen million dollars. And, according to industry surveys, seventy-five percent of that total sum came directly from the pockets of children themselves. Sticky dimes and ice-cream money were building another uniquely American entertainment industry.

1943: THE FUNNY-ANIMAL MENAGERIE

By now other publishers had taken notice of Dell's rapidly growing line of "funny animal" comics, like *Walt Disney's Comics and Stories* and *New Funnies.*

Better Publications added three new animated cartoon titles to its line this year: *Real Funnies* (January 1943), *Goofy Comics* (June 1943), and *Happy Comics* (August 1943).

Marvel Comics came out with one of the first super-powered "funny animals," called *Super Rabbit* (Fall 1943), who also appeared with Gandy Goose and Sourpuss in *All Sur-*

Walt Disney's Comics #33, © 1943 Walt Disney Productions

Crime Does Not Pay #22, © 1942 Lev Gleason Publications

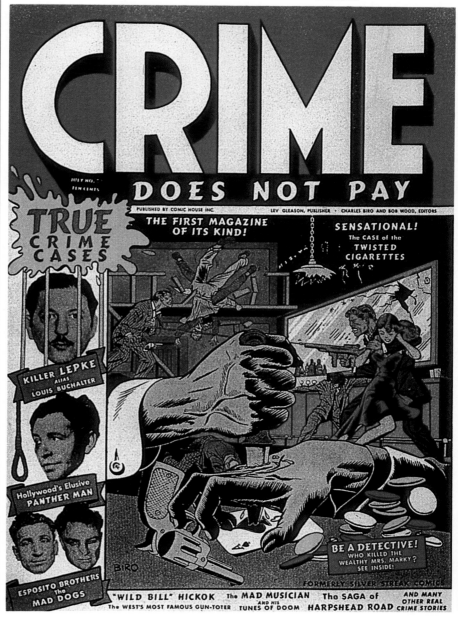

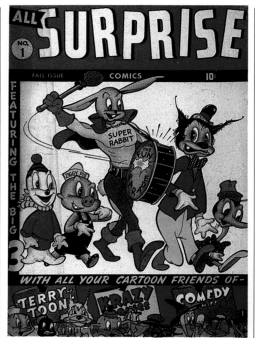

All Surprise #1, © 1943 Marvel Entertainment Group, Inc.

prise Comics (Fall 1943). Marvel's other new humor title featured a naive prizefighter with a heart of gold, *Powerhouse Pepper* (1943), who was both written and drawn by Basil Wolverton.

The American Comics Group (ACG) became a new publisher, with two comic books that were drawn by cartoon studio animators, *Giggle Comics* and *Ha Ha Comics*, both cover-dated October 1943.

Archie Comics published its first funny-animal character, Super Duck, in *Jolly Jingles #10* (Summer 1943). Initially powered by special vitamins, Super Duck later became a suburbanite foil and beleaguered parent.

The Dell Publishing Company title that had started the funny-animal trend, *Walt Disney's Comics and Stories*, now began a twenty-five-year-long series of original Donald Duck stories written and drawn by the man acknowl-

Shield-Wizard Comics #11, © 1943 Archie Comic Publications, Inc.

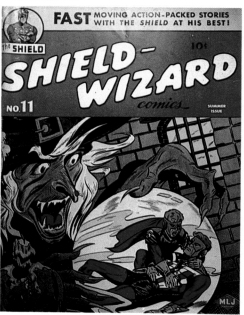

edged to be the greatest funny-animal artist of all time, Carl Barks, whose writing critics admired as much as his art.

DC Comics's only new title for 1943 was *All Funny Comics* (Winter 1943), a humor anthology. For the first time in five years, there was no new DC superhero title.

The superhero boom was far from over, however. Quality Comics gave *Plastic Man* (Summer 1943) his own book as well as continuing his starring role in *Police Comics*. Archie Comics also granted the *Black Hood* (#9, Winter 1943) his own title.

Hillman Publishing introduced such bizarre superheroes as Micro-Face, Nightmare, and Zippo in its *Clue Comics* (January 1943).

Don Winslow of The Navy #8, © 1943 Fawcett Publications, Inc.

Harvey Comics stuck with detectives and heroes like the Red Blazer and Scarlet Phantom for its *All New Comics* (January 1943).

Marvel Comics was encouraged enough by the response to its team title, *All Winners*, to come out with a second superhero anthology called *All Select* (Fall 1943). The Young Allies, Marvel's junior superheroes, also found a second home in *Kid Komics* (February 1943).

Fawcett Publications's only heroic title this year was *Ibis the Invincible* (February 1943), the super magician from *Whiz Comics*. The company also began publishing comic books based upon two already popular characters, *Don Winslow of the Navy* (February 1943) and *Hopalong Cassidy* (February 1943).

In comparison to the previous year, there were actually two fewer comic-book titles on the newsstands this year, for a total of 141. Only three new publishers—ACG, Flying Cadet Publications, and William Wise Publishing—started up this year.

Again, the seeming inertia in the industry was due to the war. Shortages of paper and labor limited how quickly the young industry could grow.

Yet the war actually helped the growth of the comic-book industry by increasing the number of American servicemen who became comic-book readers. To show the underlying strength of the 1943 comic-book market, Fawcett Publications alone sold nearly forty-seven million comic books—more than double its sales of the previous year.

1944: THE HEROIC PEAK

After a phenomenal five-year period of constantly increasing sales, the superhero titles hit their peak circulations in 1944. The most popular superhero comic book of that year, Fawcett's *Captain Marvel Adventures*, reached its all-time high circulation of 14,067,535 issues—almost three million more than the previous or succeeding year.

But for all their strong sales, publishers were looking elsewhere for new titles and the next trend.

Marvel Comics had been noticing the growing success of the Archie titles and decided to test the teenage comic-book market with *Junior Miss* (Winter 1944), *Tessie the Typist* (Summer 1944), and *Miss America* (1944).

There were a few new superhero appearances in *Blue Circle Comics* (June 1944), a comic book from new publisher Enwill Associates, as well as in E. Levy's *Yellowjacket Comics* (September 1944). Except for the *Green Lama* (December 1944), however, few of the new superheroes were memorable.

DC Comics was still exploring the humor market with its first funny-animal anthology, *Funny Stuff* (Summer 1944). Its other new humor title was *Buzzy* (Winter 1944), the continuing adventures of an Archie-type teenager who first appeared in *All Funny Comics*.

Magazine Enterprises (ME) was the only major new publisher. It began with a single title, *A-1 Comics*, which would serve as a

All Select #8, © 1944 Marvel Entertainment Group, Inc.

Happy Comics #4, © 1944 Nedor Publishing Company

Classics Illustrated #16, © 1944 Gilberton Company, Inc.

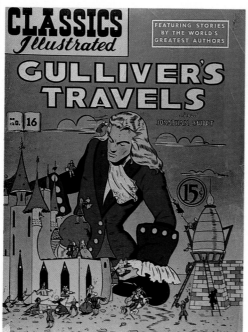

Blue Circle Comics #2, © 1944 Rewl Publications

showcase for various try-out characters and titles.

A few small publishers appeared and disappeared in 1944. R. B. Leffingwell issued a strange hero/war-fantasy comic called *Jeep Comics*, while U.S. Camera Company published *Camera Comics*, a comic book that was usually about fifty percent photographs. William H. Wise started up *It Really Happened*, another real-life adventure comic.

Although few new publishers and titles came out this year, comic books had successfully established themselves as a permanent part of American culture. The December 1944 issue of the Journal of Educational Sociology examined comic books and surprised many adults by concluding that they did an excellent job of supplying children's needs for fantasy and imaginative reading matter!

Like last year, the number of titles on the newsstands again declined—this time from 141 titles to only 130 titles, the lowest number since the decade began. The war years and paper allocation would soon end, however, and this would be the last time for ten years that the number of newsstand titles would decrease from the previous year.

1945: WOMEN AND ANIMALS FIRST!

During World War II, American women assumed a more visible role in society and this was reflected in the comics, as well.

Fawcett's *Mary Marvel* (December 1945), a Captain Marvel derivative and second only to Wonder Woman in the super-heroine popularity contest, received her own book after

Crack Comics #39, © *1945 Comic Magazines, Inc.*

starring in *Wow Comics* for a year or so.

Marvel Comics began three women-oriented comics that year with *Patsy Walker*, *Millie the Model*, and *Nellie the Nurse*. These cartoon "career girls" humorously portrayed the American woman in the workplace with a heavy dose of innocent, romantic fun.

Also ending the war year were such super-girl titles as Archie's *Miss Liberty* and Holyoke's *Miss Victory*. Together with Marvel's *Miss America*, these stars-and-striped women whipped up any fading patriotic fervor. *Miss Cairo Jones* was a comic book about a tough woman "private eye," a theme repeated in the first comic book from Avon Comics: *Molly O'Day, Super Sleuth* (February 1945).

Along with more women in the comics, there were suddenly more animals—funny animals, that is. With the grimness of war fading, America was ready for laughs and plenty of innocent mindless fun. Cartoon animals were in demand now, and new titles were appearing like Novelty Press's *Frisky Fables* (Spring 1945) and Fawcett's *George Pal's Puppetoons* (December 1945). Marvel Comics added even more cartoon-animal titles to its already sizable humor lineup, like *Funny Frolics* (Summer 1945), *Silly Tunes* (Fall 1945), and *Animated Movie Tunes* (Fall 1945).

Superheroes, however, were still a big draw on the newsstands. Fawcett featured its three most popular heroes, Captain Marvel, Captain Marvel Jr., and Mary Marvel, in a new title called *Marvel Family* (December 1945).

Harvey Comics gave strongman and prize-fighter *Joe Palooka* (November 1945) a home for the next sixteen years.

A number of minor short-lived publishers also sprang up in this post-war year. Typical among them was Enwill Associates, or Rural Home, which published a mishmash of humor, adventure, and superhero titles like *Red Circle Comics* (January 1945), *Red Band Comics* (February 1945), *Cannonball Comics*

Miss Cairo Jones #1, © *1945 Croydon Publishing Co.*

Red Circle #1, © 1945 Enwill Associates Inc.

New Funnies #96, © 1945 Dell Publishing Company

(February 1945), *Laffy Daffy Comics* (February 1945), *Mask Comics* (February 1945) and *Eagle* (February 1945).

This was also the year that comic-book godfather Max Gaines sold his superhero properties and broke with DC Comics. He formed his own company, Educational Comics (which was best known, after a name change to Entertaining Comics a few years later, as EC). Gaines wanted to pursue his long-time dream of using comic books for educational purposes.

Gaines already had developed *Picture Stories from the Bible* while at DC. He used that comic to form the basis of an educational comic-book series that eventually contained such titles as *Picture Stories from American History*, *Picture Stories from Science*, and *Picture Stories from World History*.

As paper restrictions eased with the ending of the war, the comic-book industry could resume its delayed growth. There were 157 comic-book titles published this year—the highest number since the industry began twelve years earlier.

1946: EVERYBODY READS COMICS!

By 1946, comic-book reading was an established habit—some might say an addiction—among almost all children of the time. Nine out of every ten children between the ages of eight and fifteen read comic books regularly.

As a result of this popularity, the comic-book habit was debated pro and con by educators and the media, such as in Mutual Broadcasting System's forum called "The Influence of Comics on Children."

Regardless of praise or damnation, comic books prospered. There were now approximately forty million comic books being published every month. The "Comic Magazine

Publishing Report" listed 157 active titles in 1946, with the leading publishers DC Comics, Fawcett Comics, Parents' Institute, Marvel Comics, Dell Publishing Company, Street and Smith, Famous Funnies, Quality Comics, United Features, and Educational Comics. These ten publishers accounted for over sixty percent of all the comic-book sales.

It's also interesting to notice what kind of new comics were introduced this year. Except for Marvel's *Blonde Phantom* (Winter 1946), there were almost no new superhero titles for the first time since 1939.

Educational comics were popular. DC Comics brought out *Real Fact* (March 1946), and George A. Pflaum launched his successful *Treasure Chest Comics* (March 1946) for Catholic-school students.

Funny-animal comics were still in demand.

Fairy Tale Parade #87, © 1945 Oskar Lebeck

"Starting in the 1940s there was a dramatic rise in the number of working girl comics published. The trend might be seen as a reaction to the maleless conditions brought about by the Second World War. . . . Whatever the reason for her appearance on the scene, the new careerwoman found a perfect home in the comics. The beautiful but dumb concept was rejected in favor of an image of the complete woman."
—CARL MACEK,
comic-book critic and historian

DC Comics issued *Animal Antics* (March 1946); EC Comics had *Animal Fables* (July 1946); and Fawcett added *Animal Fair* (March 1946) to the funny-animal stable.

The most welcomed new funny-animal title of 1946, however, was Walt Kelly's *Pogo Comics* (April 1946). From their beginning in *Animal Comics*, Pogo Possum, Albert the Alligator, Howland Owl, Churchy LaFemme, and all the other residents of Okefenokee Swamp now had a real home of their own.

Dell Comics, through Western Publishing, also began a long and successful series of promotional comic books called *March of Comics*. The half-size comic books featured popular Dell characters and usually were given away as promotional items by department and shoe stores.

Famous Funnies, the first newsstand comic book, hit its all-time peak in annual circulation with nearly six million copies. There were clouds on the horizon, however, for the newspaper-reprint comics. In the next two years, *Famous Funnies* would experience a sixty percent drop in circulation. By 1949, it would sell barely a million and a half copies—about one quarter of its 1946 sales.

By the end of 1946 it seemed as if the industry had reached a plateau with super-heroes and other types of comics. The time was right for something new.

Millie The Model #2, © 1946 Marvel Entertainment Group, Inc.

Captain Marvel #66, © 1946 DC Comics, Inc.

Blackhawk #13, © 1946 Comic Magazines

Atomic Comics #2, © 1946 Green Publishing

million from the year before that. As the public's fascination with costumed characters faded in the postwar years, superheroes could no longer carry the industry.

Jack Kirby and Joe Simon, superhero creators in their own right, were searching for alternatives to the costumed comic-book hero. They wanted to reach an older and more adult reader, so they came up with the idea of a romance comic that would appeal to young women. Entitled *Young Romance* (September

Milt Gross Funnies #1, © 1947 Gross Publications, Inc.

1947), it was the first romance comic book and set the tone for hundreds of imitators.

This was also the year that William Gaines, the son of Max Gaines, took over as publisher of EC Comics following his father's death in a boating accident. Like his father, the younger Gaines was an innovator. He slowly began transforming his father's educational animated-cartoon comic books into a whole new line of ground-breaking titles. By the following year, Gaines would set the trend for the industry by introducing a series of crime, western, and love comics.

By the end of 1947 the future was starting to reveal itself: Superheroes were on the way down, and the new comic-book stars would be criminals, cowboys, and young lovers.

1947: ROMANTIC BEGINNINGS

The comic-book industry was still going strong in 1947. There were 198 comic-book titles published, an increase of over twenty-five percent from the previous year.

Charlton Comics and St. John Publishing began their successful comic-book publishing careers this year, and several other minor publishers began testing the waters.

There was, however, a sense of unease among comic-book makers. Circulation figures on almost all the superhero titles were falling. *Captain Marvel*, a good bellwether of the superhero market, had a drop-off of nearly a million from its annual circulation of the previous year, and a whopping two-and-a-half

1948: COWBOYS AND CRIMINALS

Guns erupted in 1948, as "shoot 'em ups" became the hot new trend in comic books.

Before this year, only a handful of western comics and just three crime comic books dotted the market. But between 1947 and 1948, Fawcett's western title *Hopalong Cassidy* doubled its annual circulation from over four million to more than eight million copies.

Quick to recognize a trend, DC Comics

"There was a need for adult oriented comics. I remembered back to my childhood to the love magazines, like *True Confessions*, that my parents used to read. That stuck with me; how popular this type of material was. That's what led to realistic romance comics."
—JOE SIMON, co-creator of *Young Romance Comics*

> "Sexy, wanton comics should not be published. No drawing should show a female indecently or unduly exposed and in no event more nude than in a bathing suit commonly worn in the United States."
> —Code of The Association of Comics Magazine Publishers (1948)

Phantom Lady #17, © 1948 Fox Features Syndicate

published *Western Comics* (January 1948) and *Dale Evans Comics* (September 1948). Next, it converted *All American Comics*, a superhero title, into a western comic called *All American Western* (November 1948).

Movie-star cowboys were popular as well. Besides *Tim Holt Comics* (1948) from Magazine Enterprises (ME Comics), there also was Fawcett's *Tom Mix Western* (January 1948). Marvel Comics preferred to rely upon original cowboy heroes, like its popular *Kid Colt Outlaw* (August 1948) and *Two Gun Kid* (March 1948).

Yet the growth in cowboy comics was dwarfed by the crime-comic boom this year. In 1947 the three crime comic books made up about one and a half percent of all comic-book titles published that year. By 1948, however,

thirty-eight crime comics suddenly represented fifteen percent of all comic-book titles! (From this peak, the number would drop to thirty-three titles the next year, then down to only ten by 1950.)

Lev Gleason's popular titles, *Crime Does Not Pay* and *Crime and Punishment*, reached their all-time high in sales in 1948, with over one and a half million copies sold each month.

Every publisher ran to climb on the crime-comic bandwagon. A small sampling of the new crime titles this year includes Ace's *Crime Must Pay the Penalty* (February 1948), Fox's *Crimes by Women* (June 1948), EC's *Crime Patrol* (Summer 1948), Hillman's *Crime Detective Cases* (March 1948), St. John's *Authentic Police Cases* (February 1948),

Marvel's *All-True Crime Cases* (February 1948), and DC's *Gang Busters* (January 1948).

Just about every publisher, no matter how big or small, published a crime comic in 1948. Even mild-mannered Dell Comics had its criminal entry with the first regular issue of *Dick Tracy Comics* (January 1948).

The rapid growth of crime comics soon attracted the attention of the media and educators. In 1948, *Time* magazine mentioned several "copycat" crimes by kids who had read these comics. The crime comics supposedly were implicated in several juvenile crimes, including a burglary, a hanging, and a murder by poisoning.

Dr. Frederic Wertham, senior psychiatrist for the New York Department of Hospitals, presided over a symposium called "The Psychopathology of Comic Books." The doctor concluded that comic books glorified crime and violence, terming them "abnormally sexually aggressive."

This same year an ABC radio broadcast, called "What's Wrong With Comics?", was another of the many factors which prompted the formation of citizens' groups to push for regulation and, in some cases, the banning of certain comic-book titles from local newsstands. There were even a few comic-book bonfires on school grounds!

In response to the criticism of their comic books, publishers Bill Gaines (EC), Leverett Gleason (Lev Gleason), Harold Moore (Famous Funnies), and Rae Herman (Orbit), plus distributors Irving Manheimer and Frank Armer, formed the Association of Comics Magazine Publishers (ACMP) in July 1948.

The ACMP set up a code of standards for decency in comic books. Any comic book which met those standards could carry the ACMP seal as a stamp of approval. The idea was that all publishers would self-regulate the contents of their comics.

This early attempt at setting an industry code quickly failed, however, because it could not gain industry-wide support. The major publishers simply boycotted the ACMP, and the smaller publishers, some of whom relied on cheesecake and blood to sell their books, certainly were not interested either.

But for all the murder and mayhem this year, love also was afoot. Marvel Comics published the second romance title, *My Romance* (September 1948), the same month Fox released *My Life* (September 1948). Fawcett's *Sweethearts* (October 1948), along with Prize's original *Young Romance*, brought the total number of romance comics to four.

Crime, cowboys, and lovers—the comic-book industry was picking up steam. Some 239 titles were published this year, over twenty percent more than the previous year and fifty percent more than the year before that.

Murder Incorporated, © *1948 Fox Features Syndicate*

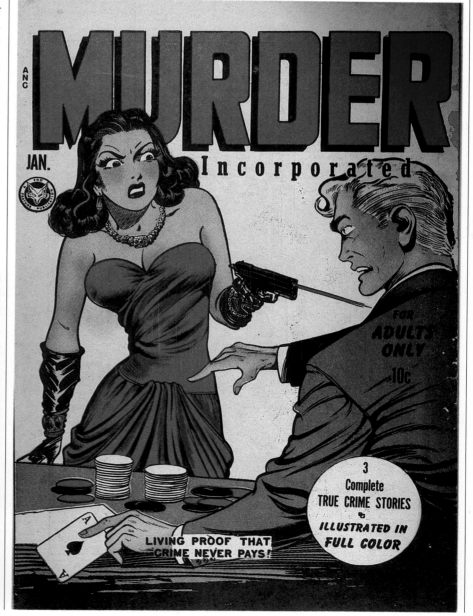

Crime Does Not Pay #60, © *1948 Lev Gleason Publications*

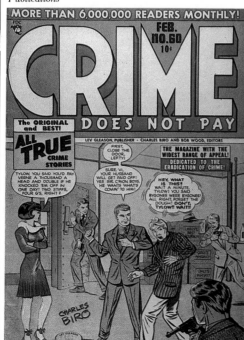

Gangsters Can't Win #3, © 1948 D.S. Publishing, Inc.

Young Love, © 1949 Crestwood Publishing Co., Inc.

1949: LOVE FOR SALE

Love triumphed in 1949. Romance comics suddenly became big—very big. By June, nine publishers were putting out twenty-one romance-comic titles. Before the end of the year, there would be ninety-nine romance comics issued by twenty-two publishers!

Romance comics became the fastest growing comic-book genre of all time. By mid-1949 Fox Comics alone accounted for eighteen romance titles. Marvel eventually had over thirty romance comics in its stable.

Soon romance comics were merging with and replacing other genres of comics. Prize Comics married the cowboy to the cowgirl in its *Real West Romance*. Marvel Comics axed the Human Torch, Blonde Phantom, and Sub-Mariner, so that their books could be turned into *Love Tales*, *Lovers*, and *Best Love*, respectively.

Not all superheroes were in disfavor, however. DC gave *Superboy* (March 1949) his own book, although it was about the only new superhero title this year.

Now western, crime, and romance comics were accounting for the majority of sales. Teenage humor comics also were booming. *Archie's Pal Jughead* got his own comic that year, as did the clothes horse and glamour girl, *Katy Keene*.

The comic-book business continued to grow at a breakneck pace. The 301 titles published this year represented another twenty-five percent increase over the previous year.

All was not rosy, however. The media was giving comic books increasingly unfavorable attention. *Parents Magazine*, for example, published the 1949 findings of a Cincinnati Committee on the Evaluation of Comic Books. This stated that seventy percent of all comic books contained objectionable material—

First Love #1, © 1949 Harvey Features Syndicate

Superboy #1, © 1949 DC Comics, Inc.

"I remember a little epic called 'The Sewer Monsters.' It got to be a contest to see how many running sores you could get on a guy's body before you lost your lunch."
—**HOWARD NOSTRAND,**
1950s horror artist

from scenes of sadistic torture to suggestive and salacious actions.

And, as a result of such attention, some thirty-two bills or resolutions introduced in sixteen states directly affected the sale of comic books to children.

1950: GASP! CHOKE! IT'S EC!

If nothing else happened this year but the birth of EC Comics, that would be enough. In 1950 William Gaines, along with Al Feldstein, decided to launch a whole new line of comic books under the imprint of Entertaining Comics (EC).

Their first three titles, *Vault of Horror* (April 1950), *Crypt of Terror* (April 1950), and *Haunt of Fear* (May 1950), launched the 1950's boom in horror comics. Their two science-fiction titles, *Weird Fantasy* (May 1950) and *Weird Science* (May 1950), featured some of the best comic-book artwork and stories of the decade.

Along with these titles, Gaines also issued the most adult crime comic, *Crime Suspenstories* (October 1950), as well as the world's most carefully researched war comic, *Two Fisted Tales* (November 1950). For the next four years, EC Comics would set standards, spawn imitators, and develop a fierce loyalty among its readers.

Still, most of the new books introduced this year were romance or westerns. But some interest was beginning to be shown in other genres as well. Marvel's *War Comics* (December 1950) heralded the coming boom in war comics. New science-fiction comics also started to appear, like DC's *Strange Adventures* (August 1950) and Youthful's *Captain Science* (November 1950) drawn by EC science-fiction artist, Wally Wood.

THE OLD WITCH   THE VAULT-KEEPER   THE CRYPT-KEEPER

© *William M. Gaines*

> "Horror comic books assume their readers to be little monsters with the brain of a child, the sex drive of a satyr and the spiritual delicacy of a gorilla."
> —DR. LAWRENCE AVERILL,
> *The New York Times*
> (December 28, 1949)

> "We never underestimated our audience and we always wrote to *our* level. . . . We were writing for teenagers and young adults; we were writing for the guys that were reading it in the Army. We were writing for ourselves at our age level, and I think perhaps that was responsible for the level we reached."
> —AL FELDSTEIN,
> editor and writer, EC Comics

Crime comic books, however, were still on the public's mind. In 1950, a Senate Committee report investigated the effects of crime comic books upon juvenile-delinquency rates from 1945 to 1950. The findings were inconclusive to say the least, although the report mildly slapped comic books which glorified crime and made criminals into heroes.

Besides comparing crime comics and juvenile-delinquency rates, the report contained some very interesting findings about comic-book readership in general this year. For example, a Dayton, Ohio, study uncovered these facts:

• Nearly forty percent of everyone over the age of eight had read a comic book in the past four months.

• Almost thirty-five percent of the entire population had read a comic book within the past thirty days.

• Fifty-four percent of all comic-book readers were adults over twenty years of age, a slight increase in adult readers from a similar survey taken two years before.

• Every comic book was read by three to four different readers.

• The average number of comic books read by each person during the previous month was about fifteen comics.

Cowgirl Romance, © 1950 Fiction House, Inc.

LOVE IS WHERE YOU FIND IT

Master Comics #115, © 1950 Fawcett Publications, Inc.

• Although children read more comic books than adults, the average adult reader read about eleven comics each month.

• Adult comic-book readers varied little according to education or occupation, but white-collar workers read more comics than any other group.

• The division of readership among both adults and children was nearly equal, with fifty-two percent male and forty-eight percent female.

The findings show two things. First, a substantial proportion of all people from all backgrounds and ages read comic books in 1950. Second, they read a *lot* of comic books, and read them regularly.

By 1950, fifty million comic books were being published every month—over a half billion a year—for an annual industry revenue of nearly forty-one million dollars.

1951: ADVENTURES INTO TERRIFYING HORROR

Horror comics suddenly became the next new trend. Before EC published its three horror comics in 1950, ACG's *Adventure into the Un-*

known had been the only regularly published horror comic book. In 1951, ACG added a companion title, *Forbidden Worlds* (July 1951), featuring its standard lineup of ghouls, zombies and werewolves.

Marvel Comics, which had been publishing horror comics sporadically since 1949, began its longest running horror title this year with *Strange Tales* (June 1951).

Harvey Comics came out with two titles, which were more than coincidentally similar to the EC horror line. Both *Witches Tales* (January 1951) and *Chamber of Chills* (June 1951) featured horror hosts and plots very similar to the EC books.

Haunt of Fear #8, © 1951 William M. Gaines

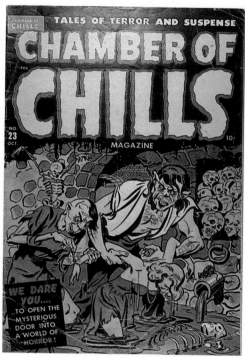

Chamber of Chills #23, © 1951 Harvey Features Syndicate

Strange Mysteries #1, © 1951 Superior Publishers Ltd.

The horror genre would attract many smaller publishers, as well. Superior Comics, a Canadian publisher, began exporting thrills and gore galore in its two new books, *Strange Mysteries* (September 1951) and *Adventure into Fear* (1951). Story Comics's *Mysterious Adventures* (March 1951) and Aragon's *Mr. Mystery* (September 1951) also were splashing plenty of blood and bones around the newsstands.

Once EC showed other publishers how to do them, science-fiction comics also became more popular. DC's entry was called *Mystery in Space* (April 1951), while Avon launched several versions, including *Earthman on Venus* and *Space Detective* (July 1951).

Victor Fox, a publisher who probably would have enjoyed exploiting both the horror and science-fiction genres, instead went out of business this year—taking with him a large chunk of the romance- and crime-comic titles.

For almost everyone else, however, the boom years were just beginning.

1952: THIS MEANS WAR!

The Korean War began in 1950. For the first time in six years, the United States was again preoccupied with war and combat. Teenage boys and young men were especially interested in learning more about war and Korea, even if only through the pages of comic books. The comic-book publishers quickly obliged them, by launching a blitz of war-comic titles that probably contained more casualties than the entire Korean "police action."

Marvel Comics showed present and potential servicemen what war was all about, at least comic-book style, in its issues of *War Adventures* (January 1952) and *War Action* (April 1952). DC fought World War II again, as well as the Korean War, in *Star Spangled War Stories* (August 1952) and *Our Army at War* (August 1952). The year saw almost all

Baseball Thrills #2, © 1951 Ziff-Davis Publishing Co.

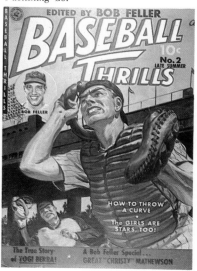

I GUESS HAND TO HAND COMBAT WAS STRICTLY FOR THE OLDEN DAYS WHEN EVERYONE FOUGHT WITH SWORDS AND KNIVES! NOW WITH ALL THE LONG RANGE WEAPONS, WE CAN KILL PRETTY GOOD BY REMOTE CONTROL! AND WE NEVER GET CLOSER'N A MILE TO THE ENEMY!

Two-Fisted Tales #25, © 1952 William M. Gaines

the publishers produce dozens of war titles, like *War Heroes*, *War Fury*, *Battle Cry*, and *Fighting Leathernecks*.

The year was also a peak period for both romance comics and horror comics. Taken to-

Combat #5, © 1952 Marvel Entertainment Group, Inc.

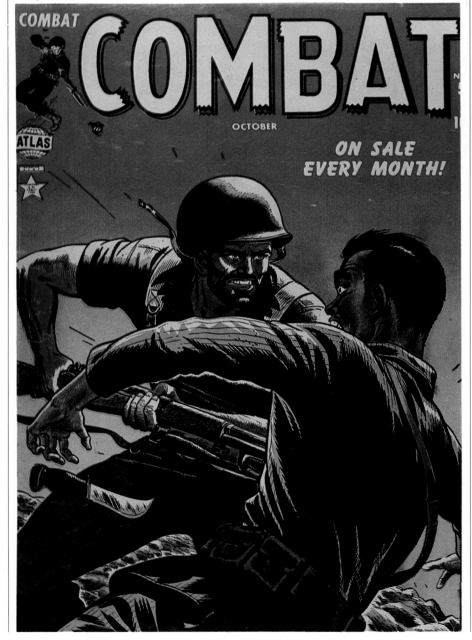

gether, romance and horror comics made up nearly half of all comics published in 1952.

Crime comics were slowly being phased out in favor of more horror titles. Marvel changed its *Amazing Detective* (March 1952) from a crime to a horror format, and Hillman joined both genres together in *Monster Crime Comics* (October 1952).

Another trend-setting comic book this year was the first issue of *Mad* (October 1952), later converted to the magazine format we know today. *Mad* magazine would be responsible for spawning dozens of imitations and

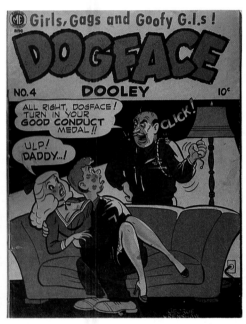

Dogface Dooley #4, © 1952 Sussex Publishing Company

also blamed for ruining the young minds of an entire generation.

Although most superheroes were in semi-retirement, DC's "Superman" titles were still strong sellers and prompted the premiere of the "Superman" television show that year.

For now, the comic-book industry was on a runaway train ride. Crime, horror, western, romance, teen, humor, war—almost any type of comic book was being published, bought, and read. In fact, a new title was being introduced almost every three days by publishers old and new.

1953: COMIC BOOKS THAT JUMP OFF THE PAGES

In the flush of ever-expanding growth, the comic-book industry was ripe for new gimmicks and innovative ways to sell even more books.

In 1953, Joe Kubert and Norman Mauer, childhood friends who had cartooned together and were now working as comic-book artists, came up with the idea of three-dimensional comic books—images that would jump right off the pages when viewed through blue and red cellophane glasses.

They took the idea to St. John Publishing,

Super-Duperman from Mad #4, © 1953 William M. Gaines

which achieved the distinction of being the first 3-D comic-book publisher. *Three Dimensional Comics* (September 1953) starred a Mighty Mouse that flew right out of the comic when you wore the accompanying 3-D glasses. Although priced at twenty-five cents, fifteen cents more than the usual price, the first printing of one-and-a-quarter million sold out quickly, and a second printing was done the next month.

The following month, St. John published seven 3-D comic books, and other publishers started taking notice. By December, sixteen publishers were putting out thirty 3-D comic books. Almost none of the 3-D comics made it past their first issue, however, and by February 1954 the 3-D fad was completely over.

World's Finest #64, © 1953 DC Comics, Inc.

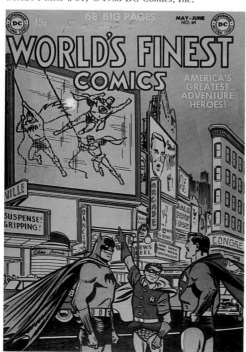

The superhero era officially ended this year, as well. Fawcett Publications published its last issue of *Captain Marvel* in November 1953, axed by a twelve-year-old DC Comics's lawsuit alleging copyright infringement of Superman. The Marvel Family of superheroes was no more. DC Comics's Batman, Superman, and Wonder Woman were the only major surviving superheroes from the 1940s.

Almost every other type of comic book, however, was still selling phenomenally well. During the first three months of 1953, Dell Comics alone printed two hundred fifty million comic books—an all-time high for any comic-book publisher before or since.

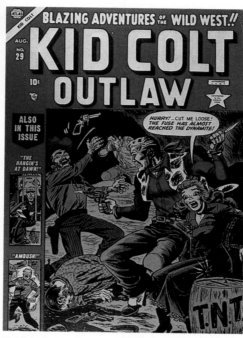

Kid Colt Outlaw #29, © 1953 Marvel Entertainment Group, Inc.

By September of 1953, there were over five hundred comic-book titles on sale—far more than any previous time in history. The average monthly circulation of the comic books this year was sixty-eight million copies—four times higher than ten years before. As incredible as it sounds, the next year would be even better!

1954: SEDUCTION OF THE INNOCENT

Three significant things happened in 1954. Dr. Frederic Wertham, a long-time vociferous critic of the comic-book industry, published *Seduction of the Innocent*, a book which detailed the allegedly ill effects upon children of reading comic books containing crime, sex, and violence.

Next, the U.S. Senate Subcommittee to Investigate Juvenile Delinquency in the United States held public hearings on the deleterious effects of comic books on children.

Finally, in October 1954, comic-book publishers established the self-regulatory Comics Code Authority which imposed a strict set of

Fantastic Fears, © 1953 Farrell Comics, Inc.

"I did a lot of horror for Timely [Marvel]. It's strange how weird some of that stuff got. I didn't notice it at first because it got progressively more bizarre until you had all this rotting flesh falling off ribs. It was all meant in the spirit of fun."
—RUSS HEATH,
Marvel and DC Comics artist

Spellbound #20, © 1954 Marvel Entertainment Group, Inc.

industry standards upon comic books. All these events would change comic books forever, and not necessarily for the better.

Wertham's *Seduction of the Innocent* is usually hailed as a classic example of research based upon anecdote as fact and guilt by association: Abnormal and delinquent kids read comic books; therefore, comic books cause abnormal behavior and delinquency! No matter that over ninety percent of *all* children read comic books at this time, with surprisingly few ax-murderers among them.

Still, the extracted pictures from some of the crime and horror comics which Wertham used to illustrate his book were powerful images, especially out of context. It was not a

good year to be a comic-book publisher.

It was an especially bad year if you happened to be William Gaines, the publisher of perhaps the best known horror and crime comics, EC Comics. At the aforementioned Senate investigation, Gaines was put in the uncomfortable position of having to defend how much blood could be shown dripping from a severed woman's neck before the comic would be unsuitable for children to read.

The Senate's report on "Comic Books and Delinquency" said in its conclusions that "this country cannot afford the calculated risk involved in feeding its children, through comic books, a concentrated diet of crime, horror, and violence." The report further con-

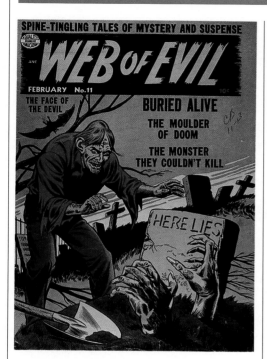

Web of Evil #11, © 1954 Comic Magazines

Code. The company went out of business this year, along with other smaller publishers like Comic Media, Timor Publishing, and Stanhall Publications.

The distribution system for comic books also underwent radical changes this year, and a major shakeout in distributors and news-stand agents was forthcoming. The real blood-bath, however, would occur in the next two years, as the industry was to feel the full and depressing effect of the Comics Code.

1955: THE GREAT CHANGE

With publication of the March 1955 issues, almost all major publishers had the Comics Code Authority "seal of approval" embla-zoned on the covers of their comic books. Many scrambled to make the last-minute changes in their books that the new Code re-quired. Artists frantically inked over plunging cleavage and erased away blazing guns so that stories already produced could be published

cluded that there must be a standard for comic books in the form of a code which would eliminate everything in a comic story that could demoralize youth or even "*potentially* exert detrimental effects."

A backlash by comic-book distributors and retailers hammered the final nail in the coffin.

The result of this whirlwind of bad publicity was the establishment of the Code of the Com-ics Magazine Association of America on Oc-tober 26, 1954. The Comics Magazine Asso-ciation of America, which consisted of all comic-book publishers that wanted to get their comic books distributed, drafted one of the strictest codes of any entertainment industry. The Code's emphasis was on eliminating all traces of crime, horror, violence, and sex in the comic books, with some minor provisions regarding acceptable advertising and treat-ment of religious figures.

For many comic-book readers, the new Code effectively gelded their favorite titles. Horror and crime comics almost vanished (they learned to rely more on suspense than slaughter), romance comics became less adult, westerns had less gunplay, and even the funny-animal comics had to tone down their rambunctious byplay. EC Comics had to re-name and reorganize its entire line of comics in order to get them distributed.

Before the Code was established at the end of October, there had been six hundred fifty titles published this year—an all-time high—with an amazing one hundred fifty million issues published *every* month. The industry was enjoying an annual revenue of ninety mil-lion dollars on a product that cost ten cents.

With the coming of the Code and the public outcry about comic books, the bubble burst. Fiction House Comics, whose beautifully en-dowed women and violent fighting men ap-peared on every comic-book cover, could no longer publish its material under the new

Space Adventures #12, © 1954 Charlton Comics, Inc.

True Crime #2, © 1947 Magazine Village

"All scenes of horror, excessive bloodshed, gory or gruesome crimes, depravity, lust, sadism, masochism shall not be permitted."
—The Code

under the new Code restrictions.

William Gaines at EC Comics responded to the new Code by replacing his horror comics with titles like *Psychoanalysis*, *Extra*, and *Impact*. These "New Direction" comics dealt with material that fell within the Code's guidelines, but distribution problems would kill off the entire EC comic-book line within the year.

Stanley P. Morse, another publisher who had depended heavily upon horror comics, shut down all four of his comic-book publishing companies. Star Publications, Sterling Comics, Toby Press, United Feature, and Eastern Color also went out of business this year. While most of the failed publishers were somewhat small, both United and Eastern had been successful in the field since its inception.

Marvel Comics finally retired its superhero division this year with the last issue of *Sub-Mariner Comics*. Marvel had revived the Sub-Mariner, along with the Human Torch and Captain America, a few months earlier for a 1950s Cold War comeback. Not even Marvel's most popular heroes, however, could spark new interest in superhero comics. Other minor 1950s superheroes, like Avenger, Strong Man, Captain Flash, and Black Cobra, also went under this year.

There were some new titles, however, among the gravestones. DC Comics modified its existing science-fiction and suspense comics so that they would meet with Code approval. It also added a new mystery title, *My Greatest Adventure* (January 1955), in an effort to appeal to the horror-comic fan who was now without his or her favorite titles. Charlton Comics, too, reached for the ex-horror-comic reader with its *Unusual Tales* (August 1955).

In this uncertain year DC Comics was also willing to test a new type of comic book. *Brave and Bold* (August 1955), an anthology of medieval superheroes, featured stories of the Viking Prince, the Silent Knight, and Robin Hood.

Dell Comics, perhaps the publisher least affected by the Comics Code, was prospering.

Sub-Mariner #42, © 1955 Marvel Entertainment Group, Inc.

Its chief mainstays of funny-animal and western comics were ideally suited to the times, and readership remained fairly steady.

For the most part, however, the Code seemed to have had a chilling effect on the comic-book industry. Although publishers brought out more romance, western, and humor comics to replace their horror and crime comics, the overall effect was a big drop in the number of titles.

From an all-time industry high of six hundred fifty titles in 1954, there were now barely more than three hundred titles—a fifty percent-plus drop. Artists and writers left the

Lorna Jungle Girl #16, © 1955 Marvel Entertainment Group, Inc.

Tonto #18, © 1955 Lone Ranger, Inc.

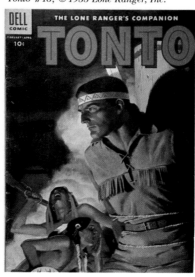

Impact #1, © 1955 William M. Gaines

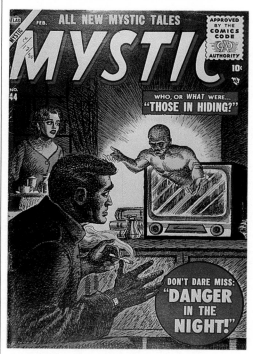

Mystic #44, © 1956 Marvel Entertainment Group, Inc.

field, publishers closed their doors, and circulation fell.

1956: DYING EMBERS, NEW BEGINNINGS

Many comic-book publishers, who had struggled through a year of declining sales after the inception of the Comics Code, finally gave up in 1956.

EC Comics shut down its post-Code line of comic books and became a one-publication company with *Mad* magazine. Quality Comics, a leading publisher all through the 1940s, sold its war and romance titles, along with *Blackhawk*, to DC Comics, then went out of business. Lev Gleason, whose crime comics could arguably be cited as one of the major reasons for the Comics Code, also went under this year. Others among the dying and dead were Ace Comics, Avon Publications, Premier Magazines, Superior Comics, and Premier Publishing.

For the first time since 1934, not one new comic-book publisher could be found. It was truly the industry's nadir.

Yet among these dying embers a few flames still burned steadily and even began to flare up over the old ground. DC, Marvel, Charlton, Archie, and Harvey Comics remained surprisingly strong and able to take advantage of the shakeout in the industry.

Besides buying up some of the Quality Comic titles, DC even added to its growing line of mystery comics with *Tales of the Unexpected* (February 1956) and *House of Secrets* (November 1956).

Marvel Comics, too, saw opportunities in the science-fiction and suspense comic fields. This year they issued *Mystical Tales* (June 1956), *World of Suspense* (April 1956), *World*

of Fantasy (May 1956), and *World of Mystery* (June 1956).

Charlton Comics also joined the fantasy "worlds" with *Out of This World* (August 1956) and *Mysteries of Unexplored Worlds* (August 1956). In addition, Charlton checked out the strength of both the romance market, with *Brides in Love* (August 1956), and the superhero market, with *Nature Boy* (March 1956).

Harvey Comics launched one of their long-running and successful characters with *Baby Huey* (September 1956), a duckling behemoth in diapers.

Finally, in the early fall, DC Comics published the comic book that would resuscitate the dying industry. *Showcase #4* (October 1956) introduced a brand-new superhero: Flash, the fastest man alive. The 1956 Flash, by Gardner Fox (writer) and Carmine Infantino (artist), actually was a revival and revision of the original 1940s DC superhero.

This sparked one of the most significant trends in comic-book history: the revival and updating of the original 1940s superheroes for a new audience. Flash launched the Second

Showcase #4, © 1956 DC Comics, Inc.

Walt Disney's Comics #200, © 1957 Walt Disney Productions

Man in Black #3, © 1957 Harvey Features
Syndicate

Heroic Age ("Silver Age") of comics and assured the future of comic books.

1957: A SHOWCASE OF HEROES

As soon as DC was able to digest the fat sales
figures of the *Showcase* appearance of the new
Flash, it quickly brought him back for a second appearance in *Showcase #8* (June 1957).

Showcase had now become DC's testing
ground for potential new characters and titles.
Two issues earlier, Jack Kirby had created a
team of heroic adventurers called the Challengers of the Unknown for *Showcase #6* and
#7 (February/April 1957). Superman's girl
friend, Lois Lane, also got her title tryout in
Showcase this year.

Noticing DC's success with its revival of the

Flash, Harvey Comics reached back to the
1940s and updated Bob Powell's *Man in Black*
(September 1957), a mysterious figure who
served as host for the book's suspense stories. Harvey also made use of Jack Kirby's
talents with a new science-fiction anthology called *Alarming Tales* (September 1957).
And, for the kiddies, Harvey gave *Hot Stuff*
(October 1957), the baby devil in diapers, his
own book.

Marvel Comics made 1957 the year of
the Kid Cowboy, with *Kid from Texas* (June
1957), *Kid from Dodge City* (July 1957), and
Kid Slade Gunfighter (January 1957).

Meanwhile, Charlton Comics was engaging
in both love and war with *First Kiss* (December 1957) and *Battlefield Action* (November 1957).

Westerns, war, romances, teen titles, and
humor comics still formed the backbone of the

comic-book industry. With the second appearance of the Flash, however, the superhero revival was one giant step closer.

1958: FLASH AND THE LEGION OF SUPERHEROES

It seems as though DC could not believe its good fortune. After introducing the Flash two years earlier, it waited until this year to bring him back for third and fourth "tryout" appearances in *Showcase #13* and *#14* (April, June 1958). DC still was not certain if the Flash would pull in enough readers to justify his own book.

The decision to give *Lois Lane* (March 1958) her own title was made easier because of the overall strength of the Superman family of comics, under editor Mort Weisinger. DC also felt that the *Challengers of the Unknown* (April 1958), under the hands of their creator, Jack Kirby, would prosper in their own book.

This year saw the introduction of the Legion of Super Heroes in *Adventure Comics #247* (April 1958). The Legion was a team of twenty-sixth-century teenage superheroes who developed a rich history and fan following that peaked in the '80s.

Harvey Comics was exploring the science-fiction field with *Race for the Moon* (March 1958), which featured art by Jack Kirby, Al Williamson, and Bob Powell. The title lasted three issues.

Gilberton, the publisher of *Classics Illustrated* comics, added another title to its line of educational comics. Called *The World Around Us* (September 1958), each issue focused on a topic such as Indians, horses, space, or prehistoric animals.

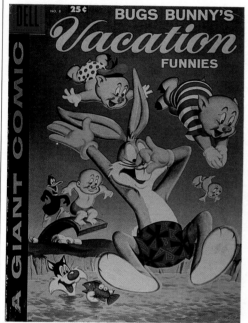

Bugs Bunny's Vacation Funnies #8, © 1958 Warner Bros. Pictures
Race for the Moon #3, © 1958 Harvey Features Syndicate

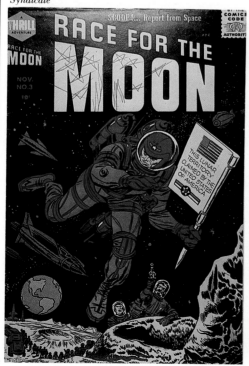

Lois Lane #5, © 1958 DC Comics, Inc.

> "Evolution transformed my race so we could eat *anything* without being harmed! No matter where or how a foe imprisons us, I could always *eat* our way to freedom!"
> —MATTER-EATER LAD,
> member of the Legion Of Super-Heroes, *Adventure Comics #303*

Showcase #22, © 1959 DC Comics, Inc.

This year also marked the demise of the few remaining marginal publishers from the 1940s and 1950s. Magazine Enterprises (ME), Farrell Comics Group, and St. John Publishing, which had been surviving on reprinted comics and recycled characters, vanished. With their passing, the way was clear for a new era of comics to begin.

1959: THE RETURN OF THE SUPERHEROES

DC Comics was sufficiently impressed by the Flash's performance in the four *Showcase* issues to give him his own book with *Flash #105* (March 1959), a continuation of its original 1940s title.

Julius Schwartz, the editor responsible for the revival of the Flash, next turned to another superhero character he had edited during the 1940s, the Green Lantern. Like the Flash, the new Green Lantern was a complete overhaul

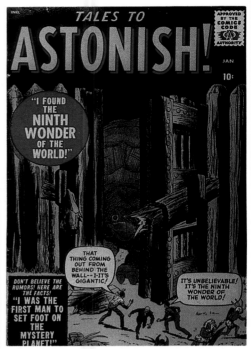

Tales to Astonish #1, © 1959 Marvel Entertainment Group, Inc.

Tales of Suspense #1, © 1959 Marvel Entertainment Group, Inc.

of his Golden Age namesake. Drawn by Gil Kane and written by Gardner Fox, the Green Lantern first appeared in *Showcase #22* (October 1959) for what would be a successful three-issue tryout.

Two other popular *Showcase* characters were also given their own regular series. Adam Strange, a twentieth-century space traveler, began his adventures in *Mystery in Space #53* (August 1959). Drawn by Carmine Infantino, the artist of the *Flash*, Adam Strange was perhaps DC's best science-fiction series. Another spaceman from *Showcase*, the Space Ranger, got his series in *Tales of the Unexpected #40* (1959). His adventures tended more toward space opera and bug-eyed monsters than the more cerebral Adam Strange *Mystery in Space* episodes.

The other big news at DC Comics this year was the first appearance of Supergirl in *Action Comics #252* (May 1959). The teenage cousin of Superman usually appeared in romantic adventures aimed at young girls. The popular series ran in various titles for twenty-five years.

The first comic-book publisher to take notice of DC's success with its new superheroes was Archie Comics. Archie Comics engaged the services of Jack Kirby and Joe Simon, the creators of Captain America, to revive their patriotic superhero of the 1940s, the Shield. Simon and Kirby updated the Golden Age hero and featured the new Shield in a comic book called *The Double Life of Private Strong*

(June 1959). The title referred to the Shield's dual secret identity as a serviceman, but it must have been too obtuse for the 1959 newsstand market. The comic lasted only two issues.

Undaunted, Simon and Kirby next tried their hands at creating a brand-new superhero for Archie Comics. This time they were more successful. The *Adventures of the Fly* (August 1959) featured a superhero who derived his insect-like powers from the fly world. Later renamed the *Fly Man*, the popular hero would survive for over twenty years.

For the time being, Marvel Comics ignored the superhero efforts of DC Comics and Archie Comics. Since Marvel's better selling books last year had been science-fiction and mystery titles, they added two more this year: *Tales to Astonish* (January 1959) and *Tales of*

The Fly #2, © 1959 Archie Comics Publications, Inc.

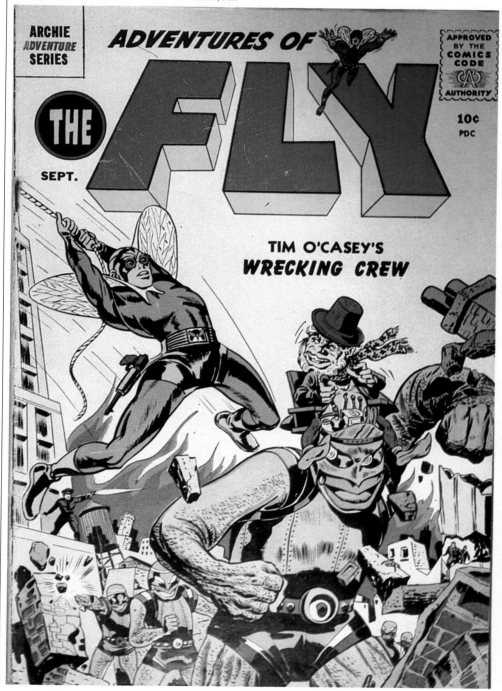

House of Secrets #21, © 1959 DC Comics, Inc.

> "As far as the Justice League of America stories were concerned, there were so many characters and so little space to devote to each one, the marvel of it is that we could finish the story in the allotted number of pages."
> —GARDNER FOX,
> writer and creator of the
> *Justice League of America*

Brave and Bold #28, © *1960 DC Comics, Inc.*

Suspense (January 1959).

Both books had a standard four-story format with a fairly consistent lineup of artists. Jack Kirby was one of those artists—the same Jack Kirby who was developing new superheroes for Archie Comics this year, as well. Soon the mixture of Jack Kirby, superheroes, and Marvel Comics would percolate and explode. For now, however, the superhero comic book again belonged to DC Comics.

1960: THE WORLD'S GREATEST HEROES

It had worked twenty years ago. DC Comics had put all of its 1940 superheroes into one title, *All Star Comics.* Now with 1960's revival of the Flash and Green Lantern, DC had enough superheroes to form a new team title. Superman, Batman, Wonder Woman, Flash, Green Lantern, and the Martian Manhunter teamed up to form the Justice League of America in *Brave and Bold Comics #28* (March 1960).

Two more tryout issues followed, then the "world's greatest heroes" were awarded their own title with *Justice League of America* (October 1960). The comic was extraordinarily popular, and as additional DC superheroes arrived throughout the 1960s, they were also inducted into the title.

Meanwhile, DC had already given *Green Lantern* (August 1960) his own title. *Flash*

Although ostensibly a career woman, Lois Lane would shamelessly debase herself at any opportunity in order to entrap Superman in marriage. *Lois Lane #19,* © *August 1960 DC Comics, Inc.*

Comics became another fertile ground for 1960 superheroes. Kid Flash, a teenage version of the adult Flash, appeared in *Flash #110* (January 1960). Two issues later, a stretchable sleuth called the Elongated Man debuted in *Flash #112*. Bearing more than a resemblance to the old Quality Comics's Plastic Man, the Elongated Man was one of the first superheroes to go public with his secret identity.

Charlton Comics was the third publisher to enter the superhero market. Steve Ditko, who was drawing monster stories along with Jack Kirby for Marvel Comics, also had been drawing science-fiction stories for various Charlton titles like *Space War* and *Outer Space*. For *Space Adventures #33* (March 1960), Ditko created an atomic-powered superhero called Captain Atom. Captain Atom thrived for over a year before Ditko left Charlton to do more work for Marvel Comics.

ACG, the publisher of *Forbidden Worlds* and *Adventures into the Unknown*, decided that the time was right for a third science-

Jughead's Fantasy #1, © *1960 Archie Comic Publications, Inc.*

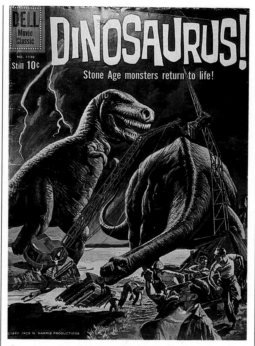

Dinosaurs #1120, © *1960 Western Publishing Co.*

fiction title. *Unknown Worlds* (August 1960) continued the ACG tradition of gentle ghost tales and moralistic space fables.

Although its arrival was not as dramatic as the new wave of superheroes, Harvey Comics's *Richie Rich Comics* (November 1960) would eventually spin off more than forty associated Richie Rich titles over the next twenty-five years!

1961: THE WORLD'S GREATEST COMIC MAGAZINE

The next one of DC's 1940s heroes up for revival was Hawkman from the old *Flash Comics*. Julius Schwartz assigned the art chores to former Hawkman artist, Joe Kubert, who updated the hero for *Brave and Bold #34* (March 1961).

Next, DC reincarnated the 1940s Atom in *Showcase Comics #34* (October 1961). Whereas the old Atom was merely a midget-sized superhero, the new Atom could shrink all the way down to subatomic size.

Flash #123, © *1961 DC Comics, Inc.*

"I won't tell you any lies. I might fantasize. I might dramatize, and I might make my characters with a little more flourish, but they'll never lie to you. They'll always be the truth. You'll find that element in them and you'll accept them."
—JACK KIRBY,
co-creator of the Fantastic Four

Fantastic Four #1, © 1961 Marvel Entertainment Group, Inc.

Schwartz was so busy editing his new superhero titles that his two other titles, *All Star Western* and *Western Comics*, were canceled. The cycle was now complete. *All Star Western*, which had bumped DC's greatest team of superheroes from *All Star Comics* in 1951, was now a victim of the return (or revenge) of the superhero.

Meanwhile, Archie Comics brought out another superhero to keep the Fly company. The *Adventures of the Jaguar* (September 1961) featured a jungle superhero who could communicate with animals and fly through the air.

Earlier that year, Marvel Comics added *Amazing Adventures* (June 1961), a science-fiction title, to its lineup. Before the end of the year, it would be renamed *Amazing Adult Fantasy* and feature stories exclusively by Stan Lee and Steve Ditko.

Near the end of the year, Martin Goodman, the publisher of Marvel Comics, noticed that

All Star Western #118, © 1961 DC Comics, Inc.

Justice League of America was one of the industry's best selling titles. He gave writer Stan Lee the go ahead to develop a team of superheroes for Marvel as well. Lee, with co-creator Jack Kirby, his chief artist at the time, devised a team of original superheroes: a scientist who could stretch, a teenager who burst into flame, an invisible girl, and a monstrously ugly strongman. The four characters debuted as the *Fantastic Four* (November 1961), a comic which would later bill itself as the "World's Greatest Comic Magazine!"

The Fantastic Four were different from the DC superheroes. They weren't perfect or godlike. The Fantastic Four, and other Marvel heroes, had problems that surpassed the soap

Fantastic Four #3, © 1961 Marvel Entertainment Group

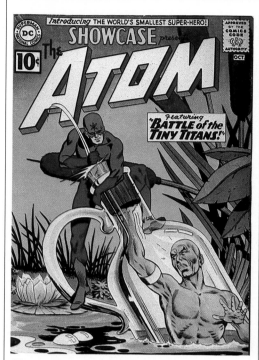

Showcase #34, © 1961 DC Comics, Inc.

operas. They behaved more like human beings who happened to be superheroes than heroes who happened to be human.

Nevertheless, 1961 belonged to DC Comics, especially as far as the fans were concerned. This year marked the beginning of annual fan awards, given by the newly formed Academy of Comic Book Arts and Sciences. These awards, called "Alleys" after Alley Oop, arguably the first comic-strip "superhero," went to the best comics of the year.

For 1961, the best title was *Justice League of America*, while Green Lantern was lauded as best hero. The best comic book of the year, however, was acclaimed to be *Flash Comics #123*, which featured the re-introduction of the 1940s Flash and the beginning of a revival of the original DC Golden Age superheroes.

1962: MIGHTY MARVEL

Both DC Comics and Marvel Comics were amazed by the reader response to their superhero revivals. For the first time in years, readers were actually writing to comic books! Letter columns were started to handle the new fan interest.

This was also the year that both Marvel and DC raised their cover prices from ten to twelve cents, and Dell went up to fifteen cents.

Encouraged by the reader response to the *Fantastic Four*, Stan Lee and Jack Kirby created the second Marvel Age superhero, the *Incredible Hulk* (May 1962). Transformed by gamma rays, Dr. Bruce Banner turns into the Hulk, a rampaging green brute. (The Hulk bore a faint resemblance to the giant monster characters that Jack Kirby also was drawing for Marvel's science-fiction books this year.)

Reaching back into the past, Lee and Kirby brought back the Sub-Mariner in *Fantastic Four #4* (1962). Now a super villain, the Sub-

Mariner was romantically attracted to Sue Storm, the Invisible Girl of the Fantastic Four.

The most significant comic book of 1962 was *Amazing Fantasy #15* (August 1962), a failing science-fiction anthology whose last issue featured a superhero called Spider-Man. Drawn by Steve Ditko, Spider-Man eventually became the most popular comic book character of the 1960s.

That same month, Lee and Kirby turned to another former science-fiction title, *Journey into Mystery*, and introduced a Norse god hero called Thor (*#83*, August 1962). For *Tales to Astonish*, Lee and Kirby created Ant-Man (*#35*, September 1962). The Human Torch was deemed the most popular member of the Fantastic Four and was given a solo strip in *Strange Tales #101* (October 1962).

By the end of 1962, Marvel had replaced most of its "monster from space" stories with exciting new superheroes. The Academy

Amazing Fantasy #15, © 1962 Marvel Entertainment Group, Inc.

**"Puny humans!"
—THE HULK,**
The Incredible Hulk #1 (March 1962)

12¢ **THE INCREDIBLE**

APPROVED
BY THE
COMICS
CODE
AUTHORITY

HULK

4
NOV.

2 FEATURE-LENGTH HULK THRILLERS IN THIS ISSUE!

"the MONSTER and the MACHINE!"

"MONGU!! GLADIATOR FROM SPACE!"

FANTASY AS YOU LIKE IT!

Incredible Hulk #4, © 1962 Marvel Entertainment Group, Inc.

Brave and Bold #42, © 1962 DC Comics, Inc.

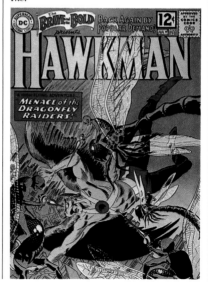

voted the *Fantastic Four* the best title of the year. DC Comics, however, still swept all the rest of the awards for 1962, with Hawkman as best hero, *Mystery in Space #75* as the best single comic, and *Brave and Bold #42* as the best cover this year.

DC Comics gave the *Atom* (June 1962) his own title after his *Showcase* appearances. Gil Kane, the artist for Green Lantern, continued drawing the adventures of the "world's mightiest mite."

The next tryouts for *Showcase #37* (April 1962) were the Metal Men, a team of automatons with human feelings. The Metal Men called Gold, Lead, Platinum, Iron, Mercury, and Tin would undergo destruction every issue, then be resurrected by their creator,

Dr. Magnus. By the next year they would earn their own book.

Although the Legion of Super Heroes had appeared irregularly in the "Superman" family of comics, they were granted a regular series beginning in *Adventure Comics #300* (September 1962). The Legion was composed of Superboy and other teenage superheroes like Lightning Lad, Saturn Girl, Colossal Boy, Bouncing Boy, Triplicate Lass, and Matter Eater Lad.

Gold Key, a new comic-book publisher, entered the field after splitting off from Dell Publishing. Gold Key's first comic book was *Dr. Solar, Man of the Atom* (October 1962), an atomic-powered superhero.

Adventure Comics #300, © 1962 DC Comics, Inc.

1963: SUPER TEAM-UPS

If one superhero was good, then a dozen must be better. Both Marvel and DC brought out several new superhero teams and groups all throughout 1963.

DC Comics brought back the first team of superheroes from the 1940s, the Justice Society of America, in a guest appearance in *Justice League of America #21* (August 1963). DC also gave the *Metal Men* (April 1963) their own book.

Another DC team of superheroes, the Doom Patrol, made its first appearance in *My Greatest Adventure #80* (June 1963). The Doom Patrol was a team of self-proclaimed freaks— Negative Man, Robotman, and Elasti-Girl— led by a wheelchair-bound doctor.

Marvel Comics now had enough heroes for a team title of its own. *Avengers* (September 1963) featured the Hulk, Thor, Ant-Man, and Iron Man. The membership of the Avengers would change over the years, yet the title always remained a showcase for Marvel's top team of superheroes.

That same month Marvel brought out another team of superheroes called the *X-Men* (September 1963). Jack Kirby and Stan Lee created the Angel, the Cyclops, the Beast, the Ice Man, and Marvel Girl, the first team of teenage mutants.

The last team title from Marvel this year was *Sgt. Fury and His Howling Commandos* (May 1963). An action-packed war comic with likeable characters and snappy writing, *Sgt. Fury* attracted both superhero and war-comic

Sgt. Fury #1, © 1963 Marvel Entertainment Group, Inc.

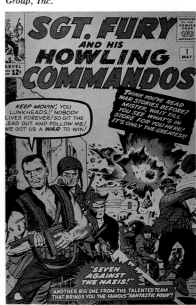

readers.

Marvel's last fantasy title, *Tales of Suspense*, became the home for a new armorplated hero called Iron Man (*#39*, March 1963). Dr. Strange, the Master of the Occult, began his transdimensional adventures in *Strange Tales #110* (July 1963).

The Amazing Spider-Man (March 1963) began his own comic book as well, and received 1963 Alley awards for both best hero and best title of the year.

1964: CAPTAIN AMERICA RETURNS!

By 1964, the Second Heroic Age was firmly established. Both Marvel and DC had launched new characters and titles that would

Tales to Astonish #39, © *1963 Marvel Entertainment Group, Inc.*

Avengers #1, © *1963 Marvel Entertainment Group, Inc.*

set the direction for both companies for the next twenty years.

With both the Human Torch and Sub-Mariner born again, Marvel brought back Captain America, the last of its big 1940s superheroes. In *Avengers #4* (March 1964), Captain America, frozen in suspended animation since the war years, thaws out and joins the Avengers. Appropriately enough, Jack Kirby drew the return of the superhero that he first created twenty-three years earlier.

The last major Marvel superhero of the early 1960s was *Daredevil* (May 1964), the Man Without Fear and, incidentally, without vision as well. The blind superhero relied upon his highly developed radar sense and acrobatic ability to foil super villains.

DC's big new book of the year was *Hawkman* (May 1964), who finally got his own title after bouncing around in *Brave and Bold* and *Mystery in Space* for years. Drawn by Murphy Anderson, Hawkman and Hawkgirl were the first married superheroes.

With all the success enjoyed by Julius Schwartz's revival of the Flash, Green Lantern, Atom, and the Hawkman, DC next gave Schwartz the task of revitalizing Batman, a character who had been engaged in lackluster battles with space aliens for the last half-dozen years. The "new look" Batman and Robin appeared under Schwartz's editorship in *Detective Comics #327* (May 1964). The updated Batman became a thinking man's hero as his stories became better plotted and executed with a more polished artistic style.

Charlton Comics brought back the *Blue Beetle* (June 1964), an old Fox superhero from

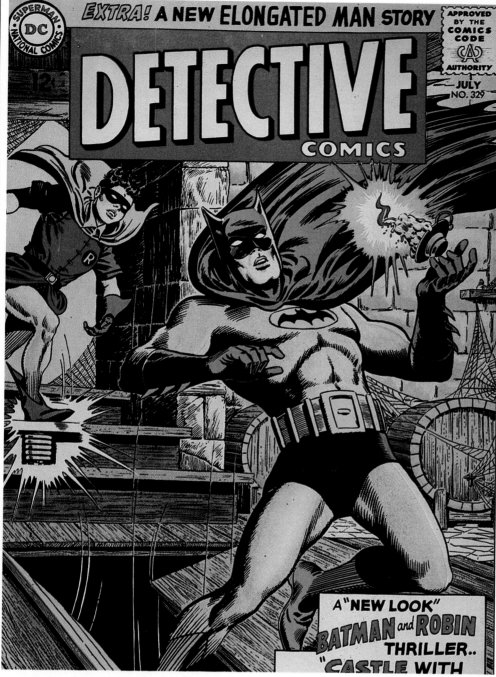

Detective Comics #329, © 1964 DC Comics, Inc.

"When I took over Batman in 1964 . . . I did a story about the Riddler. A gentleman about to take an airplane flight had nothing to read, and he happened to pick up that comic. He was very fascinated with the Batman story, and with the Riddler. His name was William Dozier. He became producer of the *Batman* TV series."
—JULIUS SCHWARTZ,
DC Comics editor

the 1940s, for a second try at a revival (the first occurred in 1955). The comic was so poorly drawn and written, however, that by the following year it would be acknowledged by fans as the worst comic book on the newsstands.

ACG, the publisher of *Forbidden Worlds* and *Unknown Worlds*, still resisted the temptation to enter the superhero field. It did, however, give *Herbie* (April 1964) his own comic book after the inscrutable fat fellow wowed the readers with his magical lollipops and supernatural powers.

James Warren, publisher of *Famous Monsters* magazine, entered the comic-book field with a black-and-white magazine-size comic book called *Creepy*. Unhampered by the need to meet with Code approval, the comic maga-

zine featured horror stories drawn by former EC artists such as Frank Frazetta, Reed Crandall, George Evans, and Wally Wood.

For the first time, Marvel Comics swept the Alley awards. Spider-Man was voted best hero and title, while the single best comic book of the year was *Avengers #4*, with the return of Captain America.

1965: SUPERHEROES FOR EVERYONE!

Marvel and DC continued to build upon the enormous success being enjoyed by their new superheroes. Responding to growing interest in their 1940s superheroes, DC revived Starman and Black Canary in *Brave and Bold #61* (July 1965), Dr. Fate and Hourman in *Showcase #55* (April 1965), and the Spectre in *Showcase #60* (January 1966). They even rewrote Wonder Woman so that her stories were now set in the 1940s.

Marvel Comics was busy creating new characters for the 1960s, such as the new *Avengers*, with Hawkeye, Quicksilver, and the Scarlet Witch. Its most significant new character this year, however, was the Silver Surfer, a galactic heavyweight with a Shakespearean speech pattern and a cosmic surfboard. The Silver Surfer first appeared in the *Fantastic Four #44* (November 1965), then starred in several Marvel books including his own.

This was the year that all the other comic-book publishers brought out their superheroes. Charlton Comics hired Steve Ditko back from Marvel, and assigned him the art chores on his old superhero, *Captain Atom* (December 1965).

Archie Comics came up with the *Mighty Crusaders* (November 1965), a team of campy, revived 1940s superheroes like the Web, the Shield, the Hangman, Steel Sterling, and Captain Flag.

Wally Wood lent his artistic talents to the emerging Tower Comics line from 1965 to 1967. Dynamo was a T.H.U.N.D.E.R. Agent—a secret team of superheroes who protected us civilians. *T.H.U.N.D.E.R. Agents #4,* © *April 1966 Tower Comics, Inc.*

Showcase #56, © *1965 DC Comics, Inc.*

Harvey Comics brought back the Man in Black in *Thrill-O-Rama* (October 1965) and created new characters like Tiger Boy and Jack Frost for *Unearthly Spectaculars* (October 1965).

Tower Comics made its debut as a publisher with the best new comic of 1965, at least as far as many fans were concerned. *T.H.U.N.D.E.R. Agents* (November 1965), an anthology of superhero agents, featured excellent artwork by such artists as Wally Wood, Reed Crandall, and Steve Ditko.

All the superhero activity in late 1965, however, was merely a prelude to the madness that was just around the corner.

Tarzan #155, © *1965 Edgar Rice Burroughs, Inc.*

1966: POW! ZAP! BAT-SHOW WOWS NATION!

The single event that had the greatest impact on comic books this year was a television show—the "Batman" television show, to be precise.

Batman and Robin aboard the Batcycle. *"Batman"*™ © *DC Comics, Inc. This Illustration* © *1966 20th Century-Fox Film Corporation. All rights reserved.*

Almost immediately after the January 12 premiere of "Batman," the entire country went Bat-crazy. The show achieved tremendous ratings and was broadcast twice a week. Sales of all comic books rose as a result, and the *Batman* comic book reached nearly an all-time high circulation of close to nine hundred thousand copies, certainly the largest circulation of any superhero comic book since the 1950s. Soon Batman was featured prominently on all DC comic-book covers, and he was given a permanent guest spot in *Brave and Bold*.

For the most part, both DC and Marvel were content to ride the new wave of super-

Plastic Man #1, © *1966 DC Comics, Inc.*

X-Men #31, © *1966 Marvel Entertainment Group, Inc.*

House of Mystery #160, © *1966 DC Comics, Inc.*

hero popularity that the Batman show brought on. There were few new superheroes, however. DC did bring back *Plastic Man* (November 1966) for the first of several revival attempts, and Marvel finally gave *Thor* (March 1966) his own title.

Tower Comics expanded its superhero line by giving two *T.H.U.N.D.E.R.* agents, *Dynamo* (August 1966) and *Noman* (November 1966), their own books.

Harvey Comics added *Jigsaw* (September 1966) and *Spyman* (September 1966) to its superhero lineup. It also introduced a new generation of comic readers to Will Eisner's *The Spirit* (October 1966) in a two-issue series.

"Television has a greater sense of reality than the comics. Although in the comics you never lose sight of the fantasy, you can lose yourself in your fantasy. I think in that sense, comics have more power than television in that the reader plays a greater part. It engages their imagination."
—JERRY ROBINSON,
1940s *Batman* artist

Flash Gordon #1, © 1966 King Features Syndicate

Jim Steranko made a splash with late 1960s Marvel comic readers with his multiple- and split-panel storytelling techniques. *Nick Fury, Agent of Shield #2, © July 1968 Marvel Entertainment Group, Inc.*

King Comics entered the field, but not as a publisher of superhero comics. Instead, it came out with comics based upon perennially popular King Features characters like Flash Gordon, Mandrake, and Beetle Bailey.

The Caped Crusader from Gotham City gave a shot of adrenalin to an already hyped-up comic-book industry. Sales of all superhero comics shot up. *Justice League of America* garnered a four hundred thousand-plus circulation, and even non-superhero comics like *Tarzan* and *Walt Disney's Comics* were selling a third of a million copies each month.

Mighty Crusaders #4, © 1966 Archie Comic Publications, Inc.

1967: THE BEGINNING OF THE END

Although the Second Heroic Age of comic books, the "Silver Age," is said to have begun in 1956, it is difficult to determine exactly when it ended. Nevertheless, 1967 might be as good a year as any to mark the beginning of the end of the second superhero boom.

Almost every comic book published in 1967 had lower sales than the previous Bat-Year. *Batman* fell in circulation by nearly one hundred thousand copies and many other titles experienced a ten-to-twenty percent drop in sales. Most of the Marvel comics managed to maintain or slightly improve their circulations.

Even so, DC Comics had nine of the top ten best selling comic books of the year: *Batman, Superman, Superboy, World's Finest, Jimmy Olsen, Lois Lane, Detective, Action,* and *Adventure*. All these titles featured either Batman or Superman. The fourth best selling comic of 1967 was *Archie Comics*, with nearly a half-million circulation.

Marvel's top selling title, *Spider-Man*, was fourteenth but climbing. Both *Tarzan* and *The Man from U.N.C.L.E.* were still outselling

Blue Beetle #3, © 1967 Charlton Comics Group

Zap #1, © 1967 R. Crumb

"The first two issues of *Zap* . . . I still really like when I look at [them]. But all that stuff was coming totally out of acid [LSD] visions. There was no doubt. I sat down and it just drew itself, so it has a certain power. There wasn't a lot of ego interference or qualms or doubts about what I was doing."
—ROBERT CRUMB,
underground-comic cartoonist

Spider-Man and the other Marvel titles, and *Betty and Veronica* had more readers than the *Fantastic Four*.

Charlton Comics had thirteen of the fifteen poorest selling comic books on the stands, with *Texas Rangers* holding down the cellar position with a circulation of 110,615.

Of the approximately one hundred comic-book titles on the stands in 1967, there were thirty-two superhero comics, twenty humor comics, fourteen romance comics, eleven teen comics, eight war comics, six science-fiction comics, four western comics, and four comics based upon television series.

Iron Man #1, © 1967 Marvel Entertainment Group, Inc.

Perhaps a greater sign of the impending troubles in the comic-book industry was that ACG (American Comics Group) went out of business after almost twenty-five years of publishing. Another comic publisher, Milson Publishing Company, began and ended its brief career all in the span of six months.

Meanwhile, outside the traditional comic-book industry, the first popular underground comic book, *Zap #1*, was published and sold by its creator, Robert Crumb, on the streets of San Francisco—the home of many of the best underground-comic creators.

These books were light years from mainstream comics, reflecting as they did the

Captain Pureheart #4, © 1967 Archie Comic Publications, Inc.

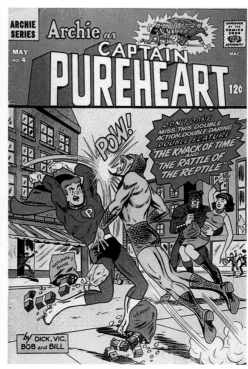

"I was always paid per story, at so many dollars per page. The rate of pay went up from one dollar per page in 1938 to fifteen bucks a page in 1968."
—GARDNER FOX,
comic-book writer

new freedom of the late '60s. Instead, they explored themes and subjects heretofore untouched—like sex, drugs, and the "counter-revolution"—through the unique visual images of talented writer/artists such as Crumb, Gilbert Shelton, Victor Moscoso, Rick Griffin, S. Clay Wilson, and Kim Deitch.

While the monetary impact of the underground comics on the industry was negligible, their influence as liberating pioneers would be widespread.

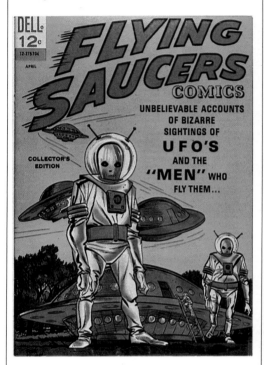

Flying Saucers Comics #1, © 1967 Dell Publishing Company

1968: THE MARVEL EXPLOSION

In 1968, Marvel Comics acquired a new distributor for its comic books, which allowed the company to add more titles.

Beginning in the spring, *Captain America* (April 1968), *Incredible Hulk* (April 1968), *Iron Man* (May 1968), *Sub-Mariner* (May 1968), and *Dr. Strange* (June 1968) were given their own titles after having had to double-up during the previous years. Marvel also gave the *Silver Surfer* (August 1968) his own book, and came out with a new superhero with an old name: *Captain Marvel* (May 1968).

Since Marvel was now associated with a distributor who could assure better newsstand distribution, the publisher experimented with a magazine-sized comic book called the *Spectacular Spider-Man* (July 1968). Originally published in black and white, the second (and last) issue was in color but still did not attract the regular Marvel comic-book buyer.

Steve Ditko, who had worked for Marvel Comics, Charlton Comics, and Tower Comics, now created a hero for DC Comics called the Creeper in *Showcase #73* (April 1968). After seven years without publishing a western comic, DC tried an offbeat, anti-hero ap-

Captain Marvel #1, © 1968 Marvel Entertainment Group

Showcase #73, © 1968 DC Comics, Inc.

proach to the Old West with *Bat Lash* (October 1968). Another unusual 1968 comic was DC's *Brother Power the Geek*, a "flower child" mannequin that came to life. DC also published the first toy-related comic book, with *Captain Action* (November 1968), a boy's action-figure doll.

Gold Key, the third-largest comic-book publisher at the time, raised the price of its comics from twelve to fifteen cents and turned to mostly reprints, as well. Classics Illustrated, which had long sold its comics for fifteen cents, increased its cover price to twenty-five cents.

The "Batman" television show delivered its

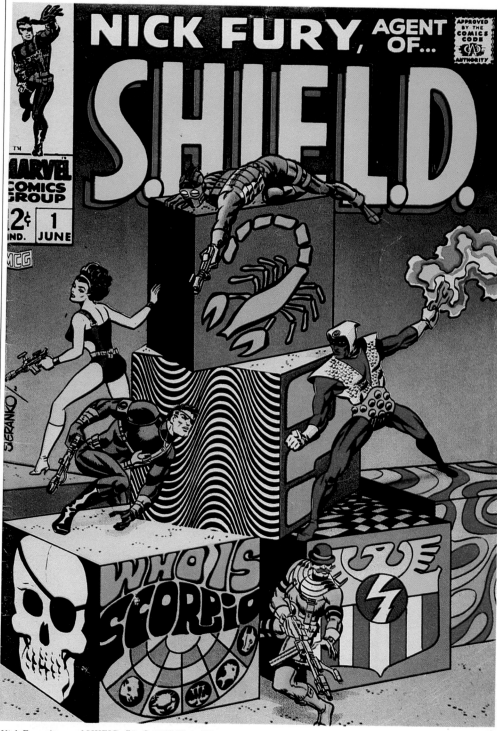

Nick Fury, Agent of SHIELD #1, © 1968 Marvel Entertainment Group, Inc.

last "zap-pow-biff" on March 14—perhaps a fitting R.I.P. date for the end of the Second Heroic Age of comic books.

1969: THE END OF A DECADE

By 1969, comic-book publishers were looking for the next trend. Superheroes had peaked and were declining. War comics had lost readers along with the growing unpopularity of the Vietnam War. Romance comics were having a difficult time reaching their female readership, and western comics had been out of style for years.

Both Marvel and DC believed that science-

fiction and mystery comics would be part of the next popular cycle. DC Comics published *The Witching Hour* (February 1969) and Marvel came out with *Tower of Shadows* (September 1969) and *Chamber of Darkness* (October 1969). All three titles were anthologies of suspense and horror stories.

Archie Comics produced *Archie's TV Laugh-Out*, a comic book tied in with its new Saturday morning animated television show. Harvey Comics's *Fruitman* (December 1969) pretty well typified the condition of the superhero comic by the end of the 1960s—a weakened parody of its former self.

Nine years after their last price increase, both Marvel and DC raised the prices of their

Brother Power the Geek #1, © 1968 DC Comics, Inc.

Teen Titans #21, © 1969 DC Comics, Inc.

Conan #2, © 1970 Conan Properties, Inc.

comic books from twelve to fifteen cents. The rest of the publishers soon followed suit.

Declining sales, increasing prices, a lack of direction, and almost no new titles or characters made 1969 the most disappointing year of the decade for comic books. Many of the long-time artists and writers who had been working in the field since the 1940s seemed to be producing their most uninspired work. The only bright spots of the year were those new writers, like Denny O'Neil and Roy Thomas, and artists, like Neal Adams and Jim Steranko, who were trying to infuse excitement and innovation into a stagnating medium.

1970: SAVAGE BARBARIANS

By 1970, most of DC Comics' old stable of writers from the 1940s and 1950s were gone. Two new talents, writer Denny O'Neil and artist Neal Adams, were assigned to *Green Lantern*, one of DC's faltering superhero titles. Beginning with their first issue (#76, May 1970), O'Neil and Adams turned the comic book into a running commentary on such ills as prejudice, drug abuse, overpopulation, and ecological waste. Unfortunately, their new approach at realism, although critically acclaimed, was not the solution to the declining interest in the superheroes.

Bypassing superheroes entirely, Marvel Comics reached back to the pages of a 1930s fantasy pulp magazine, *Weird Tales*, for its big new book of 1970. Roy Thomas wrote and Barry Smith adapted Robert E. Howard's *Conan the Barbarian* (October 1970). The sword-and-sorcery fantasy of Conan was exactly right for the post-superhero readership. *Conan* became one of Marvel's most successful books of the 1970s and inspired more than a dozen similar barbarian comics over the

next six years.

Although DC Comics and Marvel were unquestionably the major publishers in 1970, they did not have the highest selling comic book that year. That honor belonged to Archie Publications whose *Archie Comics* was selling 515,356 copies per issue.

With Batman's decline in popularity, DC's top-selling title was now *Superman* (511,984). Marvel's number one comic book was *The Amazing Spider-Man* (373,303), followed by the *Fantastic Four*. *Dennis the Menace*, however, still outsold most superhero comics with 318,557 copies. Gold Key's best-selling comic was *Tarzan* (283,968), followed by Charlton's top seller, *Popeye* (205,015).

Archie #199, © 1970 Archie Comic Publications, Inc.

Fruitman #1, © 1969 Harvey Features Syndicate

1971: THE FOURTH WORLD

After abruptly leaving Marvel, Jack Kirby developed an entirely new universe of comic-book characters and concepts for DC Comics, which had offered him greater creative control over his own books. He came up with three titles, *New Gods* (March 1971), *Forever People* (March 1971), and *Mr. Miracle* (April 1971), to create what he called a "Fourth World" of comics. The books formed a cosmological epic, complete with its own mythology and rich characterization.

Meanwhile, Marvel was busy following up Conan's success with another Robert E. Howard sword-and-sorcery hero, *Kull the Con-*

Forever People #1, © 1971 DC Comics, Inc.

queror (June 1971). Conan also was now appearing in a second title, *Savage Tales* (May 1971), one of the first Marvel black-and-white comic magazines.

Perhaps the most interesting DC and Marvel comic books of 1971, however, were *Spider-Man* (#95–97, April/May/June 1971) and *Green Lantern* (#85 & #86, September/November 1971). Both comics featured anti-drug stories, reflecting the new social consciousness of the young writers and artists working on the books. But because of Code prohibitions against any portrayal of drug use, the *Spider-Man* comic was distributed without the approval of the Comics Code Authority.

Green Lantern #85, © 1971 DC Comics, Inc.

"When I saw Neal Adams's artwork, it exceeded my expectations. I think that provided the impetus for a lot of our subsequent success. . . . We were feeding off of each other and the tremendous amount of enthusiasm. And having a sense that maybe we were doing something with the format that hadn't been done before . . ."
—DENNY O'NEIL,
writer of *Green Lantern*

"There's a balance to be struck with doing comics. . . . If you're doing it too fast, you're hacking. If you take too much time, you're being too precious. . . . But there's a balance somewhere in between of just really being hot, knowing you're hot and getting on with it."
—BERNI WRIGHTSON,
original artist for *The Swamp Thing*

However, as a result of the industry's desire to present anti-drug messages, the Comics Code reviewed its 1954 standards and modified them so such topics could be treated. At the same time the Code relaxed the prohibition against the use of horror in comics, such as werewolves, vampires, and zombies. The results of these changes would be truly "monstrous" next year.

1972: MONSTERS!

Suddenly it seemed twenty years earlier. Vampires, werewolves, ghosts and monsters appeared all over the newsstands. Horror comics were back again, and this time with the approval of the Comics Code. One of the better done horror comics was Marvel's *Tomb of Dracula* (April 1972), written by Marv Wolfman and drawn by Gene Colan for seven years to come.

Other Marvel monster offerings this year included a teenage werewolf in the "Werewolf by Night" series in *Marvel Spotlight #2* (February 1972) and Ghost Rider, a flaming skeletal motorcyclist, again in *Marvel Spotlight #5* (August 1972). Besides its new horror titles, Marvel recycled some of its horror stories from the 1950s in such titles as *Chamber of Chills* (November 1972) and *Supernatural Thrillers* (December 1972).

DC's only entry into the monster market this year was the highly acclaimed *Swamp Thing* (November 1972) by Len Wein and Berni Wrightson, although it did add a gothic-horror anthology comic book, *Forbidden Tales of Dark Mansion* (May 1972).

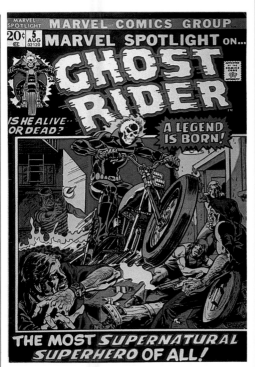

Marvel Spotlight #5, © 1972 Marvel Entertainment Group, Inc.

Also at DC, Jack Kirby introduced what would be his most successful 1970s character, *Kamandi* (October 1972). Then DC obtained the rights to publish *Tarzan* (#207, April 1972), a title which had been very successfully published by Dell/Gold Key for twenty-five years. DC's major superhero title this year was *Supergirl* (November 1972), who received her own book after years of yeoman duty in *Action* and *Adventure* comics.

Marvel Comics still had a strong base of

Marvel Spotlight #2, © 1971 Marvel Entertainment Group, Inc.

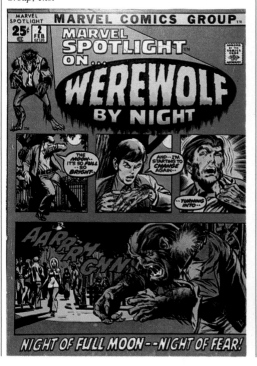

Swamp Thing #1, © 1972 DC Comics, Inc.

superhero books to build upon. From its pool of minor superheroes came the *Defenders* (August 1972), a team title similar to the *Avengers.* Also appearing that month was a cosmic-minded superhero called *Warlock* (August 1972), written by Roy Thomas and drawn by Gil Kane.

By the end of 1972, Marvel Comics's flood of both new and reprint titles was now challenging DC Comics for the number-one spot on the newsstands.

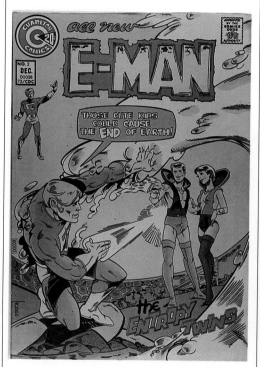

E-Man #2, © 1973 Charlton Press, Inc.

1973: SHAZAM! THE WORLD'S MIGHTIEST MORTAL

The year 1973 marked the eagerly awaited return of the most popular superhero of the 1940s: Captain Marvel. DC Comics, whose lawsuit had spelled an end to Fawcett's Captain Marvel in the 1950s, now had obtained the rights to publish the character itself. Marvel Comics was already publishing a comic book called *Captain Marvel,* although this character had no relation or resemblance to the original Captain Marvel. To avoid confusion, DC published the new adventures of its Captain Marvel under the title, *Shazam!* (March 1973).

Initially drawn by C. C. Beck, the popular Captain Marvel artist of the 1940s, *Shazam!* still could not recapture the glory of its past years. Turning again to past heroes for inspiration, DC came up with a well-drawn revival of the *Shadow* (October 1973), written by Denny O'Neil and drawn by Mike Kaluta.

Marvel, meanwhile, followed up last year's horror titles with *Monster of Frankenstein* (January 1973), *Vault of Evil* (February 1973), and *Worlds Unknown* (May 1973). It also

produced a separate line of black-and-white magazine-size monster and horror comics, like *Vampire Tales, Dracula Lives, Tales of Zombies,* and *Monsters Unleashed.*

Charlton Comics managed to get out one of the few new and interesting superhero comics of the year with the cartoony-style *E-Man* (October 1973).

While Marvel and DC were seesawing back and forth for dominance in the field, Dell Comics, which at one time had been the largest publisher of comic books in the world, ended its thirty-seven-year history of comic-book publishing. (Some of Dell's more popular titles, like *Donald Duck, Bugs Bunny, Tarzan,* and *The Lone Ranger,* remained in print, as Gold Key had bought the rights and assumed publication in 1962.)

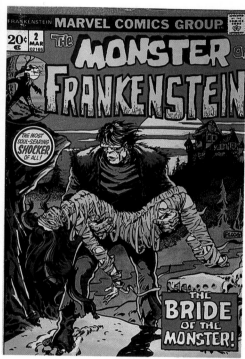

Monster of Frankenstein #2, © 1972 Marvel Entertainment Group, Inc.

1974: AND THEN THERE WERE SIX

By 1974, there were only six comic-book publishers—the fewest since 1936.

Marvel, DC, Archie, Charlton, Gold Key, and Harvey Comics collectively published a total of two hundred fifty titles that year. That amount included forty-five superhero titles, forty mystery or monster titles, nineteen funny-animal comics, ten war comics, eight jungle comics, nine westerns, and nine romances. The rest were miscellaneous adventure, humor, and teen titles.

Although there were more superhero comics than any other genre, the number of mystery and monster books had grown the most rapidly over the previous two years.

Marvel Comics established Kung Fu comics as a viable genre this year, by publishing

Shazam #1, © 1973 DC Comics, Inc.

"As an illustrator I could, in the old days, make a good story better by bringing it to life with drawings. But I couldn't bring the new [Captain Marvel] stories to life no matter how hard I tried. They just lay there on my drawing board like corpses which I was making pretty for their final burial."
—C.C. BECK,
Shazam! and Captain Marvel artist

"**The X-Men are very real people to me, and I live with them 24 hours a day. They are always on the fringes of my thoughts, no matter how much I try to divorce myself from them. It's a very awkward situation, because it inhibits the writer from doing those things to characters which must be done to keep the book dramatically viable. You don't want to kill anyone off; you don't want to break their hearts; you don't want to hurt them. They're your friends!**"
—CHRIS CLAREMONT,
writer of *The X-Men*

Master of Kung Fu (April 1974) and the magazine-format *Deadly Hands of Kung Fu* (April 1974). Both comics reflected the growing popularity of the "chop-socky" Bruce Lee movies.

Master of Kung Fu #17, © 1974 Marvel Entertainment Group, Inc.

Marvel also began its most successful black-and-white comic magazine, *Savage Sword of Conan* (August 1974). Since a magazine did not have to carry the Code seal of approval, *Savage Sword* became a more mature version of the *Conan* comic book.

DC Comics published several oversized facsimile reprints of its number one issues,

The Shadow #6, © 1974 DC Comics, Inc.

such as *Action Comics #1* and *Detective Comics #27*, in a series called *Famous First Editions*.

Meanwhile, Harvey Comics was becoming more of a one-character company, with such new titles as *Richie Rich Gems* (September 1974), *Richie Rich and Casper* (August 1974), *Richie Rich and Dot* (October 1974), *Richie Rich Billions* (October 1974), *Richie Rich Cash* (September 1974), *Richie Rich Vaults of Mystery* (November 1974), and, most appropriately, *Richie Rich Profits* (October 1974).

1975: THE NEW X-MEN

By the early 1970s, Marvel Comics had allowed its *X-Men* comic book to lapse into a reprint title of 1960s stories. No new X-Men adventures appeared until the summer of 1975, when Marvel decided to revive a few of the original X-Men and toss in a few new mutant characters. These "new" X-Men appeared in the *X-Men Giant Size* (Summer 1975) annual by Len Wein and Dave Cockrum, and began a series of adventures in *X-Men #94* (August 1975).

The new *X-Men* became one of Marvel's most successful comic books. Within a few years, the book would be its best selling title and would spawn teams of other mutant teenage superheroes.

Wulf the Barbarian #1, © 1975 Seaboard Periodicals

Teamwork was the key word at Marvel this year. It also launched two other superhero team titles, the *Invaders* (August 1975), which was a revival of 1940s Marvel heroes, and the *Champions* (October 1975), a title in the tradition of the *Avengers* and the *Defenders*.

Marvel and DC also teamed up on their first collaborative effort, an over-sized comic-book adaptation of the *Wizard of Oz.*

Charlton Comics was still busy in the comic-book backwaters, coming out with such titles as *Beyond the Grave* (July 1975) and *Monster Hunters* (August 1975). The company did have a surprisingly original title, *Doomsday + 1* (July 1975), which featured early artwork by John Byrne.

In January of this year, Chip Goodman, son of former Marvel publisher Martin Goodman, began a new comic book company called Atlas/Seaboard. By February, it had published twenty-three comic books in every popular comic-book genre: horror, western, romance, teenage, superheroes, and barbarians.

However, by the end of the year Atlas/Seaboard would be out of business, due to poor distribution and to competition from the new flood of comic books on the newsstands from Marvel and DC Comics.

Engaged in a battle for newsstand dominance, Marvel and DC each tried to outdo the other with a proliferation of new titles. Over the next three years, both companies would publish nearly one hundred new titles.

Quantity was certainly no guarantee of quality, however. Over half of the new books would fail within a year, and less than a third would still be in publication two years later.

1976: QUACK! QUACK!

The new book that made the biggest impact this year was Marvel Comics's *Howard the Duck* (January 1976), created by writer Steve Gerber and artist Frank Brunner. Howard was a duck from another world whose book was a mixture of funny-animal parody and social satire. The title was immensely popular among college students, even inspiring a movie almost ten years later.

Marvel tried a more serious new comic book with *Nova* (September 1976), a teenage superhero in the tradition of Spider-Man. It also gave the company's number one superhero his second comic book, called *Peter Parker, Spectacular Spider-Man* (December 1976).

Jack Kirby returned to Marvel and began a new cosmological mythology with the *Eternals* (July 1976). The other notable new Marvel title this year was *Marvel Classics Comics*, a line of literary adaptations similar to the old *Classics Illustrated* comics.

DC's most significant new title of the year was *Warlord* (January 1976), a sword-and-sorcery adventure series that would last for

X-Men #96, © 1975 Marvel Entertainment Group, Inc.

Howard the Duck #6, © 1976 Marvel Entertainment Group, Inc.

twelve years. DC also tried to recapture past greatness by reviving such titles as *Blackhawk* and (once more) *Plastic Man*. It also brought back the original Justice Society of America to star in the reincarnated title, *All Star Comics #58* (January 1976).

1977: THE REVOLUTION BEGINS

The major comic companies were relatively quiet in 1977. Yet some of the social issues of the counter-culture revolution of the 1960s and 1970s were felt in some of the new titles this year.

Marvel's feminist heroine, *Ms. Marvel* (January 1977), carried the subtitle, "This Female Fights Back!". Black superheroes were featured in Marvel's *Black Panther* (January 1977) and DC's *Black Lightning* (April 1977).

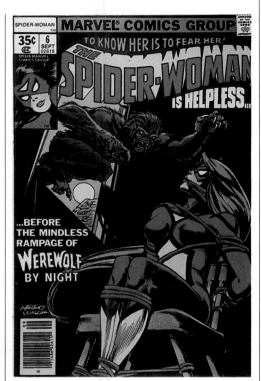

Spider-Woman #6, © 1978 Marvel Entertainment Group, Inc.

Heavy Metal, © 1977 Les Humanoids Associes-Paris

1978: THE COMIC IMPLOSION

The rapid expansion of the previous three years caught up with Marvel and DC in 1978. Marginal titles were dropped as both companies tried to tighten up their lines. DC Comics was especially hard hit. Declining sales caused it to overhaul its distribution process and cut back on titles so drastically that the phenomenon became known as the "DC Implosion." Of the more than fifty new titles begun by DC in the previous three years, only six would be spared the ax.

Jim Shooter, a comic-book writer since barely a teenager, became Marvel's editor in chief, a position he would hold for the next ten years.

But outside the traditional comic-book field, history was being made. The first graphic novel, or extended comic book, was published by a major book publisher, Berkley Books. Written by established science fiction novelist Samuel R. Delany and drawn by Howard Chaykin, *Empire* was distributed in bookstores as well as through traditional comic-book outlets.

Francoise Mouly and veteran underground artist Art Spiegelman began publishing *Raw*, an avant-garde comic magazine that encouraged experimentation and innovation by comic artists. *Raw* produced the first appearances of Spiegelman's "Maus," an autobiographical look at both his life as a cartoonist and his father's Holocaust experiences which featured anthropomorphic animals as Nazis and their victims.

Although dozens of titles were buried this year, the stage was being set for a new growth and revitalization of the industry.

Peter Parker the Spectacular Spiderman #1, © 1976 Marvel Entertainment Group, Inc.

The real revolution in comics began, however, with the publication of *Heavy Metal* by National Lampoon, Inc. *Heavy Metal*, the first Euro-style American comic magazine, consisted of reprints of modern European comic artists. But it became the biggest influence on developing comic-book artists since the underground comics of the 1960s.

Another significant event this year was the appearance of *Cerebus the Aardvark* (December 1977), a parody of the "barbarian" comics. Although only two thousand black-and-white copies of the comic were printed and distributed, it was the first regular comic book to be independently published and distributed outside of the regular comic-book industry. Its continuing success over one hundred issues would pave the way for a flood of small and independent comic-book publishers in the years ahead.

Micronauts #7, © 1979 Marvel Entertainment Group, Inc.

1979: MINI-SERIES AND TOY COMICS

DC Comics introduced a new concept in comics this year called the "mini-series." A mini-series consisted of a set of three or four issues of a comic book which made up a complete story. DC's first mini-series was *World of Krypton* (July 1979), which was limited to three issues. Mini-series would become increasingly popular among fans because all the issues in a series could be easily collected.

Another popular idea born this year was adapting toys into a comic-book series, since the audiences for both often overlapped. Marvel Comics based its *Micronauts* (January 1979) upon a set of miniature toy characters. Sales of the comic were helped by the kids who also bought the Micronaut toys. Both mini-series and "toy comics" would continue to grow over the next decade.

A relatively new artist, Frank Miller, captured the interest of comic-book readers with his version of Marvel's *Daredevil* (beginning with *#158*, March 1979). Miller's Daredevil ignited the imagination of superhero fans and set the stage for a revival of interest in the 1960s superheroes.

1980: I WAS A TEENAGE SUPERHERO

Teenage superheroes were suddenly the focus of the hot new comic books. *X-Men Comics*, about the lives and loves of a group of super-powered teenage mutants, became one of the best selling titles of the year.

DC Comics took notice, and brought back

its original team of teenage superstars, the *Legion of Super Heroes* (*#259*, January 1980). DC also updated its original teenage super-heroes from the 1960s, the Teen Titans, into the *New Teen Titans* (November 1980). Joining Kid Flash, Wonder Girl, and Robin were the Changeling, Starfire, the Raven, and Cyborg.

Detective Comics celebrated publication of its five hundredth issue, making it the oldest continuously published comic book in existence.

Distribution problems and inflation, however, were undermining the recovery efforts of the comic-book companies as they struggled out of the 1970s. Many of the traditional comic-book outlets were vanishing, and comics were being displayed less frequently on magazine racks. Gold Key actually suspended the newsstand sale of its comics, due to the unprofitably high returns of unsold books. In-

> "From the Titans, we are working from the inside-out. We know the characters as individuals; we have a lot of ourselves in there. So we work from what the gut feeling is, to their reaction, and then the character develops."
> —GEORGE PEREZ,
> artist of *The New Teen Titans*

New Teen Titans #1, © 1980 DC Comics, Inc.

"Anybody who has really looked at and studied them has discovered that comics are a unique form of communication which occasionally become art."
—DENNY O'NEIL,
comic-book editor and writer

stead, it went to a system of selling comics packaged three in a bag.

Marvel and DC Comics had to raise the price of their comics for the sixth time in ten years. Comics went from forty cents to fifty cents, and lost a few readers along the way.

1981: THE NEW COMIC-BOOK MARKET

By 1981, an interesting and most welcome phenomenon occurred in the distribution and selling of comic books. A network of several hundred specialty comic-book stores, selling almost exclusively comics and comic-related items, had spread out across the United States. These shops were being supplied by comic-book distributors, instead of the traditional newsstand distributors.

This development allowed for a distribution network and comic-book market to grow outside of the traditional newsstand market. Indeed, one reason for the growth and success of these new comic-book stores was the gradual attrition of many traditional comic-book distribution outlets in drug and grocery stores.

Marvel Comics used a first issue of a new comic book, *Dazzler* (March 1981), to test the strength of this new comic-book specialty-shop market. They sold *Dazzler #1* only through the comic-book shops, and were astounded to discover that they sold more than four hundred thousand copies—nearly twice as many as sales of the average comic-book title of the day.

Many of the issues were bought by collectors speculating that the book would achieve some collectible value, which it did not. But the comic book proved that this new network

Dazzler #1, © 1981 Marvel Entertainment Group, Inc.

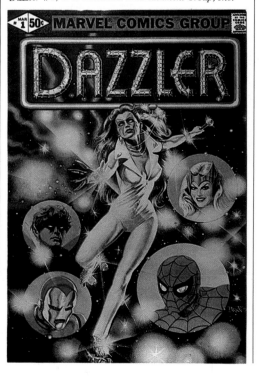

Captain Victory #2, © 1981 Jack Kirby

of comic-book distributors and specialty shops could provide a strong financial base at a time when traditional markets were shrinking.

The major event of the year—and perhaps the most significant event in the industry in the '80s—happened later this year. A California-based company called Pacific Comics decided to sell directly and exclusively to this new market of comic-book stores. Pacific Comics published *Captain Victory and the Galactic Rangers* (November 1981) by Jack Kirby. It became the first major independent comic-publishing effort by a new publisher and the first creator-owned original comic character published by a company (instead of being self-published).

The success of Pacific Comics later encouraged a flood of independent comic books produced exclusively for this new collector's market—and changed the entire face of the business.

1982: THE INDEPENDENT COMIC-BOOK COMPANIES

As the number of specialty comic-book stores grew, a market developed that could support small press runs of comic books aimed at collectors. Eclipse Comics, which had produced books sporadically for the comic collectors' market, published its first regular comic book, *Sabre* (August 1982), for this new independent market. Another start-up comic company, Comico, also tested the waters of the new collectors' market with the amateurish *Primer*. Although sales of these comics were much lower than any Marvel, DC, or Archie comic, there were still enough collectors to

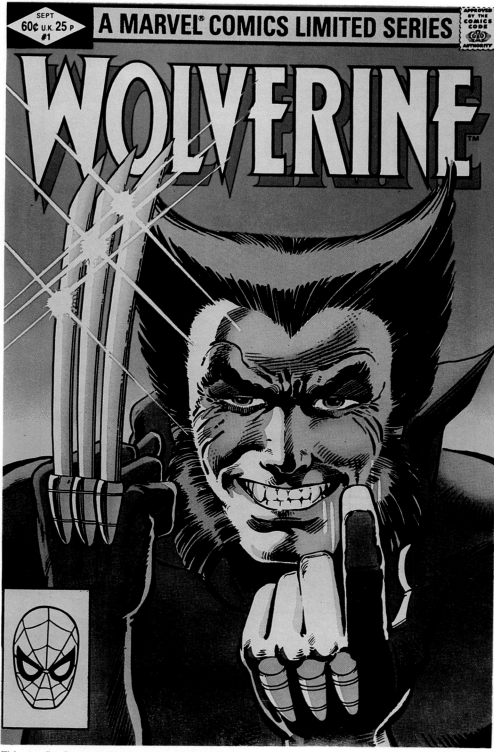

SEPT 60¢ U.K. 25 P #1 — A MARVEL® COMICS LIMITED SERIES

WOLVERINE™

Wolverine #1, © 1982 Marvel Entertainment Group, Inc.

"It's very comforting to know that there's a god-like figure going around making things right. That's a lot of what super heroes are about. Particularly with children, finding themselves in a world that frequently makes no sense whatsoever, where their parents and teachers are often arbitrary in their actions, where it's impossible to understand why they do the things they do or why they're so cruel. To have moral concepts worked out on paper, and a world where people fight for them . . . I think that's a lot of what draws our audience to comics."
—FRANK MILLER,
artist of *Daredevil* and *Batman*

support these early efforts by smaller independent comic-book companies.

DC Comics also was taking stock of the collectors' market which already had made their "mini-series" so successful. DC decided that the next step would be a "maxi-series," or a limited series of twelve issues instead of just three or four. *Camelot 3000* (December 1982) was the first such maxi-series. In addition, DC took advantage of the strong collector interest in the *New Teen Titans* title by issuing a mini-series called *Tales of New Teen Titans* (June 1982).

Marvel was the next major publisher to aim

at collectors with a mini-series featuring *Wolverine* (September 1982), the most popular member of the new X-Men.

1983: NEW KIND OF COMICS

By 1983, the direct comic-book market (comic-book specialty stores catering to collectors) had become so well established that a number of new independent publishers decided to try their hands at comic books. Many of these small publishers were former fans and collectors who financed their new companies

> "It's funny, it's nasty, and it's about a character who continues not to be your average comic book character. He's not the nicest guy in the world, and he doesn't have to be because he's in charge."
> —HOWARD CHAYKIN,
> artist and creator of *American Flagg!*

out of their own pockets.

First Comics came out with *Warp* (March 1983), its first comic book, and followed this up with an adult science-fiction comic called *American Flagg* (October 1983) by Howard Chaykin. Other independent comic publishers, such as Americomics and Capital, joined Eclipse, Pacific, Comico, and First Comics to carve a niche in the collectors' market. Unlike Marvel and DC, the independent comic-book publishers bypassed the newsstands completely and distributed exclusively to the collectors' market.

Kitchen Sink Press, known as an underground comic-book publisher, entered the collectors' market by offering Will Eisner's *The Spirit* to a new generation of readers.

The Spirit #2, © 1983 Will Eisner

Eagle Comics was another new publisher that distributed its books exclusively to comic-book stores and collectors. Its first title was *Judge Dredd* (November 1983), a popular British comic strip repackaged for American audiences.

Another foreign-influenced comic was Frank Miller's *Ronin*, a limited series published by DC, which reflected the influence of Japanese and European comics on the new American comic books.

Archie Comics revived its 1940s/1960s superheroes under the Red Circle line of comics. Encouraged by the growing collectors' market, it published eight titles, such as *The Black Hood* (January 1983), *The Fly* (March 1983) and *The Shield* (June 1983).

There were now more new styles and influences than at any time in the past twenty-five years. Although the independent comic books were limited in circulation, they revitalized and strengthened the entire comic-book industry. Moreover, they helped establish a di-

Secret Wars #1, © 1984 Marvel Entertainment Group

rect collectors' market for comic books, a market that eventually would be responsible for nearly half of all the industry's sales.

1984: THE COLLECTORS TAKE OVER

The comic-book market was gradually changing over from one dominated exclusively by newsstand distribution to one that also depended heavily upon the specialty comic-book network and collector dollar, not the casual reader. Pacific Comics, the first major independent publisher, had now introduced

The Outsiders #1, © 1985 DC Comics, Inc.

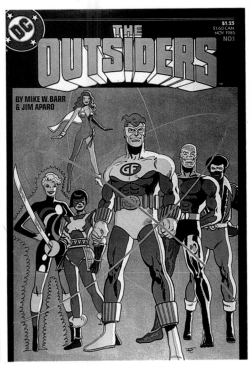

over twenty-five titles for the direct market since beginning three years earlier.

Marvel's *Secret Wars* (May 1984), a limited series which featured most of the company's characters in crossover appearances, was aimed exclusively at the comic-book-store patron and collector. It was a tremendous success—Marvel's best seller ever—and sales of all Marvel comics went up across the board.

At the same time, Whitman (Gold Key) ceased publishing, partly because it could not successfully compete in the collector market and partly because its distribution was dismal in the traditional marketplace, as well.

With Whitman's demise and Harvey Comics suspending publication for an undetermined time, there now were few comic books for the beginning comic-book reader. Marvel attempted to fill the "kiddie comic" void by beginning its Star Comic line this year, featuring such characters as Dennis the Menace and Heathcliff the Cat.

1985: DC'S GOLDEN ANNIVERSARY

Fifty years earlier, DC Comics had issued its first comic book. Now the company was publishing forty titles with an average total circulation of three million copies each month.

DC observed its fiftieth anniversary by publishing a limited series called *Crisis on Infinite Earths* (April 1985). The goal of the "Crisis" series was to reorganize and simplify the DC universe—its myriad worlds and characters—for new readers. To that end, DC terminated Supergirl, the Flash, and other characters, and tied up the loose ends in its superhero mythology and history. The series was the first step in what was to become a revitalization of the company's entire line.

Meanwhile, Marvel Comics was publishing about fifty titles and outselling DC Comics. It began a third title for its top superhero, called *Web of Spider-Man* (April 1985). By now, Marvel had approximately two thousand different comic-book characters, all of whom were being detailed for collectors in the new series, the *Official Handbook of the Marvel Universe* (December 1985).

By this year, sales to the collectors' market through the more than three thousand comic-book specialty stores accounted for half of all comic-book sales. The traditional newsstand market and distribution system had now become almost an adjunct to the collectors' market.

1986: MARVEL'S SILVER ANNIVERSARY

Marking the appearance of *Fantastic Four #1* (1961) as its first comic book, Marvel celebrated the comic's twenty-fifth anniversary in 1986. Marvel observed the event by launching a new series of comic books under the name of the New Universe titles. All the comics in this series took place in so-called "real time" and were supposed to be the beginning of the second Marvel cosmology and mythology. None of the New Universe titles, however, caught the interest of collectors, and the titles were gradually phased out.

DC Comics, on the other hand, was still running high from its fiftieth anniversary party of the previous year. DC launched a major revision of its two main characters: Superman was updated in the mini-series *The Man of Steel* (June 1986), and Frank Miller remade Batman into a vigilante in his mini-series, *The Dark Knight Returns* (March 1986).

Perhaps the best new series of the year was DC's *Watchmen* (September 1986), a richly textured limited series by Alan Moore and Dave Gibbons that explored what superheroes would be like in a real world.

Marvel's most successful new titles of the

Crisis on Infinite Earths #7, © 1985 DC Comics, Inc.

> "One of the things that we've done with the *Watchmen* is to try and come up with a work of comic art that has *effects* in it which no other medium could successfully duplicate."
> —ALAN MOORE,
> writer of *Watchmen*

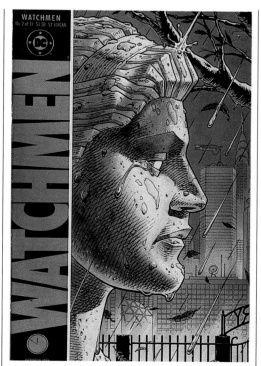

Watchmen #2, © 1986 DC Comics, Inc.

year were a retelling of the Vietnam War years in *The 'Nam* (December 1986) and an X-Men reprise called *X-Factor* (February 1986).

Charlton Comics stopped publishing altogether, after its distribution plunged and sales faded. The company sold most of its major characters to DC Comics.

Meanwhile, Gladstone Publishing entered the field with a revived line of Disney comics, which had been off the market for nearly two years. The Disney comics gave Gladstone the clout it needed to distribute successfully to both the newsstand and the specialty-collector market.

Man of Steel #1, © 1986 DC Comics, Inc.

1987: THE BUBBLE BURSTS

The past two years had witnessed the proliferation of literally hundreds of small and independent comic-book publishers. Collectors, speculators, and comic-book-store owners were buying almost any new comic book regardless of merit.

The motivation for such indiscriminate buying was that, should any of these new books suddenly become successful collectors' items, everyone wanted to profit. Since the print runs of most of these independent comic titles was around twenty thousand to forty thousand copies, even a small amount of speculative activity could sustain the market.

As small publishers started to turn out more and more comic books of questionable to poor quality, collectors and comic-book-store retailers cut back drastically on their buying. At the same time that so many marginal titles

The Punisher #1, © 1987 Marvel Entertainment Group

were being printed, several comic-book distributors failed financially, which especially hurt the smaller publishers.

Within a matter of months, the demand for independently produced comic books plummeted. Only the better produced comic books survived the fallout, while many independent comic-book publishers either cut back or suspended operations.

All was not doom and gloom, however, for the new independent publishers. First Publishing obtained the rights for an American edition of the popular Japanese comic series *Lone Wolf and Cub* (May 1987). The success of this comic encouraged other "manga" (Japanese for comics) translations, such as Eclipse's *Mai the Psychic Girl.* Another favorite on the collectors' market this year was independent publisher Dark Horse's *Concrete,* a gentle and adult comic book.

Concrete, © 1987 Paul Chadwick

1988: SUPERMAN IS FIFTY

America's first superhero celebrated his fiftieth anniversary in June 1988. Superman first appeared in *Action Comics #1* (June 1938), and DC Comics observed the occasion by re-issuing the first Superman story in a facsimile edition.

While Superman was celebrating, Batman was in mourning. DC Comics, through a telephone poll of its readers, decided to kill off Robin in *Batman Comics #428*.

Although much media and fan attention was focused on DC Comics as a result of the two events, Marvel Comics still controlled forty percent of the three hundred million dollar comic-book industry. And Marvel was issuing more comic books than anyone else— over fifty titles a month for a total circulation of more than seven million.

This year also saw a comeback by independent comic-book publishers which had survived the shakeout of the previous two years. There were now over twenty-five independent comic-book publishers, and they were providing more opportunities for creative expression and industry growth than had been seen since the early 1950s.

1989: BATMAN'S BIRTHDAY AND BEYOND

Fifty years earlier, Batman first appeared in *Detective Comics #27* (May 1939). During his Golden Anniversary, the Batman movie was released, and public interest in superheroes was again rekindled.

November 1989 also marked the Golden Anniversary of Marvel Comics. Fifty years earlier, the Human Torch, Sub-Mariner, and others had debuted in *Marvel Comics #1* (No-

vember 1939).

And although both Marvel and DC Comics now account for nearly seventy-five percent of all sales made in comic-book specialty stores, there are still over seventy-five other small and mid-size comic-book publishers turning out hundreds of titles. In January 1989 alone, more than two hundred comic-book titles were available.

More comic books, in the form of graphic novels and albums, now are being sold in bookstores than ever before, and they continue to receive critical attention and review by the media.

As the 1980s come to an end, comic books have reestablished themselves as a vital and growing medium that continues to appeal to an ever-widening and expanding audience.

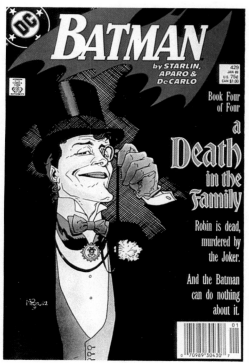

Batman #429, © 1989 DC Comics, Inc.

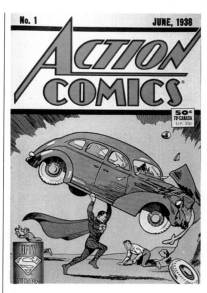

Action Comics #1, © 1988 DC Comics, Inc.

"SUPERMAN! You, who have created not only pleasure for millions of readers, but a whole new industry for thousands of my fellow editors, artists, writers, letterers, colorists, engravers, printers, etc.—we thank you publicly!"
—CARMINE INFANTINO,
former DC Comics publisher

THE
COMIC BOOK
PUBLISHERS

"What is to account for the popularity and staying power of comic book art? In the first place, it appeals to the senses: the brightly colored pages and heavily outlined figures grip the attention of the reader and, like all art, satisfy the urge of the eye to place the riotous colors of life into a balanced perspective. Secondly, it appeals to the imagination in its role as narration, and, like all literature, it satisfies the thirst for vicarious adventure into worlds and experiences outside daily reality. Finally, it appeals to the mind in its effort to create rational order out of the chaos of existence by reducing conflict and complexity into a simplified and therefore less threatening moral battle between the forces of evil and good."
—M. THOMAS ING,
Blackwell Professor of Humanities
and editor of
The American Comic Book

Comic books initially attracted publishers on the fringes, such as those who were producing "pulp" fiction, movie magazines, paperbacks, and mass-produced children's books. Such publications already were geared to the formulas, genres, and commercial considerations that would shape the developing comic-book field.

Since early comic books could be produced cheaply by reprinting existing comic strips or by hiring cartoonists at minimal rates, there were many opportunities for the beginning comic-book publisher. Printing could be done on credit, and distributors were willing to put the comics on the newsstands for future payment. As a result, many comic-book publishers originally were entrepreneurial individuals or family-owned operations.

The business of comic-book publishing was relatively simple. Artwork could be obtained from newspaper syndicates, commercial comic-book studios, or freelance cartoonists. The publisher and the editor would package the artwork and send it to the printer, who would color the art and print the comic. From the printer, the books were sent to various newsstand distributors who would put out the new issues and return the unsold issues back to the publisher for credit.

With a production and distribution system in place, comic-book publishers could churn out dozens of titles to meet the everchanging tastes of their readers.

Because comic books were viewed as packaged products with a selling life of one to two months, the publishers tended to treat their artists and writers as anonymous and interchangeable suppliers. The artists themselves may have inadvertently helped to foster this perception by working for several different publishers and turning out artwork on demand and overnight. (In some ways this was unavoidable, since the pay was so bad.)

Since artists came and went, publishers preferred to have artists remain anonymous, so the readers would not notice inconsistencies in the monthly titles.

For all the interchangeability of artists and writers, however, many comic-book publishers developed a distinctive house style, much like the movie studios of the day. The comic-book publishers, through their editors, established a theme and tone for their comic books. The characters in the comic books also were a major distinguishing feature. Dell Comics had Mickey Mouse; DC Comics published Superman; and Fawcett Publications owned Captain Marvel.

The publishers often set some degree of editorial standards, to determine what could and could not go into their comics. Dell Comics, for example, made certain that all its titles would be palatable for even the youngest comic-book reader. Other publishers, such as Victor Fox, insisted upon a certain amount of sex and violence, in order to attract an older readership.

Beyond the editorial standards (or lack thereof) different production values in packaging, coloring and printing the comics also distinguished one publisher's books from another's.

For the most part, the early comic-book publishers were located in the New York City area. Their offices often consisted of one room with a receptionist. Since the artists worked at home or at least away from the publisher's office, all most publishers needed was a traffic manager, or editor, who could route artwork back and forth to engravers and printers, and pay (or not pay) the artists and writers.

The history of comic-book publishing is made difficult by the dozens of small-scale publishers that blossomed and disappeared throughout the 1940s and 1950s. By the end of 1943, forty-five publishers had tried their hands at comic books. Ten years later, over half were out of business, yet more than twenty new publishers had taken their places.

Adding to the confusion, comic-book publishers frequently published under a variety of names and imprints. Publishers changed their names as they reorganized under new ownership or as they adopted a new image, such as the transformation of Educational Comics into Entertaining Comics. Sometimes publishers would maintain several lines of comics under different business names for legal and financial reasons. Comic-book titles and characters were passed back and forth as publishers' fortunes rose and fell.

What follows, then, is a capsule history of the most significant comic-book publishers from 1933 to 1989. There are omissions, of course, particularly during the period from 1950 to 1955, which spawned literally dozens of small publishers.

In addition, only three new comic-book publishers from the 1980s are profiled. From 1983 to 1989, there was an explosion of small press or independent comic-book companies that produced material which appeared only in comic-book specialty shops. Since many of these publishers printed comics in quantities of less than twenty thousand copies, with no circulation beyond the collectors' market, it is too early to determine the historical significance of these independent publishers.

Publishers are listed alphabetically, under the name by which they were best known, along with the years of the first and last comic books they published.

ACE MAGAZINES (1940–1956)

Aaron A. Wyn, a publisher of "pulp" fiction magazines since 1928, under the name Ace Magazines, entered the comic-book field in 1940 with *Sure-Fire Comics* (June 1940), an anthology of superheroes.

Other superhero titles quickly followed, like *Super Mystery* (July 1940), *Our Flag* (August 1941), *Banner* (September 1941), and *Four Favorites* (September 1941). Only *Super Mystery* and *Four Favorites* lasted beyond

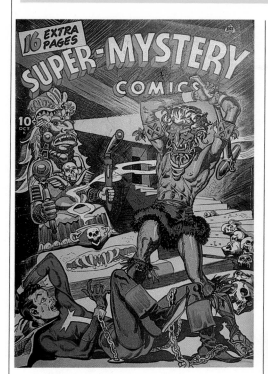

Super Mystery #2, © 1946 Ace Magazines, Inc.

1942, sustained by such heroes as Lash Lightning, Mr. Risk, and Magno the Magnetic Man.

Like many other comic publishers of the early 1940s, Ace added some humor titles to its superhero lineup, like *Monkeyshines* (Summer 1944) and *Hap Hazard* (1944).

A few years later, Ace published a string of teen comics, including *Andy* (June 1948), *Dotty* (July 1948), *Ernie* (September 1948), *Vicky* (October 1948), and *Four Teeners* (1948).

From teenagers it was only a short hop to the rapidly growing romance-comic fad. Ace promptly issued *Real Love* (April 1949), *All Love* (May 1949), *All Romances* (August 1949),

Four Favorites #22, © 1946 Ace Books, Inc.

Glamorous Romances (September 1949), *Love Experiences* (October 1949), and *Love at First Sight* (October 1949).

Crime and western comics also were coming into their own in the late 1940s and early 1950s. Ace responded with *Crime Must Pay the Penalty* (February 1948), *Men Against Crime* (February 1951), *Indian Braves* (March 1951), and *Heroes of the Wild Frontier* (March 1955). Ace also had its war title for the Korean years, *War Heroes* (May 1952).

Ace's final flurry of activity came in 1951, when it launched a line of horror comics at about the same time as a dozen other publishers. Ace's titles, *Web of Mystery* (February 1951), *Baffling Mysteries* (November 1951), and *Hand of Fate* (December 1951), were occasionally distinguished by the artwork of Lou Cameron.

After the industrywide depression in 1956,

Glamorous Romances, © 1955 A. A. Wyn, Inc.

Ace was left with one crime, one western and four romance comics. The company ceased publication by the end of that year.

AMERICAN COMICS GROUP/ ACG (1943–1967)

The American Comics Group (ACG), partially owned by Harry Donenfield of DC Comics, started publishing comics in 1943 with two of the earliest "funny animal" comic books: *Giggle Comics* (October 1943) and *Ha Ha Comics* (October 1943). The two comics, featuring such characters as Superkatt and Spencer Spook, were often drawn by cartoon-studio animators.

For the next four years ACG stuck with funny-animal and teenage comics such as

"Now I realize that you've made yourself into the kind of girl no man in his right mind would want to marry! As far as I'm concerned our date is off . . . and this is good-bye! Maybe some day you'll find some sap who will want you the way you are . . . but I doubt it!"
—from "Reigns on Her Heart," *Glamorous Romances #85* (November 1955)

"He [Richard Hughes] used dreams and dreamlike imagery to give his stories a faintly disturbing air, a sense that there's something about that simple tale that you haven't grasped consciously, but that echoes somewhere in your memories or dreams."
—GERALD JONES,
comic-book writer and co-author of *The Comic Book Heroes*

Adventures Into the Unknown #121, © 1960 Best Syndicated Features

An unlikely lu...p of flesh, Herbie Popnecker gained his supernatural powers through specially flavored lollipops. His laconic, deadpan delivery endeared him to the fans of ACG's mystery and science fiction comic books. (Ogden Whitney, artist.) *Herbie #3, © August 1964 Best Syndicated Features*

Cookie (April 1946), *The Kilroys* (June 1947), and *Hi-Jinx* (July 1947), which featured jive-talking funny-animal hipsters.

Near the end of this period, ACG came under the editorship of Richard Hughes, a writer and creator of early superheroes for Better Publications. Hughes remained at the ACG helm until its demise, and wrote most of the company's huge output of stories.

In 1948, Hughes introduced *Adventures into the Unknown* (Fall 1948), which became the first continuous-series horror comic book. For the next six years, dozens of publishers came out with their own horror comics. Hughes himself brought out a companion title, *Forbidden Worlds* (July 1951), as well as other horror titles like *Out of the Night* (February 1952) and *Skeleton Hand* (September 1952).

Unlike most other 1950s horror-comic publishers, ACG survived the 1954 Comics Code by cleaning up *Adventures into the Unknown* and *Forbidden Worlds* to conform to the new standards. The two comics would remain the company flagship titles until their demise in 1967.

During the late 1940s and 1950s, ACG also published western comics like *Blazing West* (Fall 1948) and *The Hooded Horseman* (January 1952), adventure comics like *Spy-Hunters* (December 1949) and *Commander Battle and the Atomic Sub* (July 1954), and romance comics such as *Romantic Adventures* (March 1949) and *Lovelorn* (August 1949).

By 1956 ACG had phased out most of its humor, western, and adventure titles. Only its romance and horror/mystery titles survived into the 1960s. Its first new title in four years was *Unknown Worlds* (August 1960), a companion title to the ever popular *Forbidden Worlds* and *Adventures into the Unknown*.

In the 1960s ACG experienced a minor rebirth thanks to several new characters. During the superhero craze of 1965, Hughes created

two new supernatural superheroes: Magicman for *Forbidden Worlds* and Nemesis for *Adventures into Unknown Worlds*. Both were fairly forgettable, but his third 1960s creation was not.

Herbie Popnecker, a morbidly obese kid with super powers and a penchant for magical lollipops, was designed by Hughes to be a

Forbidden Worlds #118, © 1964 Best Syndicated Features

one-time joke for a *Forbidden Worlds* story. Readers so loved the implausible fat boy with his deadpan expression and supernatural powers that Hughes gave "The Fat Fury" his own book: *Herbie* (April 1964).

As the comic-book winds shifted in 1967,

Commander Battle, © 1954 Titan Publishing

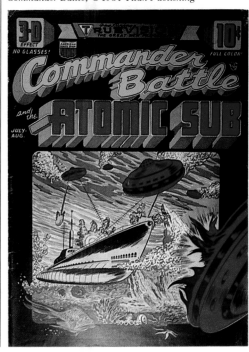

Hughes dumped his two superheroes and *Herbie* as well. He returned to his straight mystery format and added a fourth title, *Gasp* (March 1967). The title would prove to be ACG's "last gasp," as the company ceased publishing five months later.

ARCHIE COMIC PUBLICATIONS, INC./MLJ (1939–)

Archie Comics was originally known as MLJ Magazines, which took its name from the initials of the first names of its founders: Morris Coyne, Louis Silberkleit, and John Goldwater. With a background in magazine publication and distribution, the three men engaged the services of Harry Chesler to package their first line of comic books.

Within a year MLJ had released a line of superhero titles like *Blue Ribbon* (November 1939), *Top-Notch* (December 1939), *Pep* (January 1940), *Zip* (February 1940), and *Shield-Wizard* (Summer 1940). Most of their early heroes—like the Fox, the Firefly, and the Green Falcon—were eminently forgettable.

After hiring its own line of artists, MLJ

Top Notch #9, © 1940 Archie Comic Publications, Inc.

came up with better conceived heroes like the Black Hood, the Hangman, the Comet, the Wizard, and the Shield. The Shield, drawn by Irving Novick in *Pep Comics #1*, was the first patriotic superhero, predating Captain America by over a year, and became Archie's most popular superhero.

MLJ did respectably well with its superhero line, adding two more titles, *Jackpot* (Spring 1941) and *Black Hood* (Winter 1943/44). MLJ's future, however, was made with the introduction of Archie Andrews, America's Favorite Teen-Ager in *Pep Comics #22* (December 1941). Archie first appeared with his bosom buddy, Jughead Jones, and his blonde girl friend, Betty Cooper. His brunette heart-

throb, the rich Veronica Lodge, entered the picture four issues later, in *Pep Comics #26*.

Originally begun as a secondary humor strip for the MLJ superhero titles, Archie quickly catapulted into his own book, *Archie* (Winter 1942), and then stole the lead spots in *Laugh Comics* (Fall 1946) and *Pep Comics*. By 1947, the MLJ superheroes retired and let Archie and his gang at Riverdale High School have their way. And now even the company was known as Archie Comics.

Originally drawn by Bob Montana, Archie soon had a stable of artists—including Dan DeCarlo, Harry Sahle, and Bill Vigoda—who developed a house style of wholesome teen slapstick that became the Archie trademark.

By the end of the 1940s, teenage humor enjoyed a new spurt of growth across the comic-book industry. Archie Comics responded by adding two companion titles, *Archie's Pal Jughead* (1949) and *Archie's Girls Betty and Veronica* (1950). Even with five titles now de-

Archie and the Gang were always comfortably familiar—the comic books provided readers with a set of teenage pals probably a lot nicer than the kids they usually had to hang around with. *Archie Comics #120, © July 1961 Archie Comic Publications, Inc.*

"I admit I went into it [the comic book business] frankly because of Superman, Batman, and all the super heroes. They were catalysts. I thought of Superman as an abnormal individual and concluded that the antithesis—a normal person—could be just as popular. And it was."
—JOHN GOLDWATER, original publisher of Archie Comics

voted to Archie and his malt-shop gang, there was enough reader demand to warrant two additional, giant, twenty-five-cent titles: *Archie's Pals 'n' Gals* (1952) and the *Archie Giant Series* (1954), which featured a rotating lineup of Archie, Jughead, and Archie's girl friends Betty and Veronica.

Throughout the 1950s more Archie titles were added, like *Archie's Joke Book* (1953), *Archie's Mechanics* (September 1954), which gave hints for working on your car, and *Little Archie* (1956), which featured a series of adventures of Archie and the gang in their preteen years, as drawn by Bob Bolling.

Life with Archie (September 1958) was a comedy and adventure title, while *Archie's Madhouse* (September 1959) was a comedy anthology title that went for more offbeat humor and satire.

Archie Comics rarely dropped titles featuring their teen star. In the 1960s, the publisher added *Archie and Me* (October 1964), spot-

Katy Keene #55, © 1960 Archie Comic Publications, Inc.

Josie (February 1963). Suzie and Ginger faded away, but Josie caught on and eventually earned a starring role in the Archie cartoon show. The other Archie girl who made good was fashion model and clothes horse *Katy Keene* (1949).

Drawn by Bill Woggon, the Katy Keene stories encouraged readers to send in their fashion designs for the characters to wear. Pinups of Katy and her fashions were a part of every comic, and the concept was so enormously popular that *Katy Keene Fashion* (1955) and *Katy Keene Pinup Parade* (1955) helped to fill the demand. Although she lost her books in 1961, Katy Keene returned in 1983 to encourage a new generation of girls and boys to enter the world of fashion design.

After settling down with Archie in the mid-1940s, Archie Comics felt little need to follow the other trends of the 1940s and 1950s that tempted many publishers. It did have one funny-animal comic, *Super Duck* (Fall 1944), which lasted for sixteen years.

Archie Comics' only nod to the popularity of the 1940s and 1950s crime comics was *Sam Hill, Private Eye* (1950). The publisher also added the *Adventures of the Dover Boys* (1950) to its new Archie Adventure Series. Both titles faded within a year, and Archie did not revive the idea of a straight adventure comic until 1959.

During that year, Archie engaged the services of Joe Simon and Jack Kirby, comic-book packagers extraordinaire, to bring back the Shield, its most popular superhero of the 1940s. The Shield reappeared in a book suggestively titled *The Double Life of Private Strong* (June 1959). Although the book lasted only two issues, Simon and Kirby bounced back with a new superhero, *The Fly* (August 1959). *The Fly* was sufficiently interesting to last through the 1960s and to warrant a com-

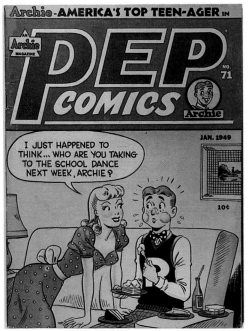

Pep Comics #71, © 1948 Archie Comic Publications, Inc.

lighting Archie's high school principal and teachers, and *Betty and Me* (August 1965), focusing on Betty's antics to snare Archie away from Veronica.

In the 1970s, Archie was licensed for a series of religious comic books, such as *Archie's Parables* and *Archie's Sonshine*. With *Archie at Riverdale High* (August 1972), the teens were back in the classroom and away from the pulpit.

Although Archie was the undisputed star of the company, MLJ/Archie Comics issued other teen titles in hopes of striking gold twice. *Wilbur* (Summer 1944) was a blonde version of Archie who never held the appeal of his red-headed counterpart, although he enjoyed a twenty-year lifespan.

The teen girls who had backup stories in earlier Archie comics were given their own chances for fame with books like *Suzie* (Spring 1945), *Katy Keene* (1949), *Ginger* (1951), and

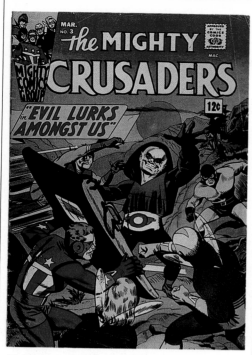

Mighty Crusaders #3, © 1966 Archie Comic Publications, Inc.

panion, the Fly Girl.

Archie tried to tap into the emerging superhero market again with *Adventures of the Jaguar* (September 1961) and *The Shadow* (August 1964). Pedestrian art and stories kept the Archie Adventure titles in the background until the peak of the superhero craze, from 1965 to 1967.

Archie began to revive many of its 1940s superheroes, like the Shield, the Comet, the Hangman, the Web, the Black Hood, and Steel Sterling, first in the renamed *Fly Man Comics* (May 1965) and then as a team in a new comic, the *Mighty Crusaders* (November 1965). Known briefly as the "Mighty Group" of superheroes, the books were a pallid imitation of Marvel's style and vanished by 1967.

Archie tried reviving its hero line again under the Red Circle imprint in 1983 with *The Fly, All New Adventures of the Mighty Crusaders,* and other titles, all of which lasted for less than two years.

But no matter—the enduring popularity of Archie, Jughead, Reggie, Betty, Veronica, Big Moose, Mr. Weatherbee, and all the others continues to make Archie Comics a favorite of its third generation of comic readers.

ATLAS/SEABOARD PUBLISHING (1975)

Martin Goodman, the original publisher of Marvel Comics, left the company after it changed ownership in 1968. In 1975 Goodman, along with Larry Lieber (a former Marvel artist and the brother of Stan Lee) and Goodman's son, Chip, introduced Atlas/Seaboard Publishing to the world. Goodman and Lieber were anxious to prove that they could compete against Marvel with their own line of comics.

Their first three comics—*Phoenix* (January

1975), *Ironjaw* (January 1975), and *The Grim Ghost* (January 1975)—came out at the beginning of the year. By the following month, Atlas was producing comic books in every popular genre: horror, western, martial arts, teenage romance, barbarians, and superheroes.

This ambitious publishing schedule flooded the newsstands with more than twenty titles, such as *Scorpion* (February 1975), *Wulf the Barbarian* (February 1975), *Weird Suspense* (February 1975), *Vicki* (February 1975), *Thrilling Adventure Stories* (February 1975), *The Cougar* (April 1975), *Targitt* (March 1975), *The Hands of the Dragon* (June 1975), and *Demon Hunter* (September 1975).

With so many titles coming out in so short a time, readers could not keep up with them; the books did not have time to develop a steady readership. Distributors, too, had difficulty fitting the company's two-dozen titles on newsstands that already were dominated by a deluge of new Marvel titles.

Before the end of the year Atlas/Seaboard went out of business—a victim of overambitious expansion and bad market timing.

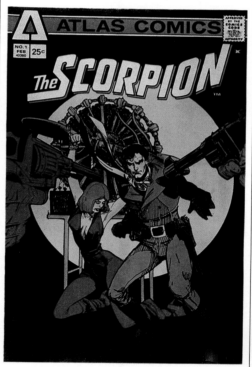

Scorpion #1, © 1975 Seaboard Periodicals

AVON COMICS GROUP (1945–1956)

Joseph Meyers, Maurice Diamond, and Henry Rebell owned the Avon Comics Group, which was part of Avon Periodicals and the Hearst Magazines Corporation. Avon was one of the first paperback-book publishers in 1941. In 1945 Avon entered the comic-book market with *Molly O'Day* (February 1945), an adventure story of a "super sleuth." Avon's next title, *The Sea Hound* (1945), was the first regularly published comic book about pirates, a genre that would become popular by 1950.

> "Comics is an escapist medium, no matter what the psychologists say. If you can entertain and make a valid social point, then all the better. But first and foremost, entertainment is our bag. And just as Atlas was a Titan in Greek mythology, so we plan to be a titan of comic books."
> —Editorial message, Atlas Comics

Iron Jaw #1, © 1975 Seaboard Periodicals

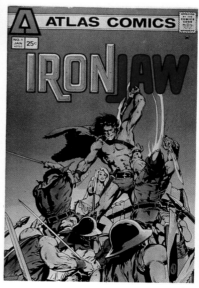

Eerie #7, © 1952 Avon Periodicals, Inc.

Avon Comics, however, is best remembered for its science-fiction titles. The company published one of the first horror comic books, *Eerie* (January 1947), three years before the boom in horror comics began. Evidently the market was not yet ready for a horror comic, because Avon suspended publication of the book after only one issue and did not resume publishing it until four years later (May 1951).

By that time, Avon had become a pioneer in the science-fiction comic-book field, with early titles like *Strange Worlds* (November 1950), *Flying Saucers* (1950), *Earthman on Venus* (1951), and *Space Detective* (July 1951). Its science-fiction books usually were distinguished by some of the best comic-book artists working in that genre: Wally Wood, Frank Frazetta, Al Williamson, Joe Orlando, and E. R. Kinstler.

Avon also enjoyed success in the other popular genres of the day: crime, romance, westerns, and war. Its *Murderous Gangsters* (July 1951) was followed by *All True Detective Cases* (February 1954) and *Sensational Police Cases* (1954). Avon's love comics, *Romantic Love* (September 1949) and *Realistic Romances* (June 1951), lasted until 1954, while its western comics like *Wild Bill Hickok* (September 1949) and *Jessie James* (August 1950) survived into late 1956. *Captain Steve Savage* (1950) was one of the very first Korean War comic books.

Avon also published heavily in the funny-animal genre, with titles like *Space Mouse* (April 1953), *Super Pup* (March 1954), *Funny Tunes* (July 1953), and its longest running comic book, Harrison Cady's *Peter Rabbit* (1947).

By late 1956, Avon fell victim to the overall industry depression and cancelled its few remaining comic-book titles.

BETTER PUBLICATIONS
(1939–1959)

(Standard; Pines)

Better Publications was run by Ned Pines, a magazine publisher since the 1920s who owned pulp magazines with titles like *Thrilling Wonder Stories*, *Thrilling Detective Stories*, *Thrilling Western Stories*, and *Thrilling Love Stories*. It should be no surprise that the longest running comic book from Better Publications would be called *Thrilling Comics* (February 1940).

Better Publications began its comic career with an oversized experimental comic book, *Best Comics* (November 1939). Because it had to be read sideways, the title quietly expired after four issues.

Exciting Comics (April 1940) and *Startling Comics* (June 1940), along with *Thrilling*, would play host to such superheroes as the Black Terror, the Fighting Yank, Doc Strange,

Best Comics #1, © 1939 Better Publications, Inc.

Pyroman, and Miss Masque. Often graced by Alex Schomberg's covers, the three titles were enough above average to last throughout the decade and to spin off other titles, as well.

America's Best (February 1942), for example, showcased superheroes from *Thrilling*, *Startling*, and *Exciting*, while two other books were devoted to the most popular Better Publications' characters, *Fighting Yank* (September 1942) and *Black Terror* (Winter 1942).

Besides superhero comics, Better Publications published a real-life adventure comic called *Real Life Comics* (September 1941). A decent imitation of the earlier *True Comics*, it proved popular enough to last for eleven years and launch a companion true-adventure title called *It Really Happened* (1944).

Recognizing the early popularity of the funny-animal and animated cartoon-type comics, Better Publications became the third comic publisher to enter that field with *Coo Coo Comics* (October 1942). The lead character in the comic, Supermouse, became the first in what was to be a long line of Superman-influenced "super animals." Better quickly added other humor titles like *Goofy* (June 1943), *Happy* (August 1943), and *Barnyard Comics* (June 1944). Four years later, Supermouse rated his own title, *Supermouse* (De-

Dennis The Menace engaged in domestic destruction and parental humiliation every issue, yet always maintained a beguiling innocence that only a six-year-old could muster. *Dennis the Menace in Hollywood #7, © Winter 1959 Hall Syndicate*

cember 1948).

By late 1949 Better terminated most of its superhero titles, like *Exciting, Startling, Black Terror* and *Fighting Yank*. The next three years also saw the end of its popular humor titles, *Coo Coo, Goofy,* and *Happy,* with only *Supermouse* surviving.

By this time Better Publications had been issuing its comics under the Standard imprint. Its great turnover in titles from 1949 to 1952 illustrates Standard's tries at several new directions and titles in those years.

Like almost every publisher at that time, Standard offered a romance line, including *Popular Romance* (December 1949), *My Real Love* (June 1952), and *Dear Beatrix Fairfax* (November 1950). Standard also jumped on the horror-comic bandwagon with such titles as *Adventures into Darkness* (August 1952), *Out of the Shadows* (July 1952) and *Lost Worlds* (October 1952).

Goofy Comics #5, © 1944 Nedor Publishing Company

Most of Standard's 1950s titles faded after a half-dozen issues. One title, however, prospered until the company's end: *Dennis the Menace* (August 1953). A consistently well-drawn and well-written comic, Dennis the Menace was the ultimate "little kid" comic that spawned dozens of imitators. Three years later Standard again changed its imprint, this time to Pines Comics.

By 1956, Better/Standard/Pines had only two strong titles: *Dennis the Menace* and *Supermouse*. With the demise of St. John Publishing in 1956, Pines quickly secured the comic-book rights to the most popular "super rodent" of them all, Mighty Mouse. He joined Supermouse in the Pines super-mice lineup with *Mighty Mouse* (March 1956).

Mighty Mouse and Dennis the Menace could pull the Pines comic-book line along for only three more years. By late 1959 Pines ceased publishing comic books, surrendering Dennis the Menace to Fawcett Publishing Company and turning Mighty Mouse over to Dell Publishing.

CATECHETICAL GUILD
(1942–1972)
(George A. Pflaum)

Although never distributed extensively on the newsstands, the comic books published by the Catechetical Guild reached millions of boys and girls in Catholic schools.

Beginning in 1942 *Topix Comics* (November 1942) featured stories on Pope Pius XII, Catholic saints, and biblical stories. Its success in the Catholic schools prompted George A. Pflaum to begin publishing *Treasure Chest Comics* (March 1946).

Treasure Chest was issued only during the school year, yet its format of wholesome adventure stories with continuing characters, combined with moral dramas and religious vignettes, kept it popular with adults and children for over sixteen years. In 1963 the magazine ran a serial entitled "This Godless Communism," which certainly did its job of indoctrinating millions of schoolchildren.

The Guild published other anti-communist comics, including *The Red Iceberg* (1960), as well as other special single-issue titles like the *Life of Christ* (1949) and *Life of the Blessed Virgin* (1950).

By 1972, *Treasure Chest Comics* no longer could hold onto its Catholic-school market. But despite its sometimes bland approach, the comic book had consistently featured wholesome and worthwhile stories.

Treasure Chest #15, © 1955 George A. Pflaum

"When I was doing horror stories for Standard [Better Publications], they had vile scenes like a man lying on a table, with rats chewing him up. I tried to figure ways of cheating around that because I didn't want to show it. In horror stories, what you don't see can be more frightening than what you do see."
—ALEX TOTH,
comic-book artist

"**Your Uncle Joe has felt for a long time that many, many boys and girls and grown-ups too would welcome a comics magazine devoted to amazing and mystery stories. Therefore, after gathering together the bestest of the best material for this type of magazine, we present it herein for your approval.**"
—JOSEPH HARDIE,
Centaur editor and publisher, in an editorial message for *Amazing Mystery Funnies #1* (August 1938)

Keen Detective Funnies #20, © 1940 Centaur Publications

CENTAUR PUBLISHING (1938–1942)

Joseph Hardie began Centaur Publishing by buying *Funny Pages*, *Funny Picture Stories*, *Star Comics* and *Star Ranger* from Ultem Publications, a short-lived partnership which had originally purchased the titles from Comics Magazine Company and Harry "A" Chesler's Studio about a year earlier. All four titles came out under the Centaur imprint in March 1938.

Hardie was very much involved with his comics, even using a letter column persona, "Uncle Joe," to address his readers.

Centaur was a whirlwind of creativity and ideas. It published twenty-two titles in four years, including *Keen Detective* (July 1938), *Fantoman* (August 1940), *Masked Marvel* (September 1940), *The Arrow* (October 1940), *Wham Comics* (November 1940) and *Stars and Stripes* (May 1941). Its comics usually featured excellent artwork and original characters, often created by the Bill Everett studio.

Half of its titles, however, lasted only three issues or less, perhaps because Centaur seemingly had an abysmal distribution system that bypassed major newsstands in favor of backwater grocery stores.

Centaur did publish two memorable and relatively long-lasting titles, *Amazing Mystery Funnies* (August 1938) and *Amazing Man* (September 1939), which featured early classic artwork by Bill Everett, Tarpe Mills, and Basil Wolverton.

Due no doubt to its poor distribution, Centaur Publishing ended its comic publishing days in 1942 with *World Famous Heroes*.

CHARLTON COMICS (1946–1986)

John Santangelo Sr., an Italian bricklayer, ar-

rived in the United States in 1923. Eight years later he began Charlton Publishing with *Hit Parader* and *Song Hits*, magazines that reprinted the lyrics to popular songs.

Santangelo laid the bricks himself for the Charlton plant in Derby, Connecticut, and converted a printing press that had been used to print cereal boxes into one that would print his new comic books. He even had his own distribution system independent of other magazine and comic-book publishers. In 1946, Charlton published its first comic book, *Marvels of Science* (March 1946).

Although always a second-string comic publisher, Charlton nevertheless published over three hundred titles in its respectable forty-year career.

During the 1940s, Charlton's modest comic output consisted of such titles as *Jack in the Box* (October 1946) and *Cowboy Western* (July 1948).

After noticing the interest in crime comics in the fall of 1950, the next spring Charlton released two crime comic books: *Crime and Justice* (March 1951) and *Lawbreakers* (March 1951). By the next year, Charlton was publishing crime, horror, and science-fiction comics like *The Thing* (February 1952), *Racket Squad in Action* (May 1952), and *Space Adventures* (July 1952).

It was not until 1954, however, that Charlton started to thrive—just as other comic-book companies were on the verge of collapsing. Charlton was able to weather the 1954-56 comic-book recession because it was a family business that also published other types of magazines. As comic-book publishers went out of business, Charlton bought their titles and added their unpublished material to its line.

Charlton obtained romance, western, and

Captain Atom #87, © 1967 Charlton Comics Group

Fightin' Army #19, © 1957 Charlton Comics Group

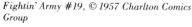

horror comics from Fawcett Comics in 1954. It also picked up titles and characters from Fox Syndicate, including the Blue Beetle, then garnered titles from four more publishers over the next two years.

Throughout the mid and late 1950s Charlton published dozens of western, romance, science-fiction, adventure, and war comics, such as *Cheyenne Kid* (July 1957), *Teen Confessions* (August 1959), *Outer Space* (May 1958), *Mr. Muscles* (March 1956), and *Battlefield Action* (November 1957). Most titles were undistinguished, except for occasional artwork by Steve Ditko, Al Williamson, John Severin, and a few other above-average artists who were willing to work for Charlton's below-average rates.

In 1960 Charlton published Captain Atom in *Space Adventures #33* (March 1960). Drawn by Steve Ditko, Captain Atom was one

Midnight Tales #3, © *1973 Charlton Press, Inc.*

of the first 1960s superheroes, appearing for over two years before Ditko's other famous hero, Spider-Man.

By the mid-1960s Charlton was being run by Santangelo's son, John Jr., who embraced the 1960s superhero revival with such titles as *Thunderbolt* (January 1966), *Peacemaker* (March 1967), *Captain Atom* (December 1965), *Judomaster* (May 1966), and *Son of Vulcan* (November 1965). None lasted beyond 1967.

In 1969 Charlton took over publishing the King line of comic characters, including Flash Gordon, Popeye, and the Phantom.

By the late sixties and through the seventies, Charlton found its niche again as a low-profile but steady supplier of genre comics (westerns, war, mystery, and romance) in a field that was dominated by superhero titles

from Marvel and DC Comics. Bowing to its dropping circulation rates, Charlton left the comic-book business in 1986 and sold its characters to DC Comics.

Star Ranger #3, © *1937 Ultem Publications*

HARRY "A" CHESLER
(1937–1948)

Harry "A" Chesler (whose middle *name* was A, not an initial) opened one of the first comic-book studios in 1936 to fulfill the needs of the new and growing industry. By advertising for artists and writers in the newspaper, he soon assembled a team that supplied materials to such early publishers as Comics Magazine Company, MLJ Publications, and Marvel Comics.

Chesler became a partner in publishing himself, putting out six issues each of *Star Comics* (February 1937) and *Star Rangers* (February 1937). By the fall of 1937 he had sold both titles to I. W. Ullman and Frank Z. Temerson (Ultem Publications). Chesler also published *Feature Funnies* (October 1937) for about a year and a half, then sold that title to the start-up Quality Comics Group.

Chesler's next published title was a premium comic book, *Cocomalt Big Book of Comics* (1938), produced for Cocomalt to give away to purchasers of its chocolate breakfast drink.

Although his comic-book studio continued to supply other publishers from 1938 to 1940, Chesler did not publish comics again until 1941. He then issued four titles in rapid succession: *Yankee Comics* (September 1941), *Dynamic Comics* (October 1941), *Scoop Comics* (November 1941) and *Punch Comics* (December 1941). The early issues contained such superheroes as Major Victory, Dynamic Man, Mr. E, Rocketman, Captain Glory, the Echo, and Yankee Doodle Jones. By the mid to late 1940s, however, the superheroes had

"His real name was Chesler, but we called him 'Chiseler.' He was a character, kind of a whimsical guy."
—WALT GIBSON,
1940s comic-book writer

taken a back seat to stories that focused on violence, crime, and soft sex. Chesler constantly pushed against the self-imposed taboos of the industry, and one of his comic-book covers featured bare-breasted women.

His later comic books, *Spotlight* (November 1944) and *Red Seal* (October 1945), also featured stories with bondage, torture, and drugs. Chesler's comic books were set in a world where evil and darkness were the norm, and even the protagonists had such names as Black Dwarf and Lady Satan.

From 1945 to 1947 Chesler gradually phased out his comic-book line until he was left with only *Dynamic Comics*, which expired in early 1948.

Red Seal #18, © 1946 Harry A. Chesler

COMIC MEDIA (1951–1954)
Artful Publications

In 1951 Allen Hardy and three other individuals began publishing comic books under the name of Artful Publications. Their first titles were romance comics: *All True Romance* (March 1951) and *Dear Lonely Heart* (March 1951). Although the quartet originally was known as Artful, they published comics under a variety of names including Harwell, Biltmore, Allen Hardy Associates, and Mystery Publishing Company. Their best-known imprint, however, was Comic Media, which appeared on many of their comic-book covers.

In addition to romance comics, the group published crime titles like *Danger* (January 1953) and *Dynamite* (May 1953), war comics like *War Fury* (September 1952), and westerns such as *Death Valley* (October 1953).

Some of their more notorious comics were their horror titles, *Horrific* (September 1952) and *Weird Terror* (September 1952). The covers of both books often featured either a

corpse's face or a leering maniac's head that had been shot, stabbed, or otherwise colorfully disfigured.

All was not death and dismemberment, however. Their humor title, *Noodnik* (1953), was originally done as a three-dimensional comic during the 1953 3D-comic craze, and lasted for another four issues as a regular comic book.

In late 1954 Comic Media continued its love and death theme by announcing that its next new titles would be *House of Horror* and *Love and Kisses*. The books never appeared, however, and Comic Media folded with the December 1954 issue of *Terrific*. By the beginning of 1955 Comic Media had sold *Terrific* and its romance-comic titles to Farrell Comics, and its western and adventure titles to Charlton Comics.

COMICS MAGAZINE COMPANY, INC. (1936–1937)

John Mahon and William Cook originally were the business manager and managing editor, respectively, of the National Allied Publications (later known as DC) comic-book line of Major Malcolm Wheeler-Nicholson. Dismayed by Wheeler-Nicholson's financial problems, Mahon and Cook left National in February 1936 to form their own comic-book publishing company, Comics Magazine Company.

Their first comic book, *Comics Magazine* (May 1936), contained a great deal of material originally intended for Wheeler-Nicholson's *New Comics* and *More Fun*. Their next title, *Funny Pages #6* (November 1936), introduced the Clock, a masked detective hero.

Their remaining titles, *Funny Picture Stories* (November 1936), *Detective Picture Stories* (December 1936), and *Western Pic-*

Funny Picture Stories #1, © 1936 Comics Magazine

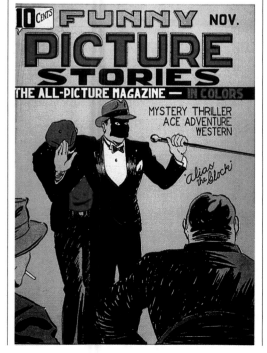

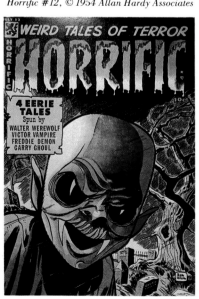

Horrific #12, © 1954 Allan Hardy Associates

Torchy was one of the beautiful women that Bill Ward drew for comic books before he became more widely known as a cartoonist for men's magazines. *Modern Comics #66, © October 1947 Comic Magazines*

ture Stories (February 1937) were all significant books. *Funny Picture Stories* was the first comic book to feature all adventure strips, and arguably the first comic book devoted to a single theme. *Detective Picture Stories* was the first mystery/detective comic, and *Western Picture Stories* tied as the first western comic book.

With publication of its June and July 1937 issues, Comics Magazine Company was sold to I. W. Ullman and Frank Z. Temerson, who combined their last names to form Ultem Publications. Ultem published *Funny Pages* and *Funny Picture Stories* until early 1938, when both titles were sold to Joe Hardie of Centaur Publications.

DC COMICS, INC. (1935–)

(National Allied Publications, National Comic Publications, National Periodical Publications)

DC Comics was begun by Major Malcolm

Wheeler-Nicholson under the name of National Allied Publications. Wheeler-Nicholson's early comics, *New Fun Comics* (February 1935) and *New Comics* (December 1935), were among the first to feature original material. In 1936 Wheeler-Nicholson formed a partnership with Harry Donenfield and J. S.

Superman #76, © 1952 DC Comics, Inc.

Funny Pages #6, © 1936 Comics Magazine

New Comics #2, © 1936 DC Comics, Inc.

Hawkman shared star billing with the Flash in *Flash Comics*. Written by Gardner Fox and illustrated here by Shelly Moldoff, the character was based upon one of the oldest wish fantasies: the ability to fly like a bird. *Flash Comics #5, © May 1940 DC Comics, Inc.*

Liebowitz called Detective Comics, Inc., which published *Detective Comics* (March 1937). By the end of 1937 Donenfield bought Wheeler-Nicholson out.

DC Comics' success was assured with publication of *Action Comics* (June 1938), which introduced Superman. This was quickly followed by *Superman* (Summer 1939) and then *Batman* (Spring 1940).

Meanwhile, M. C. Gaines joined the company in 1938 to package an independent line of comic books under the name of All American Publications. From this line came such superheroes as the *Flash* (January 1940), *Green Lantern* (Fall 1941), and *Wonder Woman* (Summer 1942).

For the next five years there would be two branches of the company, one owned by M. C. Gaines and the other by Harry Donenfield and J. S. Liebowitz. Together they would publish such heroes as Hawkman, Atom, Spectre, Sandman, Hourman, Wildcat, Starman, and others in titles like *World's Finest*, *Sensation*, *Adventure*, *All Flash*, *All American*, *All Star*, *Star Spangled Comics*, *Leading Comics*, and *Comic Cavalcade*.

In 1946 Gaines sold his interest in All American Publications to Donenfield and the company was consolidated under National Comic Publications, with the familiar "DC" emblem appearing on all the comic-book covers. The company next changed its name to National Periodical Publications in 1961, and finally to DC Comics, Inc. in 1977.

After its initial superhero explosion, DC Comics developed a humor title, *All Funny* (Winter 1943), and a funny-animal title, *Funny Stuff* (Summer 1944). As superheroes faded in popularity, DC converted two of its

Leading Comics #17, © 1945 DC Comics, Inc.

The members of the Justice Society of America always split up at the beginning of each story before they went into battle. *All-Star Comics #37,* © *October 1947 DC Comics, Inc.*

superhero titles into funny-animal anthologies, *Leading Comics* (1945) and *Comic Cavalcade* (December 1948).

DC continued to enjoy success from its humor and funny-animal comics all through the 1940s and 1950s with such comics as *Real Screen Comics* (Spring 1945), which introduced the Fox and Crow, *Three Mousketeers* (March 1956), and *Sugar and Spike* (April 1956). Sheldon Mayer, editor of the All American line and an excellent cartoonist himself, developed the last two titles for DC and drew many of DC's humor strips during the 1950s.

Although many superhero titles were dropped or transformed in the late 1940s, the Superman books always sold very well. DC's last great new superhero of the 1940s would be Superboy, who began in *More Fun Comics* and eventually starred in a series in *Adventure Comics* (April 1946) that lasted for twenty-five years. He also rated his own title with *Superboy* (March 1949).

By the end of the 1940s, however, the superhero cycle was winding down. While Batman, Superman, Superboy, and Wonder Woman survived the 1950s, most of the other DC hero titles were terminated or transformed.

For example, *All American* changed its title to *All American Western* (November 1948) and replaced Green Lantern with Johnny Thunder, a cowboy hero. Similarly, *All Star Comics* became *All Star Western* (April 1951), and superheroes were ousted by cowpunchers. *All Star Western* and DC's other western title, *Western Comics* (January 1948), lasted until 1961.

All American Western underwent another title and personality change when DC transformed it into *All American Men of War* (August 1952). That same month DC launched its war-comic offensive with *Our Army at War* (August 1952) and *Star Spangled War Stories* (August 1952). DC's other popular war titles soon included *Our Fighting Forces* (October 1954) and *GI Combat* (January 1957), an acquisition from Quality Comics.

During the lurid crime-comic fad of the late 1940s, DC maintained a dignified aloofness. Its only contribution to the genre would be restrained adaptations of two popular radio shows, *Gang Busters* (December 1947) and

All American Men of War #86, © *1961 DC Comics, Inc.*

Mr. District Attorney (January 1948). Ironically, both titles outlasted their radio namesakes by a number of years.

Two years after the first issue of Archie Comics, DC gave its favorite teenager from *All Funny Comics* his own title, *Buzzy* (Winter 1944). The next teen titles would be *A Date with Judy* (October 1947) and *Binky* (February 1948). Although DC's teen comics never developed the following of their Archie counterparts, they lasted until the late 1950s.

DC was much more successful in capturing the teenage romance-comic reader. Beginning with a base of three romance titles, *Girls' Love Stories* (August 1949), *Secret Hearts* (September 1949), and *Girls' Romances* (February 1950), DC later picked up *Heart Throbs* (April 1957) from Quality's defunct line and *Young Love* and *Young Romance,* the first romance comic, from Prize Publications in 1963. DC's romance comics sold consistently well, lasting until the early and mid-1970s.

DC's contributions to the 1950s science-fiction comic book were *Strange Adventures* (August 1950) and *Mystery in Space* (April

"Shelly [Sheldon Mayer] asked me to write a Wonder Woman story. I did the best job I could. He threw it on the floor and jumped up and down on it. I rewrote it. He threw it on the floor and jumped up and down on it. I rewrote it for the third time. He threw it on the floor and jumped up and down on it. I cursed him and I left. He called me that evening and invited me to be an editor."
—ROBERT KANIGHER,
DC Comics editor and writer

Fox and Crow #45, © *1957 DC Comics, Inc.*

"We worked hard for balance in story and art. I insisted on good, tight plots with characterization and gimmicks, but pictures with colorful locale and sweeping action had to be components. And we insisted on accuracy."
—JACK SCHIFF,
DC Comics editor from 1942 to 1967

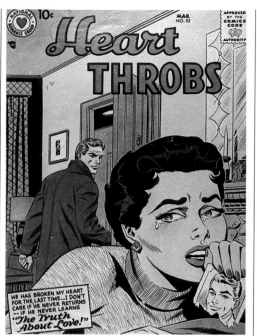

Heart Throbs #52, © 1958 DC Comics, Inc.

1951). Edited by veteran science-fiction fan and agent Julius Schwartz, the books were often written by long-time fantasy writers from the pulp magazines. DC's offering to the horror fan was *House of Mystery* (December 1951), which was remarkably tame in comparison with the other suspense and horror comics of the day.

Mystery in Space #53, ©1959 DC Comics, Inc.

Because of their restraint, however, all three titles survived the Comics Code. After the Code, DC issued *My Greatest Adventure* (January 1955), *Tales of the Unexpected* (February 1956), and *House of Secrets* (November 1956). All featured formula stories of normal individuals suddenly becoming involved with

supernatural events or alien beings. Although DC's mystery and science-fiction titles were far more sedate than their early 1950s predecessors, most managed enough story and art appeal to last for twenty years and longer.

Another interesting phenomenon of the late 1940s to early 1950s were comic books based upon movie and television stars. The first stars to receive this treatment were the Saturday-morning cowboy heroes. DC's cowboy comics were *Dale Evans* (September 1948) and *Hopalong Cassidy* (February 1954).

Jerry Lewis #69, © 1962 DC Comics, Inc.

Comedians and entertainers next caught DC's eye, and such titles as *Ozzie and Harriet* (October 1949), *Bob Hope* (February 1950), *Dean Martin and Jerry Lewis* (July 1952), *Jackie Gleason* (June 1956), *Pat Boone* (September 1959), and *Dobie Gillis* (May 1960) proved enormously successful. In fact, the *Dobie Gillis* comic continued to appear after the television show went off the air, and the *Dean Martin and Jerry Lewis* comic survived the break-up of the famous comedy team—although in 1957 it was renamed as only *Jerry Lewis Comics*.

The only nod that DC made to the superhero field in the early 1950s was to expand its always popular Superman line by giving titles to two supporting characters, *Superman's Pal Jimmy Olsen* (September 1954) and *Superman's Girl Friend Lois Lane* (March 1958).

Although the mid to late 1950s were relatively barren for new comic-book titles, DC created two significant books.

Brave and Bold (August 1955) began by featuring adventure characters like the Viking Prince and Robin Hood. It later served as a showcase for new superheroes, like the Justice League of America and Hawkman, and eventually became a team-up title for Batman and whoever was the other DC hero of the month.

The other new title, *Showcase* (March 1956), was aptly named as a proving ground for new and revived characters. *Showcase* became the starting point for many DC heroes and titles. The Flash, DC's first revived and updated Golden Age hero, made his initial appearance in *Showcase #4* (October 1956), followed by tryout appearances from the Challengers of the Unknown, Lois Lane, Adam Strange, Green Lantern, the Atom, and the Metal Men.

Interestingly enough, the first *Showcase* characters to receive their own title were *Challengers of the Unknown* (April 1958), four men who were living on "borrowed time." No doubt DC was impressed by the sales of its *Blackhawk* (January 1957) title, recently ac-quired from Quality, and felt that the time was right for another comic book featuring a team of adventurers.

The next *Showcase* alumnus to receive his own title was the *Flash* (#105, February 1959), the "fastest man in the world." A year later, the second revised Golden Age hero from *Showcase* earned his own title, *Green Lantern* (July 1960). *Showcase* also produced a title for the *Atom* (June 1962) and the *Metal Men* (April 1963), while *Brave and Bold* featured early appearances that eventually led to titles for the *Hawkman* (April 1964) and *Justice League of America* (October 1960), the superhero team title that featured most of DC's new and old heroes.

By the mid to late 1960s, the superhero fad had peaked with the "Batman" television

"I never knew a story that could develop on its own. Characterization establishes, moves the plotline, offers emotion. But don't underrate plot. A strong plot underscored with characterization is what makes a sound comic book."
—MURRAY BOLTINOFF,
senior DC Comics editor

Challengers of the Unknown #8, © *1959 DC Comics, Inc.*

Mister Miracle #1, © 1971 DC Comics, Inc.

"We were talking about doing some new things: Hey, we've got a solid revitalization for Superman . . . what about the Flash? What about Batman? What about Wonder Woman? And what about all the other major characters in the [DC] line? They sort of fell on each other in terms of revitalization. That became the company's policy, let's revitalize everything we've got before we look for something new. If we're going to publish these characters, let's make them as good as we can."
—**DICK GIORDANO,**
executive editor, DC Comics

Green Lantern #1, © 1960 DC Comics, Inc.

show and was subsiding. DC attempted a few more new superhero titles like *Teen Titans* (January 1966) and several other off-beat characters.

During the late 1960s and early 1970s, DC was paralleling Marvel's venture into supernatural comic books with titles like *The Unexpected* (February 1968) and *Witching Hour* (February 1969). DC also returned *House of Secrets* and *House of Mystery* back to their original mystery-anthology format, and launched the three weird sisters: *Weird War Tales* (September 1971), *Weird Western Tales* (June 1972), and *Weird Mystery Tales* (July 1972).

The early 1970s also saw the arrival of Jack Kirby from Marvel. Kirby's career had straddled both companies since the 1940s, and he

returned to DC this time with his own group of characters. His "Fourth World" series for DC included *New Gods* (February 1971), *Forever People* (February 1971), *Mr. Miracle* (March 1971), and *The Demon* (August 1972). His most successful title for DC, however, was *Kamandi* (October 1972), a teenage boy who matched wits in a bombed-out America with mutated talking animals.

Some of DC's other interesting 1970s titles included the *Swamp Thing* (October 1972), an homage to the Heap and EC comics as written by Len Wein and drawn by Berni Wrightson, *Shazam* (February 1973), DC's revival of Captain Marvel, and *Jonah Hex* (March 1977), an ugly western comic-book hero who was eventually killed, stuffed and mounted.

With the success of Marvel's new *X-Men*,

Adventures of Superman #424, © 1987 DC Comics, Inc.

featuring teenage mutants, DC revived an old title and added new characters to form the *New Teen Titans* (November 1980). And the entire DC line of superheroes underwent a transformation with *Crisis on Infinite Earths* (April 1985), a twelve-issue series that killed off some of DC's older characters and introduced new ones.

By the late 1980s DC launched several innovative projects. The upscale, limited-edition series, *Batman: The Dark Knight Returns* (March 1986), warranted national publicity and redefined the popular character. Alan Moore, a British writer who had already given new life to DC's *Swamp Thing*, wrote what many believe to be one of the most complex and rewarding comic-book series of the 1980s, *Watchmen* (September 1986).

DC continued its renovations and innovations with a revamped version of *Superman* (January 1987), *Wonder Woman* (February 1987), *Flash* (June 1987), and *Justice League International* (May 1987).

With over five hundred published titles, DC Comics not only is the oldest American comic-book publisher, but also publisher of the most widely recognized comic-book characters in the world.

DELL PUBLISHING COMPANY (1936–1973)

Although George T. Delacorte and Dell Publishing were early pioneers in the comic-book field with the 1929 tabloid-size *The Funnies*, it was not until 1936 that they began publishing a regular line of newsstand comic books.

The first three regular titles—*Popular Comics* (February 1936), *The Funnies* (October 1936), and *The Comics* (March 1937)—

were packaged and printed for Dell by M. C. Gaines at the McClure Syndicate offices. They followed Gaines's early format for *Famous Funnies* by using newspaper-strip reprints.

In 1938, Dell Publishing contracted with Western Printing and Lithography to prepare *original* material for its comic-book line. These comics now were being printed by Western's Whitman division in Poughkeepsie, New York, and packaged under the direction of Oskar Lebeck.

When *Super Comics* (May 1938) and *Crackajack* (June 1938) were added to Dell's lineup, they represented more original material and characters.

Dell's big break in the comic-book field came in 1940, when Helen Meyer, Delacorte's vice-president, successfully negotiated with Walt Disney Studios to produce the first issue

Batman: The Dark Knight #3, © 1986 DC Comics, Inc.

of *Walt Disney's Comics and Stories* (October 1940), as well as other comics featuring the Disney characters.

Over the next two years Dell also secured rights to publish the cartoon characters of Warner Brothers Studios (*Looney Tunes*, Fall 1941), Walter Lantz Studios (*New Funnies*, July 1942), and MGM Studios (*Our Gang*, September 1942).

As the first publisher of "funny animal" comics, Dell aggressively launched a fantastically successful line of humor comics for younger readers. These included *Animal Comics* (December 1941), which featured the first appearance of Walt Kelly's Pogo Possum, *Fairy Tale Parade* (June 1942), *Santa Claus Funnies* (December 1942), and *Donald Duck #9* (1942), the first full-length original Disney comic book.

The Donald Duck comic was the ninth issue in Dell's Four Color Series (September 1939), which would become the backbone of its comic-book line. Every month four to six new Dell comics appeared as part of the Four Color Series.

From 1941 to 1948, Dell used the Four Color Series as a home for *Bugs Bunny, Mickey Mouse, Flash Gordon, Roy Rogers,*

Looney Tunes #83, © 1948 Warner Bros. Pictures

Woody Woodpecker, Popeye, and over 200 other books featuring newspaper, cartoon, and original characters. The Four Color Series was a convenient way for Dell to try out and gauge the sales of many different books under one umbrella title, thus avoiding the overhead of publishing dozens of separate titles.

By the late 1940s and early 1950s, however, comic-book sales were so strong that Dell graduated many of its titles in the Four Color Series to separate titles of their own.

Popular movie heroes, like *Tarzan, Roy Rogers,* and the *Lone Ranger,* were all given their own books in January 1948. The ever-popular *Popeye* and *Little Lulu* both began their own series the next month (February 1948).

Walt Disney's Comics #96, © 1948 Walt Disney Productions

The Funnies #1, © 1936 Dell Publishing Co., Inc.

ALLEZ-OOP	CAPTAIN EASY	FRECKLES	MUTT & JEFF	'SPARAGUS
BECK'S "DOG'S LIFE"	CURIOUS WORLD	HAPPY MULLIGAN	NUGENT'S PUZZLE PAGE	STAMP PAGE
BEN WEBSTER	DAN DUNN	HERKY	OUT OUR WAY	STRANGER THAN FICTION
BOOTS	DON DIXON	MAJOR STRANGE	REGLAR FELLERS	TAILSPIN TOMMY
BRONC PEELER	FLAPPER FANNY	MYRA NORTH	SALESMAN SAM	TINY MITES & OTHERS

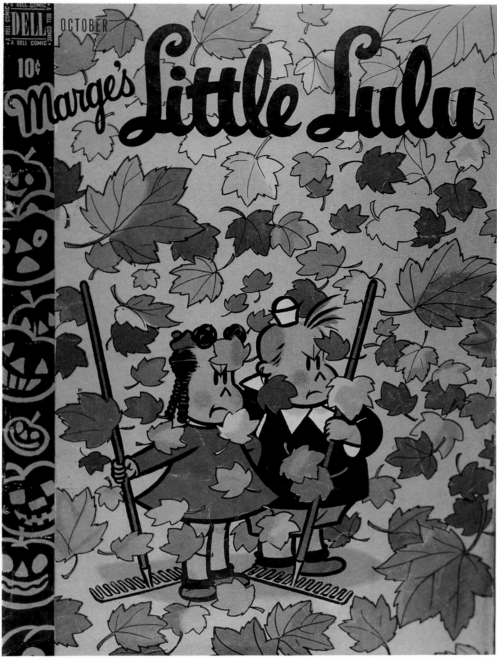

Little Lulu #16, © 1949 Western Publishing Co.

"Intelligence and wit almost invariably triumphed over violence in the *Little Lulu* comics. Time and time again, there were stories in which some physical threat was overcome by thought and Ulysses-like craft. Brutish force was shown to be ridiculous and evil; strategy was portrayed as the admirable solution to a problem."
—MAGGIE THOMPSON, comic-book historian and critic

Over the next five years, Dell would undergo an explosion of growth by moving title after title from the Four Color Series into continuing books of their own, like *Porky Pig, Donald Duck, Bugs Bunny, Woody Woodpecker, Andy Panda,* and *Uncle Scrooge.* The Four Color Series still continued strong all through the 1950s and early 1960s, with over thirteen hundred comic books appearing under its auspices.

The Comics Code, which dealt a blow to some of the comic publishers, actually enhanced Dell Comics' position in the later 1950s because of its reputation for wholesomeness and respectability. Indeed, Dell Comics was the only major publisher, other than Classics Illustrated, which did not submit its comics for Code approval; Dell already had its own rigid set of standards!

During the 1950s Dell was the largest publisher of comic books in the world. In these boom years, Dell sold over three hundred million comic books annually—more than three times as many as all the comic-book publishers in 1981 sold together! By the 1960s, however, Dell Comics underwent a drop in circulation, causing a radical change in its comic-book operations.

From 1940 through 1961, all comics published by Dell were prepared by Western Printing and Lithography. In 1961, Dell Publishing—still the sales leader in comic books—raised the price of its comics from ten cents to fifteen cents. Since the other comic publishers kept their comics priced at ten cents for several more months, then only raised their prices to twelve cents at the beginning of 1962, Dell took a beating in the marketplace.

For example, Dell's flagship title, *Walt Disney's Comics and Stories,* had been selling nearly two million copies per month in 1960.

Carl Barks begins another of his many adventure stories featuring Uncle Scrooge, Donald Duck, and his three nephews—Huey, Dewey, and Louie. *Donald Duck #189,* © *June 1948 Walt Disney Productions*

"The Dell Trademark is, and always has been, a positive guarantee that the comic magazine bearing it contains only clean and wholesome entertainment. The Dell code eliminates entirely, rather than regulates, objectionable material. That's why when your child buys a Dell Comic you can be sure it contains only good fun."

—Dell Comics' "Pledge to Parents"

With the price increase, sales fell to one million by the end of 1961, and down to half a million by 1962.

Because of licensing fees and declining sales, by mid-1961 Dell decided to produce its own comics in-house. Evidently Western felt that Dell's decision was not in Western's best interests, so Western decided to take its titles with them. In 1962 Western began publishing its own product under the new Gold Key line.

Dell Comics after 1962 differed significantly from the Western-packaged books. For one thing, the popular licensed characters like Donald Duck, Bugs Bunny, Tarzan, and the Lone Ranger were now part of the Gold Key line.

Dell Comics, now under the direction of veteran comic-book artist and designer L. B. Cole, developed several new characters to replace its lost licensed characters. As a result, Dell introduced new characters and titles

Three Stooges Meet Hercules, © *1963 Norman Maurer Productions*

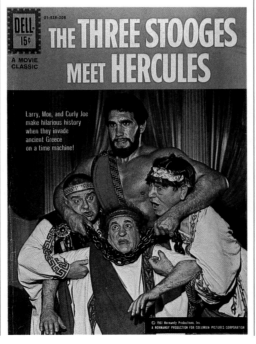

Kona #5, © *1963 Dell Publishing Company*

such as *Nukla, Melvin Monster, Brain Boy,* and a trio of prehistoric and jungle kings called *Toka, Kona,* and *Naza.*

Dell also held onto a few licensed characters such as Mighty Mouse, Felix the Cat, Heckle and Jeckle, and Mr. Magoo. They also developed several war titles (*Jungle War Stories, Combat, Air War Stories*), as well as mystery and science-fiction titles (*Ghost Stories, Tales from the Tomb, Flying Saucers, Space Man*).

The great majority of the post-1962 Dell titles, however, were television and movie adaptations. From television Dell Comics gave us *Bewitched, Perry Mason, Dr. Kildare, The Monkees, The Mod Squad, Ben Casey, The Beverly Hillbillies, Get Smart, Gentle Ben, The Outer Limits, Room 222,* and dozens more.

Dell's movie adaptations included *King of Kings, Tammy Tell Me True, Sons of Katie Elder, Beach Blanket Bingo, The Music Man, Three Stooges Meet Hercules,* and over sixty other movie titles from the 1960s.

By the 1970s, Dell was reprinting some of

its earlier 1960s titles. With a decrease in TV/movie adaptations and no strong stable of regular characters, in late 1973 Dell Publishing Company ended its long involvement with comics and closed its record of over eight hundred different titles published in thirty-seven years.

EASTERN COLOR PRINTING COMPANY (1933–1955)

(Famous Funnies, Columbia Comics)

Eastern Color Printing Company, and its later comic-publishing subsidiary, Famous Funnies, Inc., played a starring role in early comic-book history, but quickly faded into the background. In twenty-two years, Eastern Color published only three major comic-book titles.

If nothing else, Eastern Color always will be remembered as the publisher of the first modern American comic book, *Famous Funnies* (1933). For the next seven years, however, Eastern published only that one title—despite the growing boom in comic books that they themselves initiated.

In 1940 Eastern no longer could ignore the lure of the superhero explosion on the newsstands. The company introduced its second major title, *Heroic Comics* (August 1940), which featured costumed heroes such as Hydroman. The similarity between the aquatic hero Hydroman and Marvel Comics' water hero, Sub-Mariner, was no chance coinci-

Famous Funnies #4, © 1934 Eastern Color Printing Co.

Big Shot Comics #4, © 1940 Columbia Comic Corporation

Al Williamson was one of EC's premier science fiction artists. Two of the reasons—his beautiful women and his alien landscapes—are shown here. *Weird Fantasy #15*, © September 1952 William M. Gaines

"We knew EC was doing some interesting stuff, above the average comic book stuff. Different. So, in a way, it was like being above the crowd in some respects . . . It was a labor of love and fun."
—AL WILLIAMSON,
artist, EC Comics

dence. Both were created by Bill Everett, working out of the Funnies, Inc. studio which supplied original material for both *Heroic* and the early Marvel titles.

By the end of World War II, *Heroic Comics* had switched from stories of superheroes to real-life war heroes, keeping the true adventure format until its demise in 1955.

The remaining major Eastern title was *Jingle Jangle Comics* (February 1942), which it described as an "animated cartoon magazine for children ages 6 to 12." The comic book prospered for seven years under the surrealistic talents of George Carlson and his "Pie Face Prince of Old Pretzleburg" strip.

Eastern published twenty-eight titles over the years. The remaining ones usually fell into neat categories: newspaper-strip-character titles, such as *Buck Rogers* (Winter 1940), *Dickie Dare* (1941), *Mickey Finn* (November 1942), and *Steve Roper* (April 1948); humor/teenage titles, like *Juke Box Comics* (March 1948), *Sugar Bowl* (May 1948), and *Club 16* (June 1948); or romance titles, like *Personal Love* (January 1950) and *Movie Love* (February 1950).

In addition to the Famous Funnies subsidiary, Eastern also published under the Columbia Comic Corporation name. The flagship title of Columbia, *Big Shot Comics* (May 1940), featured a costumed-aviator hero, Skyman, who quickly earned his own title (*Skyman*, Fall 1941). Under Columbia, Eastern also published *The Face* (1941), *Dixie Dugan* (July 1942), *Joe Palooka* (1942), and *Sparky Watts* (November 1942). Eastern ended the Columbia Comic Corporation activity with *Big Shot #104* (August 1949).

Along with many other publishers, Eastern Color left the comic business in the mid 1950s. Its last issue was *Famous Funnies #218* (July 1955), the title that started it all.

Heroic Comics #19, © 1943 Eastern Color Printing Co.

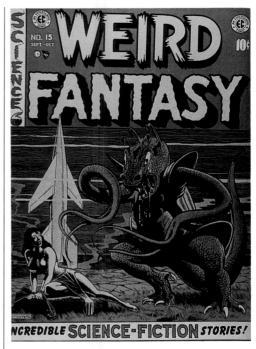

Weird Fantasy #15, © 1953 William M. Gaines

EC COMICS (1946–1956)

EC Comics earned a deserved reputation as publisher of some of the best comic books in history.

In the early 1940s Max C. Gaines, the man who started the industry with *Famous Funnies*, was packaging the All-American line of comics for DC Comics. Gaines had a vision of the new comic-book medium being used for educational purposes. While at DC, he developed *Picture Stories from the Bible* and *Picture Stories from American History*.

When Gaines left DC in 1945, he took those two books with him and used them to launch Educational Comics (EC) in 1946.

The next year he added *Picture Stories from World History* and *Picture Stories from Science* to his educational line. He also began an antiseptic line of kiddie comics, with *Tiny Tot Comics* (March 1946), *Animal Fables* (July 1946), *Land of the Lost* (July 1946) and *Dandy Comics* (Spring 1947). None sold very well.

Gaines now called his business Entertaining Comics (still EC), but his next series of 1947 titles—*International Comics*, *Happy Houlihans*, *Fat and Slat* and others—did not live up to the new name, and sales were unimpressive.

Later that year, Max Gaines died in a boating accident. His son, William M. Gaines, became the publisher of EC at the age of twenty-five. The younger Gaines reorganized the EC line, and by 1948 was publishing two crime comics (*Crime Patrol* and *War Against Crime*), two westerns (*Saddle Justice* and *Gunfighter*), and an adventure comic (*Moon Girl*).

By 1950, William Gaines had six titles, none selling fantastically well. He and his editor, Al Feldstein, decided to completely change all their titles into what they called a

Vault of Horror #28, ©1952 William M. Gaines

"New Trend" of comic books. Although not the first horror comics, EC's New Trend titles, *Vault of Horror* (April 1950), *Haunt of Fear* (May 1950), and *Crypt of Terror* (April 1950, later renamed *Tales from the Crypt*), became the best known horror comics of all time.

The EC horror comics were hosted by the Crypt-Keeper, the Vault-Keeper, and the Old Witch, who introduced and ended each twisted tale with an obligatory gruesome pun: "You might say he really AXED for it, eh kiddies?" The feature that distinguished the EC horror comics from their legion of imitators was the twist ending that always insured the reader wouldn't know what the heck was happening until the last panel.

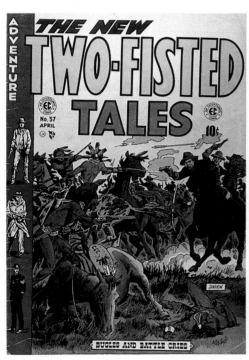

Two Fisted Tales #37, © 1954 William M. Gaines

The other New Trend books for 1950 were *Weird Science* (May 1950) and *Weird Fantasy* (May 1950), perhaps the best science-fiction comic books ever. Aimed at an older audience than the horror comics, the science-fiction titles often adapted stories by Ray Bradbury and dished out food for thought along with

their diet of bug-eyed monsters and space maidens.

Gaines's other New Trend title for 1950 was *Crime Suspenstories* (October 1950), which was a more adult version of the popular crime comics of that day. The stories usually revolved around a love triangle, with a husband or wife and his or her lover deviously murdering the spouse. The deceased spouse then returns from the grave, in graphically rendered stages of decay, to punish the conniving lovers.

At the time Gaines launched his New Trend of comic books, he viewed them as an interesting experiment—done chiefly to amuse himself and Feldstein. When he saw the amazing sales figures for the horror comics, he knew there was an audience for the types of comics he wanted to do. As a result, he used the talents of his new editor and artist, Harvey Kurtzman, to package a book called *Two-Fisted Tales* (November 1950).

Two-Fisted Tales, and its later companion

Tales from the Crypt #43, © 1954 William M. Gaines

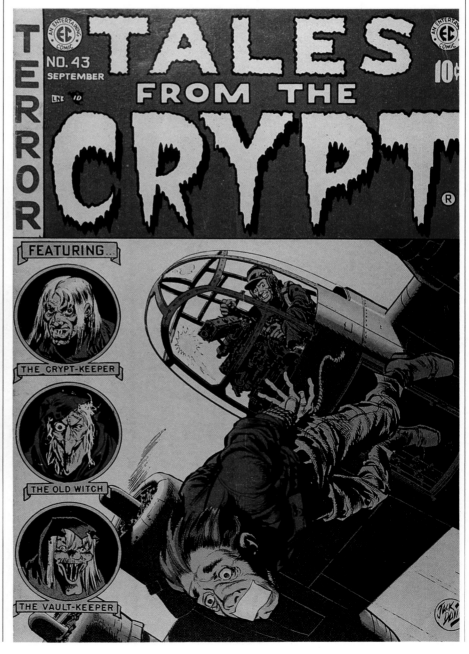

Frontline Combat (July 1951), were the most historically accurate war and adventure comic books made. If a story called for a submarine scene, Kurtzman would go down in a submarine to get the detailed accuracy he wanted in his books. The stories covered not only the Korean War, but also others like the Civil War, the American Revolution, and Roman Empire battles. They portrayed war and fighting men so realistically they became "anti-war" comics.

In 1952 Gaines added another New Trend title, *Shock Suspenstories* (February 1952). This one was hard-hitting in its treatment of such topics as racism, drug addiction, and the anti-communist "witch hunts" of the day—strong stuff for a children's comic book.

Although the EC stories by Feldstein, Kurtzman, and Jack Oleck were literate and often times provocative, it was the EC artwork that elevated the comic books far beyond their forebears, imitators, and successors.

Crime Suspenstories #21, © 1954 William M. Gaines

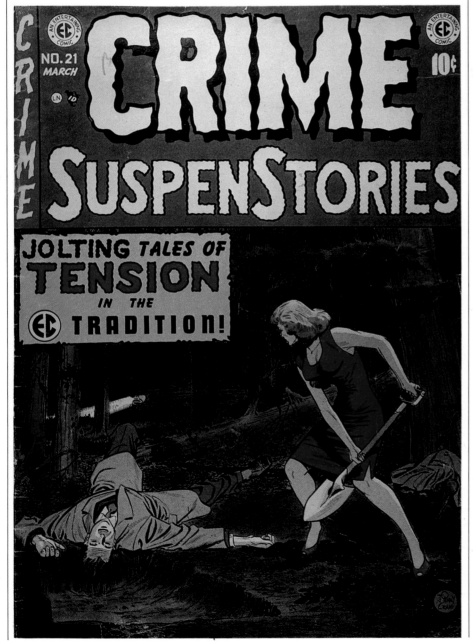

Mad #12, © June 1954 William M. Gaines

EC attracted some of the most talented artists of the day because of its uncompromising quest for quality. Wally Wood, Al Williamson, Frank Frazetta, Jack Davis, Graham Ingels, Reed Crandall, Bernie Krigstein, Johnny Craig, Joe Orlando, George Evans, and John Severin worked on many of the titles and did some of the best work of their careers for EC.

In late 1952, Gaines added his last New Trend title. Created by Harvey Kurtzman, *Mad Comics* (October 1952) forever changed the consciousness of America. *Mad* originally was a parody of other comic books of the day, with such stories as "Super-Duper Man," "Little Orphan Melvin," and "Flesh Garden." It later satirized television, movies, books, advertising, and social customs with a cynical incisiveness that forever captured a growing readership of irreverent adolescents.

The success of *Mad Comics* prompted Gaines to issue *Panic* (February 1954), a companion title edited by Feldstein which somehow never achieved the zip of Kurtzman's *Mad*.

A month after introducing *Panic*, Gaines consolidated his two poorly selling science-fiction titles into *Weird Science-Fantasy* (March 1954). By late 1954, EC Comics had forever transformed the American comic-book scene, through a modest line of only eight titles.

And then trouble began, in the form of congressional hearings on the potentially harmful effects of crime and horror comics. The public outcry against comic books, perpetuated by educators and self-styled experts, gave rise to the Comics Code Authority. This board of self-censorship was established by and for comic publishers and distributors, in an attempt to defuse the opposition to comic books.

Once the Code was in place, by early 1955 Gaines had no choice but to comply with its standards if he wanted his comics distributed. The Code's rules against gore, violence, and adult topics effectively gutted Gaines's New Trend titles. One rule in particular—prohibiting use of the words "crime," "terror," and "horror" in comic-book titles—meant that Gaines had to cease publishing or retitle *Crime Suspenstories* and *Vault of Horror*.

Gaines refused to let the Code put him out of business. Instead, he came up with a line of

Piracy #6, © 1955 William M. Gaines

"I didn't want to join it [the Comics Code] and many other publishers didn't want to join it. But you know what happened if you didn't join? The wholesalers wouldn't handle your book . . . So you had to join. And even after I joined the wholesalers still didn't want to handle my stuff, and I ultimately dropped all my magazines except for *Mad*."
—WILLIAM GAINES,
publisher of *Mad* magazine
and EC Comics

comics called "New Direction" comics. Still using the talents of his best artists and writers, the New Direction titles consisted of *Piracy* (October 1954), *Valor* (March 1955), *Impact* (March 1955), *Extra* (March 1955), *Psychoanalysis* (March 1955), *M.D.* (April 1955), and *Incredible Science Fiction* (July 1955).

Piracy and *Valor* adhered to the old *Two-Fisted Tales* adventure-anthology format, while *Impact* was a cleaned-up version of *Shock Suspenstories*. *Extra* followed the adventures of international reporters, while *M.D.* focused on heroic doctors. *Psychoanalysis*, illustrated exclusively by EC workhorse Jack Kamen, was made up entirely of stories about people in therapy.

Sales of these books were never impressive. Gaines reached his last straw in late 1955, when the Comics Code refused to approve an anti-racism story in *Incredible Science Fiction* on the grounds that it was offensive because its hero, a black man, was shown perspiring! Gaines denounced the Code, ran the story anyway with a bogus Code Approval Seal, and then shut down his New Directions comics at the end of 1955.

He tried to return to his more adult line of comics by issuing black-and-white magazine-sized comics that would bypass Code-regulated distribution channels. Entitled *Shock Illustrated*, *Confessions Illustrated*, *Crime Il-*

> "In 1977, when I began publishing comics, the independent newsstand distributors controlled the comic industry. I decided to aim the Eclipse comics at comic shops because they were the direct path to the discriminating comics fan. I felt then, and continue to feel, that the comics fan is the backbone of the industry, and will continue to support it in a way that the casual newsstand browser will not."
> —DEAN MULLANEY, publisher of Eclipse Comics

lustrated, and *Terror Illustrated*, and proclaimed "picto-fiction," the magazines featured black-and-white comic illustrations with dialogue and descriptions underneath the panels. Sales were so bad that only two issues of each title made it to the newsstands.

The experiment, however, was not without its benefits. Gaines also transformed his biggest selling comic book, *Mad*, into a black-and-white magazine with issue *#24* (July 1955). Although plagued by spotty distribution over the next three years, *Mad* eventually became one of the best selling magazines in America and the most successful humor publication of all time—an especially remarkable feat since it has never accepted advertising.

Although EC ceased its comic-book publishing in early 1956, *Mad Magazine* continues its legacy well over thirty years later.

ECLIPSE COMICS (1978–)

Eclipse Comics began its publishing career by producing one of the first graphic novels (more extended stories in comic-book format), *Sabre* (October 1978). Over the next few years, Eclipse continued to publish graphic novels that were sold in specialty comic-book stores.

By 1983 Eclipse was publishing eight comic books each month and was on its way to becoming one of the major new publishers of the 1980s.

Because most of Eclipse's comics are created and owned by the artists and writers themselves, there often is great variety in the types of comics published. For example, Eclipse has come out with opera adaptations like *Ariane and Bluebeard* (December 1988), horror comics such as *Twisted Tales* (Novem-

Miracleman #7, © 1986 Paul Gulacy

ber 1982), and superheroes like *Miracleman* (August 1985) and *Airboy* (July 1986).

Eclipse also has published American translations of Japanese comic books, such as *Mai the Psychic Girl*, as well as packaged anthologies of classic comic-book stories from the 1950s, including *Mr. Monster's High-Octane Horror* (August 1986) and *Walt Kelly's Christmas Classics* (1988).

FARRELL COMIC GROUP (1952–1958)

Robert W. Farrell began the Farrell Comic Group in 1952 with the financial support of S. Lichtenbert, an investor who also owned part of the Stanley P. Morse comic-book line. Farrell published under a variety of names, including Ajax-Farrell, Excellent Publications, and Four Star Publications.

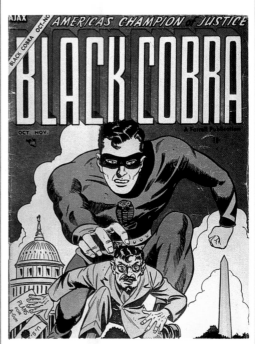

Black Cobra #1, © 1954 Farrell Comics, Inc.

Farrell launched his company at the peak of the horror- and war-comic boom of 1952 with such titles as *Voodoo* (May 1952), *Haunted Thrills* (June 1952), *Battle Report* (August 1952), *War Stories* (September 1952), *Strange Fantasy* (October 1952), and *Fantastic Fears* (May 1953).

Much of the material that appeared in the Farrell comics came from the Iger studio, which also supplied stories for several other small publishers of the day.

Although Farrell built much of its line on the horror comics, it also published westerns like *Swift Arrow* (February 1954), funny-animal comics like *Billy Bunny* (February 1954), romances like *Lonely Heart* (March 1955), and even a *Mad* imitation called *Madhouse* (March 1954).

Interestingly enough, Farrell prospered during the years that many other comic pub-

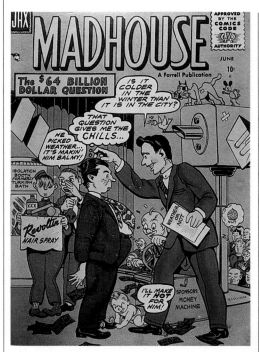

Madhouse, © 1957 Four Star Comic Group

lishers were going under. From 1954 to 1956 Farrell became the ghoul of the comic-book graveyard, feasting upon the remains of such defunct publishers as Star Publications, Comic Media, and Fox Features. From these companies Farrell purchased titles, characters, and any remaining artwork for such comics as *All True Romance* (1955), *Terrific* (1955), and *The Flame* (December 1954).

During the deepest depression of the superhero cycle, Farrell tested the market with such heroes as the *Black Cobra* (October 1954), *Samson* (April 1955), *Wonder Boy* (May 1955) and the *Phantom Lady* (December 1955); none were successful. Farrell next turned to funny-animal and humor titles, such as *Frisky Animals on Parade* (September 1957), *Mighty Bear* (September 1957), and *Mighty Ghost* (June 1958). But they, too, did not save the company.

For the most part, Farrell's titles rarely lasted long enough to attract a steady readership. The company survived as long as it did because of its penurious publishing practices and its willingness to occupy a marginal niche at the lowest end of the comic-book marketplace.

FAWCETT
PUBLICATIONS (1940–1953)

Fawcett Publications published over fifty magazine titles in the mid and later 1930s, among them *True Confessions*, *Motion Picture*, *Real Life Story*, and *Mechanix Illustrated*. In late 1939, Roscoe K. Fawcett announced Fawcett's premier comic-book title, *Whiz Comics*, to his magazine distributors. He promised them that the star of the new comic, Captain Marvel, would be "another character sensation in the comic field!"

He was absolutely right. With the first issue

of *Whiz Comics* (February 1940), Captain Marvel challenged all present and future superheroes for readership popularity.

So popular would Captain Marvel become, that he spawned a whole family of Marvel heroes: Mary Marvel, Captain Marvel Jr., three Lieutenant Marvels, and even Hoppy the Marvel Bunny! His own title, *Captain Marvel Adventures*, was in such high demand that it was published *twice* a month in 1946 and reached a biweekly circulation of nearly one and a half million copies.

The very concept of Captain Marvel appealed to young readers: simply say a magic word ("SHAZAM!"), and you could change from a powerless kid into the "world's mightiest mortal." Coupled with a steady editorial guiding hand and the strikingly simple yet appealing artwork of C. C. Beck and his assistants, Pete Costanza and Kurt Schaffenberger, the Marvel Family titles—*Whiz*,

> "There must be a blood delivery service for vampires! When Mr. Black moved, he must have neglected to notify the milkman . . . I mean *bloodman* . . . of his new address. It's the only possible explanation, Anne!"
> —*Strange Fantasy #7* (August 1953)

Haunted Thrills, © 1954 Farrell Comics, Inc.

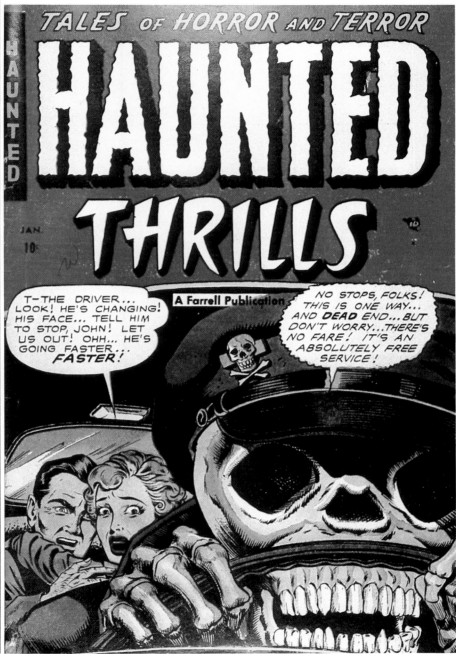

> "An injunction was ordered, forcing Fawcett to close down the Captain Marvel line. Damages per individual copied panel and instances of story plagiarism were awarded. The suit was settled for peanuts instead of the actual millions of dollars involved. Most damaging in the 1953 trial was the testimony of two Fawcett employees that they had been ordered to copy Superman."
> —JACK SCHIFF,
> DC Comics editor

Fawcett's Funny Animals #35, © 1946 Fawcett Publications, Inc.

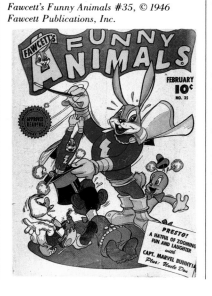

Captain Marvel #96, © 1949 DC Comics, Inc.

Captain Marvel Adventures, Captain Marvel Jr., Master, Wow, Mary Marvel, and *Marvel Family*—prospered until the end of 1953.

Fawcett produced other superhero titles as well, such as *Bulletman* (1941–1946), *Spy Smasher* (1941–1943), and *Captain Midnight* (1942–1948). And although not "super" in the same sense Fawcett's *Don Winslow of the Navy* entertained readers with his heroic exploits for eight years (1943–1951).

Although best known for Captain Marvel, Fawcett published many other memorable titles, among them western comics (*Hopalong Cassidy, Rocky Lane, Gabby Hayes Western, Tom Mix Western, Monte Hale, Lash Larue Western, Western Hero, Six Gun Heroes*), ro-

mance comics (*Life Story, Sweetheart Diary, Romantic Story, True Confidences, Love Memories, Exciting Romances, Sweethearts, True Stories of Romance, I Love You, Love Mystery, Romantic Secrets*), romance westerns (*Cowboy Love, Romantic Western*), horror and science-fiction (*This Magazine Is Haunted, Strange Suspense Stories, Beware Terror Tales, Worlds of Fear, Unknown World*), sports (*Jackie Robinson, Joe Louis, Larry Doby*), humor comics (*Fawcett's Funny Animals, George Pal Puppetoons*), and even a jungle comic (*Nyoka the Jungle Girl*).

Fawcett accounted for a significant percentage of most comic-book sales through the 1940s, with a total annual circulation of comic books ranging from around fifty million copies in 1943 through 1947 to over seventy million comics per year by the end of 1949.

By 1953, however, Captain Marvel finally fell prey to the pending lawsuit by DC Comics (initially filed in 1941) that alleged Captain Marvel infringed on the copyright of their Superman character. With both the lawsuit and the continuing decline of comic-book sales, Fawcett chose to cease publishing comic books.

Marvel Family #84, © June 1953 DC Comics, Inc.

Fawcett sold dozens of its western, romance, and horror titles—like *Lash Larue, Nyoka, Strange Suspense Stories,* and *Romantic Story*—to Charlton Publications in late 1953. Charlton continued the publication of the Fawcett titles in the spring and summer of 1954, with notably less interesting artwork and stories.

In 1958, Fawcett Publications again entered the comic field, but this time primarily as distributor of the popular *Dennis the Menace* comic book. Dennis appeared in a monthly comic, as well as in dozens of spin-off titles, annuals, and digests, keeping Fawcett's hand in the comic business until 1980.

FICTION HOUSE (1938–1954)

Fiction House, like many of the early comic-book publishers, originally published pulp adventure magazines with titles like *Action Stories, Fight Stories, Jungle Stories,* and *Planet Stories.*

But then the Eisner-Iger comic-book-art studio approached Fiction House publisher T. T. Scott with an idea for a comic called *Jumbo Comics.* Among others, it would feature a jungle queen named Sheena. Evidently Scott appreciated a beautiful woman because, from the very first issue, Fiction House comics always featured pin-up type women on its covers.

Jumbo Comics (September 1938) began a twenty-five-year run of jungle queens and goddesses, bound to stakes and staring into the eyes of crazed natives and hungry gorillas. Young men loved the comic, and Fiction House followed its success formula again with *Jungle Comics* (January 1940).

That same month Fiction House also released *Planet Comics,* the first continuously published science-fiction comic, and *Fight Comics.* With the addition of *Wings Comics* (September 1940) and *Rangers Comics* (October 1941), Fiction House established the five main titles that accounted for eighty-five percent of all the comics they published.

Other titles included *Sheena* (Spring 1942), *Wambi* (Spring 1942), *Indians* (Spring 1950), *Ghost* (Winter 1951), *Spirit* (Spring 1952), *Jet Aces* (1952) and *Monster* (1953). Invariably, all the Fiction House titles featured richly-drawn and thinly-written stories of beautiful endangered women in exotic locales.

Interestingly enough, a good portion of the Fiction House "pin-up" strips were drawn by women who used masculine pseudonyms, in deference to the male-dominated comic-book industry.

With the coming of the Comics Code, Fic-

Jumbo Comics #142, © 1949 Fiction House, Inc.

> "The Fiction House gang was able to introduce sexy ladies into every situation and locale. In their stories, you encountered amply constructed and sparsely clad young women on the land, on the sea, and in the air. Deep in the jungles, you ran into beautiful blondes wearing leopardskin undies; off on some remote planet there would be a lovely redhead sporting a chrome-plated bra."
> —RON GOULART,
>
> comic-book historian and author of
> *The Great History of Comic Books*

Jungle Comics #140, © 1952 Fiction House, Inc.

tion House's half-dressed heroines had no place to hide on the newsstand. After more than eight hundred issues, Fiction House ceased publishing comics with *Jungle Comics #163* (Summer 1954).

FIRST PUBLISHING (1983–)

First Publishing was one of the earliest and most successful of the new wave of 1980s comic-book publishers. Its first comic book, *Warp* (March 1983), was aimed at a slightly

American Flagg! #50, © 1988 First Publishing Inc. & Howard Chaykin

older reader than the average newsstand comic-book buyer. One of its more popular titles, *American Flagg!* (October 1983), was a science-fiction political fantasy complete with sex interest.

By 1985 First was becoming one of the largest new publishers with the success of such titles as *Grimjack* (August 1984), *Elric* (August 1985), *Nexus* (April 1985), and *Badger* (May 1985).

First can be credited with several "firsts" in the comic-book field. *Shatter* (June 1985) was the first computer-generated comic book, while *Lone Wolf and Cub* (May 1987) was the first successful American translation of a Japanese comic-book series.

First also has published several graphic novels, including comic-book adaptations of such literary works as *Beowulf* and the Oz series.

Forgotten Forest of Oz, © 1988 First Publishing, Inc.

By 1988 First was publishing thirteen regular comic-book titles, becoming the fourth largest comic-book publisher (after Marvel, DC, and Archie).

FOX FEATURES SYNDICATE (1939–1951)

Victor Fox, a twenty-year veteran of Wall Street, entered the comic-book business as an accountant for Detective Comics, Inc. (DC Comics) in 1938. After witnessing DC's success with Superman, Fox promptly set up his own office in the same building and published *Wonder Comics* (May 1939) which featured a made-to-order imitation of Superman.

Under threat of a lawsuit, Fox dropped Wonder Man and struck out with a series of superhero titles like *Wonderworld* (July 1939), *Mysterymen* (August 1939), and *Fantastic* (December 1939). These comics featured,

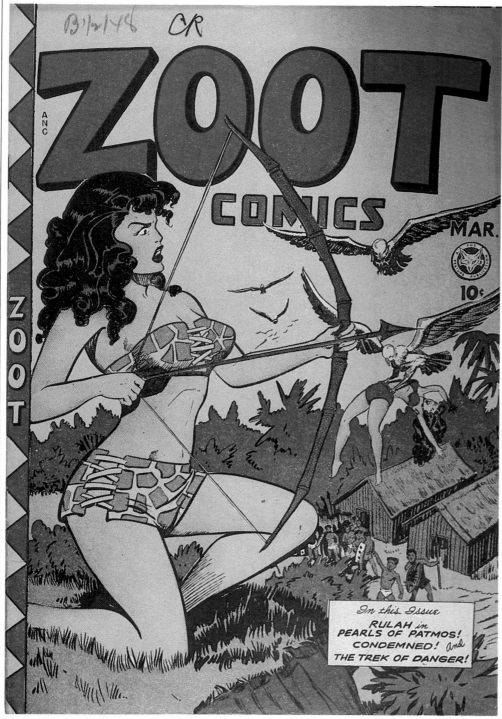

Zoot Comics, © 1948 Fox Features Syndicate

among others, superheroes who soon rated their own series, like *Blue Beetle* (Winter 1939), *The Flame* (Summer 1940), *Green Mask* (Summer 1940), and *Samson* (Fall 1940).

The early Fox issues consisted of artwork supplied by the Eisner-Iger shop and featured outstanding stories by Lou Fine, Bob Powell, and Will Eisner. After dropping the Eisner-Iger studio, Fox hired struggling freelance artists for his books. The quality declined noticeably and Fox's superhero books began to fade.

Like other small publishers of the mid-1940s, Fox began looking for the next trend in comic books. With superheroes losing ground, Fox jumped on the funny-animal and humor comic wave. He quickly issued many uniquely named but otherwise forgettable titles like *Rib Tickler* (1945), *All Top* (1945), *Jo-Jo Comics* (1945), *Zoot* (1946), *Cosmo Cat* (July 1946), and *Wotalife Comics* (August 1946). All of these titles lasted for about two years as humor comics.

In 1947–1948, Fox smelled new blood in the marketplace. The next big sellers would not be super-powered men or talking cats and rabbits; instead, Fox saw his fortune in jungle, crime, and romance comics—all featuring beautiful women and plenty of violence. *Jo-Jo Comics* became *Jo-Jo Jungle King*, and *Zoot* zipped away its funny animals and became another jungle title with barefoot white women.

"Fox would walk up and down the aisles, watching us work. He was a little guy and he had a big cigar and he'd be walking back and forth saying, 'I'm the king of the comics! I'm the king of the comics! Work faster!'"
—JACK KIRBY,
comic-book artist

Matt Baker's *Phantom Lady* was a crime-fighting lass who used a black-out ray as her secret weapon. Her working outfit provided few places for concealing any other weapons. *Phantom Lady #14,* © September 1947 Fox Features Syndicate

Fox gave the boot to Cosmo Cat and packed the Phantom Lady and Rulah of the Jungle into *All Top Comics* (November 1947). For extra measure, he threw in a revamped Blue Beetle that always seemed to rescue well-endowed women.

And speaking of well-endowed, Fox's *Phantom Lady* (August 1947) gave meaning and popularity to the slang term "headlights." Women were everything in a Fox comic, from *Zegra Jungle Empress* (October 1948) to *Rulah* (August 1948), whose legs actually hung over the panels of the page.

Fox also prominently featured women in his new line of crime comics, such as *Crimes by Women* (June 1948) and *Women Outlaws* (July 1948).

Fox's other crime comics, such as *Murder Inc.* (January 1948) and *Crimes Incorporated* (June 1950), were among the most violent, sexy, and poorly drawn of all the comic books of that time.

Even the Fox line of western comics was particularly bloody, with titles like *Western*

Fantastic Comics #10, © 1940 Fox Features Syndicate

Thrillers (August 1948), *Western Killers* (1948), and *Western Outlaws* (September 1948).

Besides jungle and crime, Fox's other big sellers of the late 1940s were romance comics. As was to be expected, Fox's love comics typically were more sordid than most others on the stands. They made up the largest part of the Fox empire at that time, with over twenty-five romance titles like *My Desire* and *My Love Secret.*

The Fox line of comics alone probably would have been enough to draw the attention and attack of the early comic-book critics in the late 1940s. When *Newsweek* magazine asked Fox in 1948 to defend the salacious and lowbrow contents of his books, Fox patiently explained to them that, "There are always

Romantic Thrills, © 1950 Fox Features Syndicate

more morons than people, you know."

Ironically enough, Fox's comics would never have to come under the scrutiny of the Comics Code that he no doubt helped precipitate. By 1951, all of the more than fifty titles he had started in the late 1940s would fail. Three years later, Fox sold the Blue Beetle to Charlton Comics and passed the Phantom Lady on to another third-string publisher, Farrell Comics.

GILBERTON PUBLICATIONS (1941–1971)

(Classics Illustrated)

Classics Illustrated are probably some of the best remembered comic books. They began

when Albert Kanter, a former manufacturer of toy telegraphs, came up with the idea of adapting literary classics into a comic-book format. With two partners, he formed Gilberton Publications and arranged for Lloyd Jacquet's Funnies Inc. shop to provide materials for his new line of literary comic books.

The first issue, an adaptation of Alexandre Dumas's *Three Musketeers* (October 1941), appeared under the imprint Classic Comics. In 1947, the name of the series was changed to Classics Illustrated and one hundred sixty-nine issues appeared over the next twenty years.

The various adaptations, such as *Robinson Crusoe*, *Macbeth*, *Gulliver's Travels*, and *Moby Dick*, proved popular with schoolchildren

> **"In a world of bad comics, we were the best. We were the cleanest, we were the most researched, and, within the limitations of our page length, as faithful to the original as humanly possible."**
> **—MEYER KAPLIN,**
> editor and writer, *Classics Illustrated*

Classics Illustrated #47, © 1948 Gilberton Company, Inc.

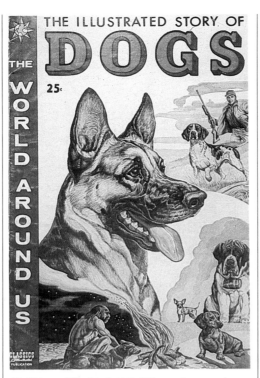

World Around Us #1, © 1958 Gilberton Company, Inc.

looking for a quick book report. Unlike other comics, Classics Illustrated were often reprinted, and some titles had more than twenty printings.

The interiors usually remained the same over the years, but after 1951 new covers were done in a painted style in contrast to the cartoon-line drawing covers of the 1940s.

The enormous success of the Classics Illustrated comic books spawned the Classics Illustrated Junior series (October 1953), seventy-seven fairy-tale adaptations for the younger set. The Junior series featured adaptations of such stories as *Cinderella*, *Paul Bunyan* and *Puss-n-Boots*, lasting for eighteen years.

Gilberton also published a Classics Illustrated Special series of sixteen books from 1955 to 1962 on such topics as *The Atomic Age*, *World War II*, *The Story of Jesus*, and *Prehistoric World*. About the same time, Gilberton produced a similar series, *The World Around Us* (September 1958), whose thirty-six issues gave the classic-comic-book treatment to such subjects as *Dogs*, *Indians*, *Railroads*, *Magic*, and *Fishing*.

The Classics Illustrated series achieved worldwide fame, when in 1948 it began issuing foreign editions in nine different languages. Over two dozen countries carried the international issues of Classics Illustrated. The European series was so popular, it added eighty additional non-U.S. titles and continued publishing original material until 1976—five years after the last American issue.

GLADSTONE PUBLISHING (1986–)

Bruce Hamilton named his company, which specializes in publishing Disney comic books,

Mickey and Donald #2, © 1988 The Walt Disney Company

after Donald Duck's incredibly lucky cousin, Gladstone Gander.

Gladstone's first four titles were *Walt Disney Comics and Stories*, *Uncle Scrooge*, *Donald Duck*, and *Mickey Mouse*, all launched in October 1986. The books continued the original Disney titles which had been in limbo since 1984.

Gladstone's comics feature a mixture of reprints from Disney comics of the previous fifty years, as well as first-time American printings of Disney material created by and for the European market. In the second year of publication some new high-quality American material also began to appear.

The perennial appeal of the Disney characters proved strong enough for Gladstone to add additional titles like *Uncle Scrooge Adventures*, *Donald Duck Adventures*, *Mickey and Donald*, and *DuckTales*. By late 1989, Gladstone lost its rights to publish the Disney comic characters.

LEV GLEASON PUBLICATIONS (1939–1956)

In 1936 Leverett S. Gleason began his career in comics as editor of United's *Tip Top Comics*. Five years later, in 1941, he joined Arthur Bernhard, who was publishing *Silver Streak Comics* (December 1939). Gleason hired Charles Biro, a veteran comic-book writer, artist and editor, to help with two new comics: *Daredevil* (July 1941) and *Boy Comics* (#3, February 1942).

Biro's savvy comic-book packaging and storytelling skills made *Daredevil* and *Boy Comics* newsstand favorites for nearly twenty-five years. The books featured continuing characters like Daredevil, Crimebuster, and the Little Wise Guys, but their real appeal was

Silver Streak Comics #1, © 1940 Lev Gleason Publications

Daredevil #47, © 1948 Lev Gleason Publications

Biro's stories of sympathetic characters with human failings.

In 1942 Gleason changed *Silver Streak Comics* into the first original, continuing comic book on crime: *Crime Does Not Pay* (#22, June 1942). The book received little notice its first year, mustering a monthly circulation of only 213,000 copies—below the break-even point for most comics of that time.

By 1943, however, *Crime Does Not Pay* was showing a profit, with a monthly circulation of 323,000. Over the next five years the number of copies sold steadily increased until it reached a million copies a month in 1948. By

Crime Does Not Pay #97, © 1951 Lev Gleason Publications

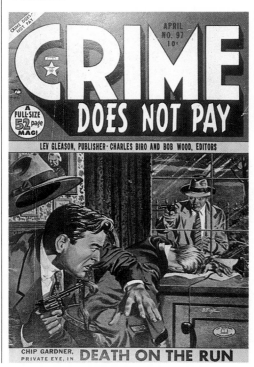

the next year the combined monthly circulation of Gleason's *Boy, Daredevil,* and *Crime* ranked tenth among *all* magazines in the nation, right behind *Life* and *Look* magazines.

For six years Gleason published only the three titles. With the emerging crime-comic boom, he finally added a companion title, *Crime and Punishment* (July 1948).

Westerns and romance comics were the other two best-selling genres of the time. For the horse lovers, Gleason added *Desperado* (June 1948), which later was renamed *Black Diamond Western* (#9, March 1949). For the romantic lovers, he offered *Lovers' Lane* (October 1949) and *Boy Meets Girl* (February 1950).

Gleason added a few other titles in the 1950s, like a movie-star adaptation, *Buster Crabbe* (December 1953), and fairy-tale comics for the younger set, *Uncle Charlie's Fables* (January 1952) and *Adventures in Wonderland* (April 1955).

By 1955 *Crime Does Not Pay* and *Crime and Punishment* had fallen prey to the Comics Code cleanup. Within a year Gleason's romance comics, *Boy Comics,* and *Daredevil Comics* all appeared for the last time.

Uncle Scrooge #105, © 1973 Walt Disney Productions

GOLD KEY (1962–1984)

(Whitman)

After its breakup from Dell Publishing Company in 1962, Western Printing Company began publishing its own books under the Gold Key imprint.

For the most part, Western took the lion's share of titles when it left Dell. Western continued publishing its more successful books, such as *Walt Disney Comics, Uncle Scrooge,* and *Bugs Bunny,* under the new Gold Key la-

"Stand back and shut up, pop! The first one to open his mouth will be swallowing bullets!"
—*Crime Does Not Pay #39*
(November 1943)

bel. Western also lowered the prices on its books from Dell's fifteen cents to twelve cents, the standard industry price at that time.

In addition to the popular Disney, Warner Brothers, and Hanna-Barbera cartoon characters, Gold Key also developed its own line of titles that would be free of licensing fees. The Gold Key universe consisted of such characters (and titles) as *Dr. Solar, Man of the Atom* (October 1962), *Magnus, Robot Fighter* (February 1963), *Mighty Samson* (July 1964), and *Dagar the Invincible* (October 1972).

Like Dell, Gold Key depended heavily upon television and movie adaptations, with such titles as *Bonanza, Twilight Zone, Man from U.N.C.L.E., Lost in Space, How the West Was Won,* and *Beneath the Planet of the Apes.*

In 1980, faced with diminishing newsstand distribution, Gold Key packaged its comic books three-in-a-bag and offered them to department stores and other non-traditional outlets. In 1981, Gold Key changed its imprint to Whitman.

Magnus Robot Fighter #15, © 1966 K. K. Publishing

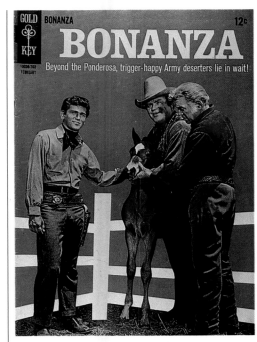

Bonanza #23, © 1967 NBC

For the next three years, Whitman futilely struggled to overcome distribution problems and finally ceased publishing comics in 1984.

HARVEY COMICS (1939–)

Harvey Comics ties with Archie Comics (MLJ/ Archie) as the third longest running comic-book publisher. Started in 1939 by brothers Leon and Alfred Harvey, the company existed under several names before settling on Harvey Comics in 1941.

In its fifty year history (with a publishing suspension from 1982 to 1986), Harvey has published nearly sixty-four hundred comic books and over two hundred fifty titles, ranging from superhero to crime to war to western

Champion Comics #4, © 1940 Worth Publishing Co.

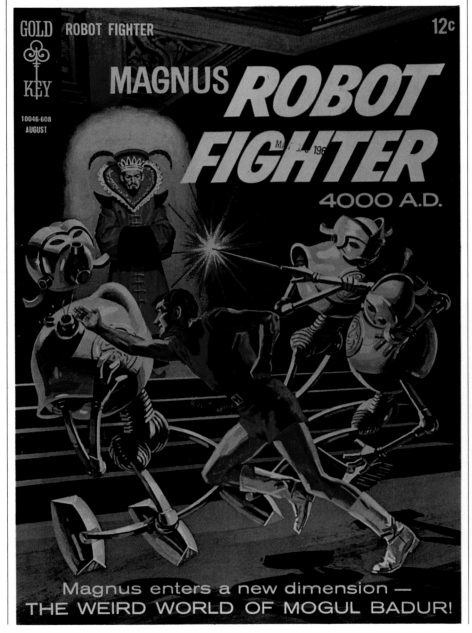

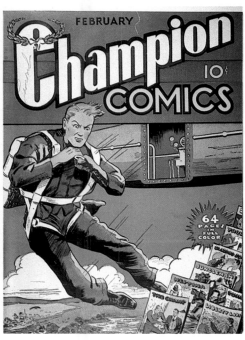

to horror comics.

In its first year, Harvey Comics published *Speed* (October 1939) and *Champion Comics* (December 1939), two adventure titles. In the 1940s Harvey became noted for such heroes as the *Green Hornet* (December 1940), which was borrowed from the radio show and ran until September 1949, and *Black Cat Comics* (June 1946), a Hollywood stunt girl and early super heroine.

From 1946 to 1950 Harvey picked up its sales with comic-strip reprints and adaptations of such characters as *Joe Palooka* (November 1945), *Terry & the Pirates* (April 1947), *Li'l Abner* (December 1947), *Kerry Drake* (January 1948), *Sad Sack* (September 1949), *Dick Tracy* (March 1950), *Blondie* (March 1950), and *Dagwood* (September 1950).

By the early 1950s Harvey had capitalized both on the romance-comic craze (*First Love Illustrated*, *First Romance*, *Hi-School Romance*, *Love Problems and Advice*, *Love Lessons*, *Sweet Love*, *Teen-Age Brides*, *True Bride Experiences*, and *True Bride-to-Be Romances*) and the horror-comics explosion (*Black Cat Mystery*, *Tomb of Terror*, *Chamber of Chills*, and *Witches Tales*).

(September 1953), *Felix the Cat* (August 1955), *Little Lotta* (November 1955), *Spooky the Tuff Little Ghost* (November 1955), *Hot Stuff the Little Devil* (October 1957), *Wendy the Good Little Witch* (August 1960), and *Richie Rich* (November 1960).

Except for a brief foray into the superhero revival of 1966–1967 (*Spyman*, *Spirit*, *Jig Saw*, *Bee-Man*), Harvey would concentrate exclusively on its "kiddie line" by publishing multiple titles of its popular characters: Baby Huey (three titles), Little Dot (three titles), Hot Stuff (three titles), Sad Sack (thirteen titles), Casper (seventeen different titles featuring the "Friendly Ghost"), and the "golden goose" of the Harvey line, Richie Rich (thirty-eight titles devoted to the world's "Poor Little Rich Boy"—more than any other American comic book character).

By 1981 Harvey had cut back its line to only Richie Rich and Hot Stuff titles. In the fall of 1982, Harvey suspended publication,

Black Cat Mystery #45, © 1953 Harvey Features Syndicate

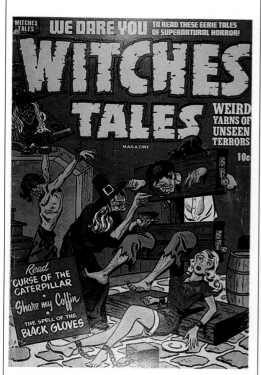

Witches Tales #5, © 1951 Harvey Features Syndicate

In a fortunate move that would assure Harvey's future, in 1952 the company acquired several of the Paramount animated characters and titles from St. John Publishing. Among these titles were *Casper the Friendly Ghost* (December 1952) and *Little Audrey* (August 1952). Also from Paramount Harvey acquired the rights to publish *Baby Huey, The Baby Giant* (September 1956).

During this same period Harvey launched several other wholesome characters aimed at a very young readership, such as *Little Dot*

Richie Rich #44, © 1966 Harvey Features Syndicate

"I think not enough respect is given to the cartoony work. Richie Rich, as I've said many times and I'm sure will say many times again, is the biggest selling character in comics history. Not Mickey Mouse, not Superman, not anybody sold as well as Richie."
—ERNIE COLON,
25-year Richie Rich artist

then reentered the market in 1986 with *Richie Rich Digest.*

HILLMAN PERIODICALS (1940–1953)

Hillman Periodicals, a publisher of movie-star magazines, became the twentieth publisher to enter the exploding comic-book field with *Miracle Comics* (February 1940).

Miracle, and Hillman's next two titles *Rocket* (March 1940) and *Victory* (August 1941), featured standard superhero fare along with a dash of war heroes. Its fourth title, *Air Fighters* (November 1941), featured all flying heroes like the Skywolf, Flying Dutchman, Iron Ace, and Airboy.

Airboy, a combination aviator and superhero, proved to be the most popular of all the Hillman characters and rated his own title, *Airboy Comics* (December 1945). The most memorable Hillman character, however, was the Heap, an undefinable mass of human decay and swamp vegetation who stalked the back pages of *Airboy.*

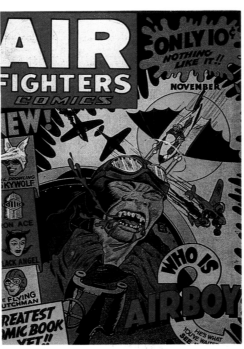

Air Fighters #1, © 1941 Hillman Publications

Clue Comics (January 1943) boasted its own bizarre litany of superheroes like Micro-Face, Zippo, and the Iron Lady. In 1947 it became one of the early crime comics with a title change to *Real Clue Crime* (June 1947). One of the more successful crime comics, *Real Clue* and its companion title, *Crime Detective Cases* (March 1948), lasted until the end of the Hillman career.

Hillman's other efforts included sports comics such as *All-Time Sports Comics* (April 1949), romance comics like *Romantic Confessions* (October 1949), and westerns like *Dead-Eye Western Comics* (November 1948) and *Western Fighters* (April 1948).

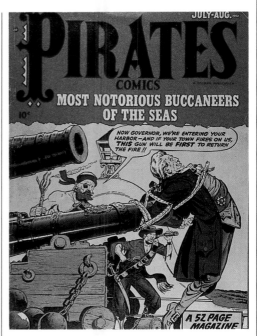

Pirates Comics #3, © 1950 Hillman Publications

By late 1952, Hillman was down to less than six comics. With the May 1953 issues it canceled its remaining titles.

HOLYOKE PUBLISHING COMPANY (1940–1946)
(Continental Publishing)

Frank Z. Temerson, a former city attorney for Birmingham, Alabama, first entered the comic-book business in 1937. He and a partner purchased both the Comics Magazine Company and Harry "A" Chesler's comic-book lineup. A few months later, in 1938, they sold their comic book business to Centaur Publishing.

Suspense Comics #9, © 1945 Continental Magazines

Temerson, under the name Tem Publishing, returned to comics with *Crash Comics* (May 1940). The next year he renamed it *Catman Comics* (May 1941) after the title's star superhero. Temerson also changed his company's name to Holyoke Publishing.

Next up were *Captain Fearless* (August 1941) and *Captain Aero* (December 1941), complete with super patriots and aviator demigods.

By 1943 Holyoke was known as Continental Publishing. It issued *Suspense Comics* (December 1943), a ground-breaking early horror and mystery comic distinguished by L. B. Cole's artwork. Continental then followed up in 1944 with such titles as *Terrific*, *Contact*, and *Power Comics*, all featuring covers by the prolific Cole.

For all its efforts, however, Continental never had more than four major titles in publication at any one time. In 1946 it canceled its remaining three—*Catman*, *Captain Aero*, and *Suspense*—and was out of the comic-book business.

IW/SUPER COMICS (1958–1964)

Israel Waldman (IW) began IW/Super Comics by purchasing the printing plates of various 1940s and 1950s comic-book titles from a Connecticut printer.

Waldman used the plates and simply made reprints of the various companies' books without obtaining permission. He put new covers on the books and bypassed the Comics Code by distributing the books through non-conventional channels. They often appeared in plastic bags at a cut rate (three for twenty-five cents) in places where comics were not usually sold—variety stores, five-and-dime stores, small grocery stores, etc.

Strange Planets #18, © 1964 I. W. Enterprises

The IW/Super Comics provide historical interest because they reprinted a wide variety of comic-book titles from the late 1940s through the early 1950s, such as *Plastic Man*, *The Spirit*, *Ziggy Pig*, *Space Mysteries*, and *Muggy Doo the Boy Cat*.

IW/Super published over one hundred twenty reprint titles, running the full gamut—from horror to war to western to romance to jungle to superhero to funny-animal titles.

KING FEATURES SYNDICATE (1966–1968)

The newspaper comic-strip characters from King Features Syndicate (a member of the Hearst group) have appeared in comic books from various publishers since 1936. During the great comic-book boom of 1966, King decided to enter the field as a publisher in its own right. William Harris served as editor of a line of comics that featured the famous King characters in all new stories.

During its first month of publication, in August 1966, King issued *Beetle Bailey*, *Popeye*, and *Blondie*. The next month, September 1966, saw the first King issues of *Flash Gordon*, *Phantom*, and *Mandrake the Magician*.

Flash Gordon #7, © 1967 King Features Syndicate

The original stories and art in all the books were uniformly competent, with several issues of *Flash Gordon* containing outstanding artwork by Al Williamson and Reed Crandall.

The King comics often were distributed by packaging either the three humor comics or the three adventure titles in a plastic bag and selling all three at once. Unfortunately, this distribution method did not work out well, and King was unable to establish itself in the now crowded comic-book field. By the end of 1967 it suspended regular publication of its titles.

"Our story conferences at Hillman were memorable to say the least. Ed Cronin [the editor] was so good at creating comic book stories because he never had a grip on reality. I remember one instance when he began, 'Airboy is about to get into his birdplane when suddenly the Empire State Building comes flying by.' And from that wild germ of an idea an entire fanciful, thrilling tale evolved."
—HERB ROGOFF, comic-book writer and editor, Hillman Publishing

"No! You must not kill! Only the law can take a life! Even *these* men have the right to a fair trial by jury!"
—*Straight Arrow*
(September 1950)

In 1968, King Features Syndicate reprinted the first issue of *Flash Gordon* as an Army giveaway comic. During the 1970s, the company again reprinted its comics as part of an educational series called the Comics Reading Library. The books were used to encourage reading in the classroom and featured a vocabulary list of words used in each comic.

For all practical purposes, however, King was out of the comic-publishing business by late 1967. In early 1969 Charlton Comics took over publishing the King characters and titles.

MAGAZINE ENTERPRISES/ ME (1944–1958)

Magazine Enterprises (ME) was started by Vincent Sullivan, a veteran of DC Comics since 1935. He had served as the editor of both *Detective Comics* (Batman) and *Action Comics* (Superman). He left DC in 1940 to become editor of Columbia Comics' new line of titles, consisting initially of *Big Shot* and *Skyman Comics*. A little over three years later, Sullivan started Magazine Enterprises and hired Raymond Krank as his editor.

Sullivan started his comic-book line with a single title, *A-1 Comics* (1944), which originally began as an anthology title of mostly forgettable humor and adventure strips like "Texas Slim" and "Inca Dinca." By 1948, Sullivan and Krank were trying out new titles under the *A-1 Comics* title.

By rotating characters, such as Tim Holt, Ghost Rider, and Cave Girl, in and out of the A-1 series, ME was able to maintain over a dozen different comic books under a single umbrella title. In an eleven-year period, ME published one hundred thirty-nine comic books under the *A-1 Comics* title, which no doubt simplified their distribution and accounting procedures.

Cave Girl #11, © 1953 Magazine Enterprises

ME published titles in many genres like war, science fiction, jungle and comedy, with titles such as *American Air Forces* (1951), *Space Ace* (1953), *Thunda, King of the Congo* (1952), and *Muggsy Mouse* (1951).

Among the better known artists who worked for ME were Frank Frazetta, Dick Ayers, Fred Meager, Frank Bolle and the prolific Bob Powell. Gardner Fox, the author of many DC comics, became the chief writer of the ME comic line.

In 1948 ME bought out its first licensed character, *Tim Holt*, a western movie star from RKO studios. The book was so successful, ME next tried comics based upon other movie personalities, such as comedian *Jimmy*

A-1 Comics #3, © 1946 Magazine Enterprises

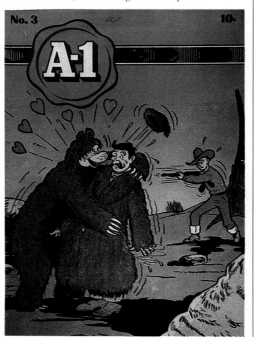

Mighty Atom #3, © 1958 Magazine Enterprises

Durante (1948) and leading screen man *Dick Powell* (1949).

These books failed, and ME soon realized that it was not just movie stars readers wanted, but *western* stars. It quickly licensed *The Durango Kid* (October 1949), a Columbia Pictures character who had appeared in sixty-five movies. ME raided the radio for its next two western titles, *Straight Arrow* (February 1950) and *Bobby Benson's B-Bar-B Riders* (May 1950). Rounding out its western lineup was Dick Ayers's *Ghost Rider* (1950), a spectral costumed cowboy who captured the imagination of horror-comic fans, as well.

By 1956 ME was publishing only a few humor comics, like *The Brain* (September 1956), *Clubhouse Rascals* (June 1956), and the *Mighty Atom* (November 1957). When it reissued a few humor titles in 1958, these were the last ME comics.

MARVEL COMICS (1939–)
(Timely, Atlas)

For most of its existence, Marvel Comics has published under several names. For three months in 1942 it was known as Timely Comics. Many comic historians still refer to all Marvel Comics from the '40s as Timely.

During the first half of 1947 and again for a year and a half between 1949–1950, the Marvel Comic symbol appeared on the comic covers. From 1951 to 1957 the Atlas globe symbol was used on the cover to distinguish Marvel Comics, and collectors often refer to these issues as Atlas Comics. Adding to the confusion, Marvel (under the Timely, Atlas, and Marvel imprints) issued comics under fifty-nine different publishing names. By 1962, however, all of the company's comics would be known as Marvel Comics.

All Winners #8, © 1943 Marvel Entertainment Group, Inc.

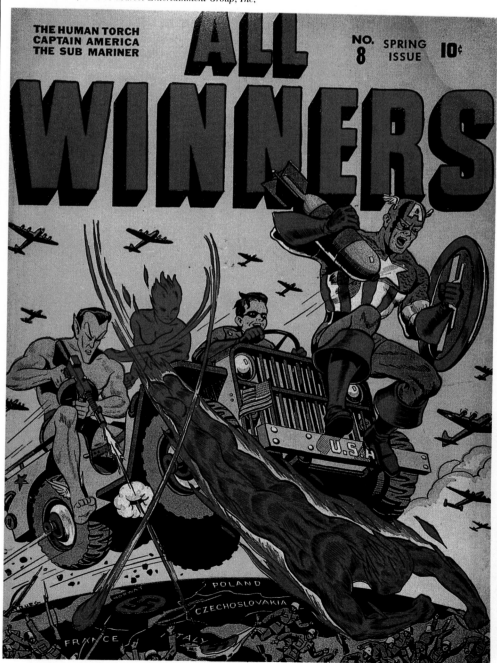

Red Raven #1, © 1940 Marvel Entertainment Group, Inc.

"During the first two decades I toiled for Timely [Marvel] the comic book business was a fairly simplistic operation. If cowboy films were the rage, we produced a lot of westerns. If cops and robbers were in vogue, we'd grind out a profusion of crime titles. If the trend turned to love stories, Timely became big in romance mags. We simply gave the public what it wanted—or so we thought."
—STAN LEE

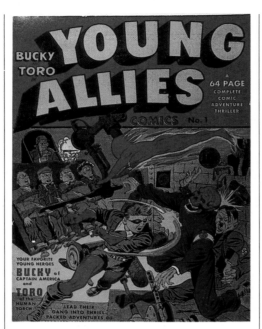

Young Allies Comics #1, © 1941 Marvel Entertainment Group, Inc.

Martin Goodman, a pulp publisher of the 1930s, began the Marvel line of comics in 1939 with publication of *Marvel Comics* (November 1939). By the second issue the title became *Marvel Mystery Comics* (December 1939).

The comic book launched a whole line of superhero comics, with the Human Torch and the Sub-Mariner as the stars of the new title. After *Marvel Mystery* came *Daring Mystery* (January 1940), *Mystic* (March 1940), and *Red Raven* (August 1940), featuring heroes like the Human Top, the Silver Scorpion, and Flexo the Rubber Man.

The Human Torch, created by Carl Burgos, and the Sub-Mariner, created by Bill Everett, quickly rated their own books, *Human Torch* (Fall 1940) and *Sub-Mariner* (Spring 1941). At

The Human Torch, © 1940 Marvel Entertainment Group

the same time the third major Marvel hero of the 1940s leapt from the pens of Joe Simon and Jack Kirby into his own title, *Captain America* (March 1941).

The next Marvel Comic, *All Winners* (Summer 1941), teamed up the Human Torch, the Sub-Mariner, and Captain America in one book. With the addition of other superhero titles like *Young Allies*, *USA Comics*, *All Select*, *Tough Kid Squad*, and *Kid Komics*, Marvel Comics covered the newsstands of pre-World War II America with its flashy heroes and lurid comic covers.

Many of those comics were written by a teenager, Stan Lee (aka Stanley Leiber), who was Martin Goodman's cousin-in-law. Lee wrote his first filler material for *Captain America #3* in 1941. By the next year, he was writing scripts for *Mystic Comics*. With the departure of Joe Simon, co-creator of Captain America, Lee was made editor of Marvel Comics. Over the next thirty years, at one time or another he would edit or write almost every Marvel comic book.

Battle #11, © 1952 Marvel Entertainment Group, Inc.

Some of Lee's early original creations were cartoon characters, like Ziggy Pig and Silly Seal, which he and other writers and artists developed for *Krazy Komics* and other new humor comics like *Comedy* (April 1942), *Joker* (April 1942), *Krazy* (July 1942), and *Powerhouse Pepper* (1943).

Marvel Comics continued its formula of superheroes and funny comics until 1948, when sales on all superhero comics plummeted. By the next year Marvel suspended publication of *Marvel Mystery*, *Captain America*, *Human Torch*, and *Sub-Mariner*.

As Marvel reorganized its line to follow the new romance trend, the *Human Torch* became *Love Tales* (June 1949) and *Sub-Mariner* changed into *Best Love* (August 1949). Other

Although crime comic books proudly proclaimed themselves to be lessons against crime, you can bet none of the readers were perusing them for moral instruction. *All-True Crime #26*, © *February 1948 Marvel Entertainment Group, Inc.*

"Marvel Comics. Not so much a name as a state of mind. Not so much a group of magazines as a mood, a movement, a mild and momentary madness."
—STAN LEE,
former editor, publisher, and writer of Marvel Comics

Marvel love comics soon proliferated, like *My Own Romance* (March 1949), *Love Romances* (May 1949), *Love Adventures* (October 1949), and *True Secrets* (March 1950).

Marvel also jumped on the western boom, with *Two-Gun Kid* (March 1948), *Kid Colt* (August 1948), *Wild West* (Spring 1948), and *All Western Winners* (Winter 1948). Many more westerns would come out through the 1950s, with Kid Colt and Two-Gun Kid lasting until the 1970s.

Crime comics also were big sellers by the late 1940s, and Marvel responded with *All-True Crime Cases* (February 1948), *Crime Exposed* (June 1948), *Crime Can't Win* (September 1950), and *Crime Must Lose* (October 1950).

By 1950 horror comics suddenly were in demand. Marvel, under its Atlas imprint, issued twenty-five titles devoted to ghouls and fiends. These almost always consisted of five or six short stories with surprise endings. Marvel's formula horror comics included *Adventures into Terror* (November 1950), *Adventures into Weird Worlds* (January 1952), and *Uncanny Tales* (June 1952).

The Korean "police action" inspired Marvel, along with many other publishers, to start a line of war comics. Of all the 1950s war comics, Marvel's were perhaps the most visible and

anti-communist. With titles like *Battle* (March 1951), *War Adventures* (January 1952), *Battle Action* (February 1952), *War Action* (April

Uncanny Tales #52, © *1957 Marvel Entertainment Group, Inc.*

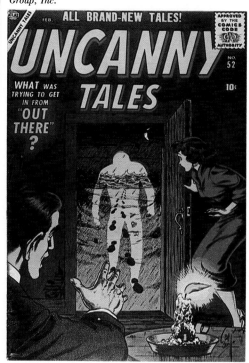

Fantastic Four #73, © 1968 Marvel Entertainment Group, Inc.

Journey Into Mystery #1, © 1952 Marvel Entertainment Group, Inc.

1952), *Combat* (June 1952), and *Battleground* (September 1954), Marvel packed its war comics full of gritty "he-man" action with a heaping helping of "blood and guts" patriotism.

After the comic recession in the mid-1950s, Marvel subsisted chiefly upon its humor and teen comics and its science-fiction titles.

Two science-fiction titles, *Strange Tales* and *Journey into Mystery*, were among the better selling Marvel comics of the late 1950s. Influenced by the 1950s science-fiction films, the comics usually featured a giant monster invader with an unpronounceable name, like Gomdulla, Grotto, Gorgolla, Zzutak, Vandoom, Moomba, and Fin Fang Foom.

Silly as it sounds, the formula worked well enough to launch three new books: *Tales of Suspense* (January 1959), *Tales to Astonish* (January 1959), and *Amazing Adventures* (June 1961). Along with *Strange Tales* and *Journey into Mystery*, these titles formed the breeding ground for Marvel's new line of 1960s superheroes.

In 1961, or so the story goes, Martin Goodman noticed the high circulation figures for *Justice League of America*, a new DC title featuring Batman, Superman, Wonder Woman and the recently revitalized Flash and Green Lantern. Goodman asked Stan Lee to come up with Marvel's own team of superheroes. Lee

Journey Into Mystery #85, © 1962 Marvel Entertainment Group, Inc.

responded with the *Fantastic Four* (November 1961).

Jack Kirby, who had recently returned to Marvel fulltime after working for DC, helped Lee create the characters for what they modestly called "The World's Greatest Comic Magazine!" Lee transformed the Human Torch character from the 1940s into a 1960s version with a new secret identity, Johnny Storm. Johnny's sister, Sue, was the Invisible Girl. The third member of the Fantastic Four was Reed Richards, also known as Mr. Fantastic because of his amazing stretching powers. The final character, Ben Grimm, was simply called the Thing.

Originally a test pilot, Grimm was blasted by the atomic radiation which had transformed the other Fantastic Four members as well. He turned into a rocky mass of orange scaly flesh, the Thing, bearing a certain resemblance to other monsters that Kirby had been drawing for books like *Strange Tales* and *Journey into Mystery*.

The *Fantastic Four* became home to many new Marvel characters, including a revitalized Sub-Mariner, their arch-enemy Dr. Doom, the Silver Surfer, and the Black Panther. The rich character development and interplay in *Fantastic Four* became the hallmark of all the 1960s Marvel comics.

Fantastic Four was so successful that Lee and Kirby immediately produced another superhero title, *The Incredible Hulk* (May 1962). Instead of dropping existing titles to make way for other new superhero characters, Lee made room in *Journey into Mystery #83* (August 1962) for his next superhero, Thor the Thunder God, whose stories were steeped in Norse mythology.

Lee next turned to *Amazing Fantasy* (formerly *Amazing Adventures*) and the artist who

was drawing all the stories for that magazine, Steve Ditko. Lee and Ditko created what was to become the most famous Marvel superhero of all time, Spider-Man, in the last issue of *Amazing Fantasy* (#15, August 1962).

Back to another monster title, *Tales to Astonish*, where Lee originally had written a science-fiction story about a man in an anthill. Lee brought the character back and gave him a name (the Ant Man), a costume, and a regular strip in *Tales to Astonish #35* (September 1962). Ant Man later gained a girl friend, the Wasp, and eventually obtained the power to enlarge to giant size—which earned him a new name, Giant Man.

The next month the Human Torch was spun off from the Fantastic Four into his own strip in *Strange Tales #101* (October 1962), where he eventually would be joined by the Thing in a comedy/adventure team-up series.

The remaining all-monster title, *Tales of Suspense* (#39, March 1963), became home to

> "I never talk about myself. My work is me. I do my best, and if I like it, I hope somebody else likes it, too."
> —STEVE DITKO, co-creator of *Spider-Man*

Amazing Fantasy #15, © 1962 Marvel Entertainment Group, Inc.

Amazing Spider-man #7, © 1963 Marvel Entertainment Group, Inc.

"If ever there was a perfect artist and co-plotter for our amazing arachnid, it had to be the dazzling Mr. D [Ditko]! His layouts and drawings set the unique illustrative style for the strip, a style that would last for many years to come, a style that made Spidey utterly distinctive among comic strip creations. His sense of pacing, his flair for action scenes, and his ability to make the most outlandish situations look totally believable after he had drawn them gave the early Spider-Man stories an impetus that helped keep them rolling until this very day."
—STAN LEE,
co-creator of *Spider-Man*

the next Marvel superhero, Iron Man. A wealthy industrialist, Iron Man Tony Stark invented his iron suit of armor to provide a support system for his weak heart.

That same month Spider-Man moved into his own title, *Amazing Spider-Man* (March 1963), after an "amazing" reader reception to his try-out appearance in *Amazing Fantasy*.

Strange Tales #107, © 1963 Marvel Entertainment Group, Inc.

The summer of 1963 would see yet more new Marvel heroes. In *Strange Tales #110* (July 1963), Dr. Strange, a supernatural hero drawn by Steve Ditko, entered other dimensions on mystical adventures that seemed to

Tales of Suspense #59, © 1964 Marvel Entertainment Group, Inc.

Daredevil #37, © 1968 Marvel Entertainment Group, Inc.

anticipate the psychedelic revolution.

By now Marvel had such a stable of superheroes that it could muster a team title, so Thor, Iron Man, the Hulk, Ant Man, and the Wasp joined together in the *Avengers* (September 1963). The Hulk left a few issues later and was replaced by Captain America, another Marvel superhero revived from the 1940s.

The other team title, issued the same month as the *Avengers*, was the *X-Men* (September 1963). Five teenagers with mutant powers, the X-Men did not reach their height of popularity until after they were refashioned into a new team in the 1970s.

The last burst of the Marvel superhero explosion came from *Daredevil* (May 1964), a blind superhero. With his finely developed extrasensory powers, Daredevil could "see" and fight his enemies more accurately than his sighted colleagues.

Although superheroes were the order of the day from 1962 to 1964, Marvel also released some other interesting titles. *Sgt. Fury and His Howling Commandos* (May 1963), with its multi-ethnic mix of World War II fighting men, resembled the Blackhawks but had more finely realized characters and snappier dialogue.

Westerns *Kid Colt Outlaw, Rawhide Kid,* and *Two-Gun Kid* received the new Marvel treatment of three-dimensional characterization. Even the remaining teen/love title, *Millie the Model*, bore the earmarks of the new Marvel house style.

In 1968 Marvel Comics and Stan Lee signed up with Curtis Distributing and Marvel eventually was bought by Cadence Industries Corporation. During this time Marvel began to challenge DC Comics for dominance in the marketplace by launching several new titles. All of the major characters in its old fantasy

Avengers #4, © 1964 Marvel Entertainment Group, Inc.

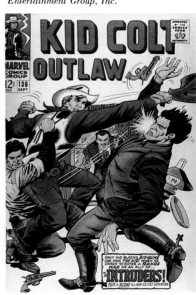

Kid Colt Outlaw #136, © 1967 Marvel Entertainment Group, Inc.

titles like *Tales of Suspense* and *Tales to Astonish* received their own comic books, including *Captain America* (April 1968), *Incredible Hulk* (April 1968), *Sub-Mariner* (May 1968), and *Iron Man* (May 1968).

By the early 1970s the second superhero cycle was winding down. Instead of new costumed heroes, Marvel launched such titles as Robert E. Howard's sword-and-sorcery hero, *Conan* (October 1970), written by Roy Thomas and drawn by Barry Windsor-Smith, and *Tomb of Dracula* (April 1972). With the relaxation of the Comics Code rule on featuring werewolves, vampires, and other monsters as main characters, Marvel followed *Dracula* with *Werewolf by Night* (September 1972),

The Monster of Frankenstein (January 1973), and nearly a dozen other original and reprint monster titles like *Chamber of Chills* (March 1972) and *Vault of Evil* (February 1973). Martial-art titles also were popular, so Marvel supplied *Master of Kung Fu* (April 1974) and *Iron Fist* (November 1975).

In 1975 as the monster titles waned, Marvel sparked a third cycle of superheroes with the introduction of the new *X-Men* (#94, August 1975, and *Giant Size #1*, Summer 1975). The new mutants (Wolverine, Nightcrawler, Storm, and others) replaced three of the five original X-Men (Angel, Iceman, and Marvel Girl), and started the most popular Marvel comic-book series ever.

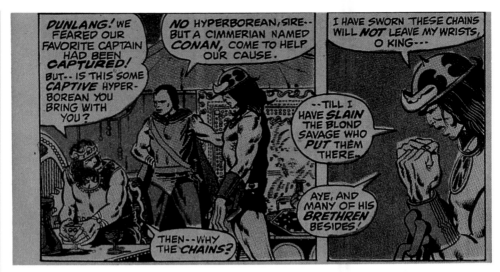

The new *X-Men* marked the beginning of a new trend in putting together teams of teenage superheroes or mutants. All through the 1970s and into the 1980s, the X-Men influence was seen in such Marvel titles as *The New Mutants* (March 1983), *Alpha Flight* (August 1983), and *X-Factor* (February 1986).

In 1982 Marvel initiated the first of three more innovations. A series of graphic novels, *Marvel Graphic Novel* (1982), featured extended stories in a comic-book-album format. A children's line, Star Comics, followed in 1984, showcasing such characters as *Heathcliff* (April 1985) and *Top Dog* (April 1985). Marvel also created a second imprint called Epic Comics, devoted to creator-owned work.

By the mid and late 1980s, Marvel was responsible for sixty percent of all comic books sold on the newsstands. It its rich history to date, Marvel has created some of the most memorable comic-book characters of all time. The more than nine hundred different titles produced in its first fifty years seems to assure Marvel Comics of the title as America's most prolific comic-book publisher.

DAVID McKAY COMPANY (1936–1951)

In 1936 David McKay Company became the fourth publisher to enter the new comic-book field, when Hearst's King Features Syndicate approached McKay with the idea of issuing a comic book consisting of King Features' newspaper-strip reprints.

King Comics (April 1936) featured a heavy dose of adventure strips like Flash Gordon, Jungle Jim, and Mandrake.

Its second entry, *Wow Comics* (July 1936), contained a healthy smattering of original material. But it died after four issues, probably because of its magazine-size format.

McKay returned to its winning combination in *King*, by bringing out a companion title, *Ace Comics* (April 1937). *Ace* leaned a little bit more toward humor than *King*, and also

King Comics #8, © 1936 King Features Syndicate

reprinted "The Phantom" and "Prince Valiant" Sunday strips during its run.

Magic Comics (August 1939) completed the McKay trio of King Features's reprints with strips of "Mandrake the Magician" and Chic Young's "Blondie."

McKay's *Feature Book* (May 1937) reprinted strips of a single major character, such as "Popeye," "The Phantom," or "Dick Tracy." This was the first series of comic books to have each issue focus on a single comic character.

McKay was neither a leader nor a follower of trends, but content to stick with its successful formula of reprinting newspaper strips all through the 1940s.

By late 1949 *Ace Comics* and *Magic Comics*, along with most of the other reprint comics, vanished. McKay held onto *King Comics*

Ace Comics #126, © 1947 King Features Syndicate

for another two years, then sold it to Standard Comics where it finally died four issues later.

M.F. ENTERPRISES, INC. (1966–1967, 1969)

M.F. Enterprises was the company of Myron Fass, a publisher and former comic-book artist from the early 1950s. In the late 1950s and early 1960s M.F. Enterprises published men's magazines such as the descriptively titled *Oogle.*

By late 1965 Fass noticed the renewed interest in comic books, "pop art," and the upcoming "Batman" television show. He returned to the comic-book field with a teenage humor comic called *Henry Brewster* (February 1966). Two months later, he rushed to cash in on the blossoming Batman fad by reviving one of the biggest superheroes of all time, *Captain Marvel* (April 1966).

Captain Marvel, © 1966 Country Wise Publications

Actually, M.F. Enterprises' Captain Marvel bore no resemblance at all to the original Captain Marvel last published by Fawcett in 1953. The new character, art, and story were eminently forgettable and a tarnished footnote to the original namesake.

The book was transformed into *Captain Marvel Presents the Terrible Five* and, along with *Henry Brewster*, expired with the September 1967 issue. In 1969 Fass put out a black-and-white magazine-size comic book, *Great West*, which lasted one issue.

MILSON PUBLISHING COMPANY (1967)

Milson Publishing Company was another short-lived 1960s comic publisher. Begun at the height of the superhero craze, Milson published only two titles and five issues.

Milson's editor, Kenneth Dennis, worked with C. C. Beck and Otto Binder, the original artist and writer of *Captain Marvel*, to produce *Fatman the Human Flying Saucer* (April 1967). Similar in tone and mood to Beck's original 1940s Captain Marvel, Fatman failed to capture a 1960s audience and lasted for only three issues.

Milson's other title was *Super Green Beret* (April 1967), which featured a teenage boy who turned into a full-grown, Commie-kicking Vietnam hero when he doffed a magical Green Beret.

Both *Fatman* and *Super Green Beret* were giant-sized sixty-four-page issues that sold for twenty-five cents, or twice as much as the regular thirty-six-page comic books. The higher cover price may have prevented Milson's books from gaining an audience, and they vanished after five months.

Fatman the Human Flying Saucer #2,
© 1967 Milson Publishing Company

STANLEY P. MORSE (1951–1955)

(Aragon, Gilmor, Key Publications, Stanmor Publications)

Stanley P. Morse owned four comic-book companies called Stanmor, Gilmor, Aragon, and Key Publications. There appeared to be little difference between any of his four companies' comic books, although the Aragon titles leaned more toward science fiction and horror while Stanmor titles tended to be war comics. The art and stories in all the series, however, were dependably bland—except for Basil Wolverton's deliciously disturbed artwork in Aragon's *Mister Mystery* (September 1951) and

Silver Kid Western #2, © 1954 Key Publications

Weird Tales of the Future (March 1952).

Morse published *Radiant Love* (December 1953), *Daring Love* (September 1953), and *Weird Mysteries* (October 1952) under his Gilmor company. Under the Key company appeared *Hector* (November 1953) and *Peter Cottontail* (January 1954), two of the decidedly milder titles, and a romance comic called *Tender Romance* (December 1953). Key also published *Weird Chills* (July 1954), a comic book full of bondage, blood draining, and torture.

Under the Stanmor label, Morse published a western, *Silver Kid* (October 1954), and a string of war comics that were among his last comics, *Battle Cry* (May 1952), *Battle Attack* (October 1952), *Battle Fire* (April 1955), and *Battle Squadron* (April 1955).

NOVELTY PUBLICATIONS (1940–1949)

(Premium Group)

Curtis Publishing Company, a large magazine publisher, owned Novelty Publications, or the Premium Group of Comics as it was also known. Its first comic, developed by Bill Everett and the Funnies, Inc. studio, was *Target Comics* (February 1940). It featured several superheroes and outstanding artwork during its early years, but became a fairly pedestrian title by the mid-1940s.

Similarly, *Blue Bolt Comics* (June 1940) and *Four Most* (Winter 1941) also began as homes for well-drawn superheroes, then degenerated into stupefying dullness within a few years.

Novelty's other titles included *Young King Cole* (Fall 1945), a funny-animal comic called

Target Comics #1, © 1940 Novelty Press

Frisky Fables (Spring 1945), and a teen comic named *Humdinger* (May 1946). Although sometimes distinguished by occasional L. B. Cole covers, most of the books' interiors were unusually bland.

Novelty took note of the growing criticism of the industry in the 1940s and decided to leave the comic-book business in late 1949. Curtis Publishing auctioned the Novelty titles and remaining inventory of artwork off to L. B. Cole, who used them as a basis to begin his Star Publications.

True Comics #33, © 1944 True Comics, Inc.

PARENTS MAGAZINE INSTITUTE (1941–1950; 1965)

George Hecht, the publisher of *Parents Magazine*, produced the first educational comic book, *True Comics* (April 1941). The comic book featured stories about real-life heroes, historical adventurers, and medical and scientific discoveries.

Evidently a lot of parents bought the comic book for their children because it immediately gained a respectable 300,000 circulation. The success encouraged Hecht to add a companion title, *Real Heroes* (September 1941), and the first comic book aimed specifically at girls, *Calling All Girls* (September 1941).

Calling All Girls was half comics and half articles on fashions, good looks, and dating tips. It was later followed by both *Calling All Boys* (January 1946) and, for the prepubescent set, *Calling All Kids* (December 1945).

Parents issued other true-type comics such as *True Aviation Comics* (1942), *True Animal Picture Stories* (Winter 1947), and *Sport Stars* (February 1946). An interesting experiment was the publication of *Negro Heroes* (Spring 1947), the first comic book to feature all black characters.

In 1950 the last five issues of *True Comics* did not even make it to the newsstands. They

Calling All Boys #1, © 1946 Parents Magazine Institute

were sent only to subscribers, as Parents' Magazine Institute left the comic-book business. The Institute returned in 1965, however, to publish two issues of *True Comics and Adventure Stories*, the first comic book to feature Vietnam War heroes.

PRIZE PUBLICATIONS (1940–1963)

Prize Publications, under the ownership of Mike Bleir and Teddy Epstein and the editorship of Maurice Rosenfeld, produced a small line of above-average comic books.

Among the fifteen new publishers to enter the comic-book business in 1940, Prize released its first comic book with the unsurprising title of *Prize Comics* (March 1940).

For three years *Prize Comics* was Prize's only title, but it was a rich one with such characters as the Black Owl by Joe Simon and Jack Kirby, Frankenstein by Dick Briefer, and the Green Lama.

Prize's next title, *Headline Comics* (February 1943), initially featured superheroes like Atomic Man and the Blue Streak, but it would later become better known as a crime/suspense comic.

The popularity of the Green Lama in *Prize Comics* eventually resulted in his own series, *Green Lama* (December 1944). This featured exquisitely rendered artwork by Mac Raboy, an artist also remembered for his work on Fawcett's *Captain Marvel Jr.*

The other *Prize* character to be given his own title was the schizophrenic *Frankenstein* (Summer 1945). Initially played as a humorous strip in the first seventeen issues of the title, Frankenstein then went into limbo for three years. He came back from the dead in 1952 as a straight monster comic book—just in time to cash in on the new boom in horror

> "We believe that by offering comic readers a magazine that looked like the others, but was informational as well as entertaining, we could fight fire with fire. In other words, parents and teachers can offer this new comic, made up of stories from history and current events, as a substitute for the less desirable comics. Psychologically, such substitution is better than a prohibition of all comics while they are so very popular."
> —GEORGE J. HECHT, publisher of *True Comics*

Prize Comics #10, © 1941 Prize Publications

"I spare you to live—to live in misery also—to watch and see the suffering and grief that I, your creation, will cause the human race. You will chase me, but never get me! I go now, always haunting and tormenting you!"
—FRANKENSTEIN,
Prize Comics #7
(December 1940)

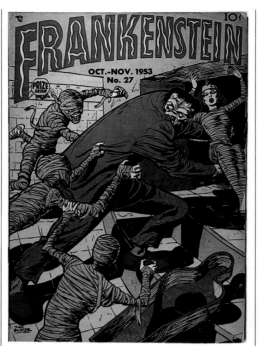

Frankenstein #27, © 1953 Feature Publications

comics. Interestingly enough, Dick Briefer drew Frankenstein in both versions and managed to excel both times.

Prize Publications made its mark as the first romance comic-book publisher with *Young Romance* (September 1947). Extremely successful, the comic quickly spawned three other imitations the next year, and one hundred twenty more romance titles by 1949! Among these 1949 entries was Prize's second romance comic, *Young Love* (February 1949). Its other romance titles included *Young Brides* (September 1952) and *All for Love* (April 1957).

By 1948 the simultaneous boom in western comics and bust in superhero titles prompted Prize to change *Prize Comics* to *Prize Comics Western* (April 1948). A dependably well-written and well-drawn comic, *Prize Comics Western* actually had a lifespan a few months longer than the original *Prize Comics*.

At the beginning of the horror-comic trend in 1950, Prize again turned to the two men who had begun the romance boom: Joe Simon and Jack Kirby. They developed *Black Magic* (October 1950), which later became one of the few horror comics of the early 1950s to struggle into the 1960s.

In 1956 Prize ceased publishing *Headline*, *Prize Comics Western*, and a romance title. As its remaining titles disappeared over the next seven years, by 1963 Prize was left with only *Young Romance* and *Young Love*. It sold both titles to DC Comics, with the June 1963 issues the last editions of Prize comics.

QUALITY COMICS GROUP (1939–1956)

Everett M. "Busy" Arnold was in the printing business. In 1936 he printed the *Funny Pages*

and *Funny Picture Stories* for the newly formed Comics Magazine Company, Inc. Over the next two years, he printed more of the new comic books, including *Feature Funnies*. By 1939 Arnold sensed that there was more money to be made in publishing comic books than in just printing them.

He formed Quality Comics Group and purchased *Feature Funnies* from Harry "A" Chesler. He renamed the book *Feature Comics* and published his first issue (*#21*) in June 1939. Two months later, he released *Smash Comics* (August 1939), followed by *Crack Comics* (May 1940), *Hit Comics* (July 1940), *National Comics* (July 1940), *Military Comics* (August 1941), *Police Comics* (August 1941), *Uncle Sam* (August 1941), *Doll Man* (Fall 1941), *Plastic Man* (Summer 1943), and *Blackhawk* (Winter 1944).

Hit Comics #1, © 1940 Everett M. Arnold

Quality Comics lived up to its name. Arnold developed a reputation as a fair publisher who paid good rates, and he attracted some of the better artists in the field: Will Eisner, Jack Cole, Lou Fine, Bill Ward, Reed Crandall. While Quality's editorial and production values were consistently high, the strength of the company lay in its memorable characters, most notably Plastic Man, Doll Man, the Spirit, and the Blackhawks.

Doll Man was the first Quality superhero, beginning in *Feature Comics #27* (December 1939) and earning his own title (*Doll Man*) in 1941, which lasted until 1953. The ability to shrink down to less than a foot in size may not seem a likely "super" power, but Doll Man bashed enough crooks and monsters to warrant a companion, Doll Girl, and a crime-fighting canine, Elmo the Wonder Dog.

While Doll Man's shrinking power might seem trivial, Plastic Man's power to s-t-r-e-t-c-h and shape his body into everything from a fire hydrant to a skyscraper dazzled his readers. Created by Jack Cole, Plastic Man first

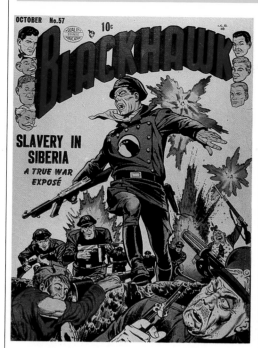

Blackhawk #57, © 1952 Comic Magazines, Inc.

Quality published its last comics in December 1956, then sold its titles and characters to DC Comics. DC continued a few of the Quality titles, among them *G.I. Combat* (January 1957), *Robin Hood* (January 1957), *Heart Throbs* (April 1957), and *Blackhawk* (January 1957)—the last an enduring reminder of a "Quality" past.

ST. JOHN PUBLISHING (1947–1958)

Archer St. John, a young and innovative publisher, entered the comic-book business as industry sales were rising to their all-time peak. His first comic books, *Comics Revue* (June 1947) and *Treasury of Comics* (June 1947), featured reprints of newspaper strips, like "Ella Cinders" or "Abbie an' Slatts."

The future of St. John's comic-book company was made, however, when he obtained the rights to publish Mighty Mouse and the Terry-Toon characters.

Police Comics #59, © 1946 Comic Magazines, Inc.

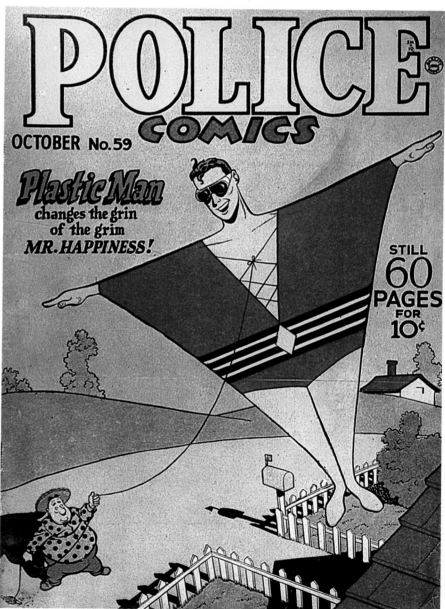

appeared in *Police Comics #1* (Summer 1941). Within two years he picked up a comic sidekick (Woozy Winks) and his own title, *Plastic Man #1* (Summer 1943).

Plastic Man, probably the most surrealistic superhero ever, delighted his readers with zany stories of comical villains and improbable scenarios, such as stretching his ear ten stories high to overhear a crook's conversation. Plastic Man stretched his Quality career out to November 1956, outliving many of his more serious superhero compatriots.

Will Eisner's Spirit, although not created for Quality Comics, appeared side by side with Plastic Man beginning in *Police Comics #11* (September 1942) and warranted his own title, *The Spirit*, in 1944. Like Plastic Man, the Spirit was a masked crime fighter with a comic sidekick, in this case Ebony, who earned the distinction of being the first regular black comic-book character.

Just before the United States entered World War II, *Military Comics* (August 1941) appeared. With its first issue came Blackhawk, another one of Will Eisner's creations. Blackhawk had an international squad of freedom fighters—Andre, Chop-Chop, Olaf, Hendrickson, Chuck, and Stanislaus—who flew around in supersonic planes to battle Nazis and, later, communists. After the war, *Military* changed its name to *Modern Comics* but Blackhawk was still the main draw. The group received their own title in 1944, and *Blackhawk* comics was published for another forty years, although not entirely by Quality.

Besides its superhero comics, Quality Comics published many other titles in the 1950s, including war comics (*G.I. Combat, Yanks in Battle*), humor comics (*The Barker*), romance comics (*Heart Throbs, Love Secrets, Love Letters*), horror comics (*Web of Evil*), and adventure comics (*T-Man, Robin Hood, Lady Luck*).

"In fact, I smell cats and I'm off to save the day!"
—MIGHTY MOUSE,
Mighty Mouse
(November 1950)

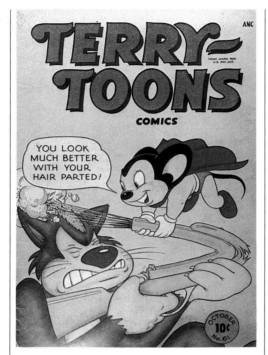

Terry Toons #61, © 1947 Metro-Goldwyn-Mayer

When St. John launched *Mighty Mouse* (August 1947) and *Terry-Toons Comics* (September 1947), he optioned several Terry-Toons animators to draw the comics. The talents of Art Bartsch, Connie Rasinski, and other studio animators elevated the St. John Mighty Mouse titles to top sellers. St. John later added other Terry-Toon titles to the line, including *Paul Terry's Comics* (March 1951), *Heckle & Jeckle* (October 1951), *Dinky Duck* (November 1951), and *Gandy Goose* (March 1953).

Throughout the rest of the 1940s and early 1950s, St. John followed the dominant comic-book publishing trends of the time: crime (*Authentic Police Cases*, February 1948), western

Kid Cowboy #14, © 1955 St. John Publishing

(*The Texan*, 1948), romance (*Teen-Age Romances*, January 1949), or horror (*Weird Horrors*, June 1952).

In 1950 St. John was selling nearly twenty million comic books per year, with an average monthly circulation of 340,000 copies per title—a very respectable amount for an admittedly small publisher.

St. John's chance to become a trendsetter occurred in the spring of 1953, when he decided to publish the world's first three-dimensional comic book. St. John had learned about a 3-D comic-book-production process just as the 3-D movie craze began.

St. John used the process on his most popular title, rushing out over a million copies of a *3-D Mighty Mouse* (September 1953) magazine. It sold over ninety-nine percent of its printing—an absolutely phenomenal occurrence!

St. John was convinced that 3-D was now the way for all future comic books to go. He began converting his publishing operations to an all 3-D line, and ordered five more 3-D comics for October and seven more for November. He hired a special staff of thirty artists and scheduled print runs three or four times his usual amount. In just three months, St. John earned the distinction of being not only the first, but the most prolific, of the 3-D comic-book publishers—producing fourteen titles in 1953.

Just as quickly as they rose, however, the novelty of 3-D comics faded. Sales for St. John's October 3-D books were fifty to seventy percent of their print run. The November batch sold as low as ten to thirty-five percent of its print run.

The 3-D collapse left St. John on the edge of ruin. Only the Mighty Mouse titles kept the company going for two more years. In late 1955 St. John surrendered the comic-book rights to the Terry-Toon characters to Pines Publishing.

St. John all but suspended publication after that, except for a brief emergence in late 1957 when he released a few intermittent titles such as *Do You Believe in Nightmares?* (November 1957) and *Double Trouble* (November 1957). By February 1958 St. John comic books were no more.

STANHALL PUBLICATIONS (1953–1954)

Stanhall Publications was owned by Michael Estrow and Stanley M. Estrow. Since Hal Seegar was chief writer and creator of many of its titles, the name of the company combined his first name with Stanley Estrow's name (Stan-Hal).

The editor for Stanhall was Adolphe Barreaux, who also edited the Estrows' Trojan Publishing line of comics.

The Stanhall lineup consisted of humor titles created by Seegar, who later went on to shape the 1965 "Milton The Monster and

Fearless Fly" television-cartoon show. The comic books included a teenage title, *Oh Brother* (January 1953); an army humor title, *G.I. Jane* (May 1953); a funny-animal comic, *Muggy-Doo, Boy Cat* (July 1953); and two innocently risque books, *Farmer's Daughter* (February 1954) and *Broadway-Hollywood Blackouts* (March 1954).

In late 1954 Stanhall transferred some of its titles to the Estrow brothers' other comic-book companies, Merit Publishing and Trojan Magazines, and Stanhall Publications itself went out of business.

Terrors of the Jungle #10, © 1954 Star Publications

STAR PUBLICATIONS (1949–1955)

L. B. Cole, a veteran comic-book artist with over fifteen hundred comic-book covers to his credit, formed Star Publications in 1951 with Jerry Kramer, a popular tax-guide author. They began the company by purchasing the titles of Novelty Publications from its parent company, Curtis Magazines.

Star Publications took over the Novelty titles with the November 1949 issues. Over the next six years, it published over four hundred titles, producing one comic book nearly every calendar day. Star's cumulative annual circulation was two hundred million comic books that included crime, horror, western, romance, funny-animal, sports, satire, teen, and adventure titles.

Despite all the comic books it published, Star never produced a single strong character or title. Instead, most of its comics sold mainly on the strength of L. B. Cole's eye-catching covers.

The previously tame and mundane Novelty titles, *Blue Bolt* (November 1949) and *Four Most* (November 1949), were repackaged as lurid horror comics. Other Star comics calculated to induce nightmares were *Startling Terror Tales* (May 1952), *Spook* (January 1953), and *Terrifying Tales* (January 1953). Even the jungle comics were scary, with *Terrors of the Jungle* (May 1952) a prime example.

Crime comics had their place in the Star line, with *Crime Fighting Detective* (April 1950), *Thrilling Crime Cases* (June 1950), and *Shock Detective Cases* (September 1952).

Star displayed a lighter side, with teen and romance titles like *Popular Teen-Agers* (September 1950) and *True to Life Romances* (January 1950), and comics for the younger set such as *Frisky Animals* (January 1951), *Fun Comics* (January 1953), and *Mighty Bear* (January 1954).

With the death of Cole's partner, Kramer, Star Publications went out of business. Cole moved on to work as art director for Classics Illustrated in the 1950s and as editor for Dell Comics in the early 1960s. Some of the Star titles eventually were sold to Farrell Comics, which briefly revived them from 1957–1958.

STERLING COMICS (1954–1955)

Martin Smith, editor of Sterling Comics, managed a line of comics that never grew beyond three titles at any one time. Almost all of the books were drawn by Mike Sekowsky, who later drew the *Justice League of America* for DC Comics.

Sterling began publication right before the advent of the Comic Code, by issuing a pair of crime-and-horror comics called *The Informer* (April 1954) and *The Tormented* (July 1954). Its next title was its most significant, *Captain Flash* (November 1954), who has the distinction of being the first new 1950s superhero.

Sterling's next three books were published

Captain Flash #1, © 1954 Sterling Comics, Inc.

> "Around 1952, Leonard B. Cole suddenly loosened up. His covers [for Star Publications], which had been ordinary at best, suddenly blossomed into hideously graphic representations of monsters with bloody fingernails, walking skeletons wearing tattered garments, and disgusting beasts rising out of swamps to dismember people, all rendered in a dark, moody, offbeat style. Imagine Aubrey Beardsley drawing with his toes under the influence of Dexamyl, and you'll have a pretty good idea of Cole's work during this period."
> —JOHN WOOLEY, comic-book writer and critic

after the Comics Code was in place. *Surprise Adventures* (March 1955) and *After Dark* (May 1955) featured watered-down horror and mystery stories. The final title, *My Secret Confession* (September 1955), lasted one issue.

STREET AND SMITH (1940–1949)

A "pulp" publisher since the nineteenth century, Street and Smith entered the comic-book business in 1940 with comic-book adaptations of the two most famous pulp heroes in history: *Shadow Comics* (March 1940) and *Doc Savage Comics* (May 1940). The two characters somehow never made a successful transition to the comics, although the *Shadow* struggled along for nine years, sustained by the popular radio show and artwork by Bob Powell.

Street and Smith next introduced *Sports Comics* (October 1940), the first sports comic book, then *Super Magician* (September 1941),

Shadow Comics #10, © 1949 Street and Smith Publications, Inc.

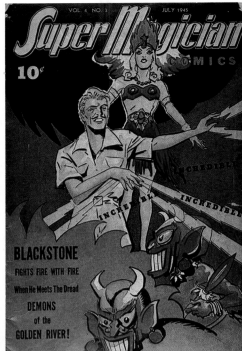

Super Magician #3, © 1945 Street and Smith Publications, Inc.

a comic book devoted entirely to magicians.

Other Street and Smith titles included *Red Dragon Comics* (January 1943), *Air Ace* (January 1944), and perhaps its most innovative creation, *Supersnipe* (October 1942), which featured "The Boy With the Most Comic Books In America!"

For the most part, however, by the time Street and Smith left the comic-book business in the summer of 1949, it had earned its reputation as one of the most ordinary comic-book publishers of the 1940s.

SUPERIOR COMICS (1947–1956)

Superior Comics originally began as Dynamic Publications in Toronto, Canada. The company was closely associated with the United States comic-book market, and it reprinted American comics for Canadian distribution while exporting its own comic books to the United States.

Superior Comics took over Harry Chesler's comic book, *Red Seal Comics*, in June 1947 and continued to print it in Canada for both domestic and U.S. audiences. In 1948 it began reprinting comic books for Canadian readers from such American publishers as EC Comics, Marvel, Avon, and Magazine Enterprises. The reprinting of American comic books occurred throughout Canada from 1948 to 1951, because comic books were on a list of five hundred import items banned by the Canadian government in an effort to improve its balance of payments.

Superior also reprinted some U.S. comic strips in comic-book format, such as *Ellery Queen* (May 1949) and *Brenda Starr* (June 1948).

Superior is best remembered, however, for

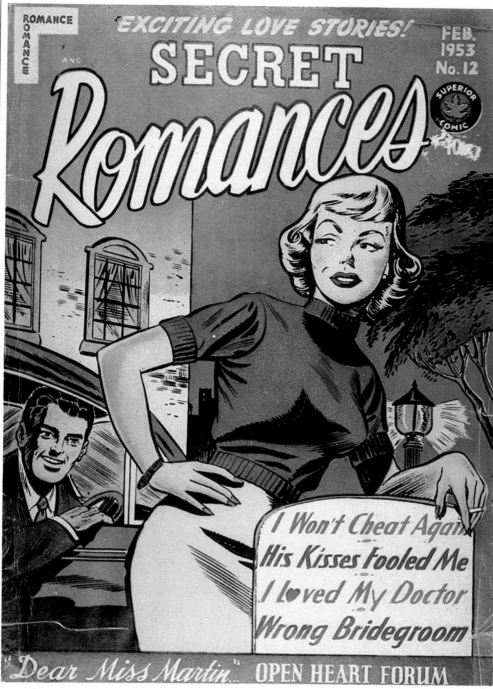

Secret Romances #12, © 1953 Superior Publishers Ltd.

Strange Mysteries #11, © 1953 Superior Publishers Ltd.

its line of original comic books, particularly the horror and romance titles which were distributed in the United States. These Superior books were put together under the supervision of Robert W. Farrell, an American comic-book publisher, and S. M. Iger, owner of a New York comic-book-art studio. Farrell and Iger continued to work together on the Farrell Comic Group line of comics throughout the 1950s.

Superior's horror comics were noted for grotesque and surreal stories that appeared in such titles as *Journey into Fear* (May 1951), *Strange Mysteries* (September 1951), and *Mysteries Weird and Strange* (May 1953). Its romance comics were equally sordid, somehow always managing to feature the heroine changing her clothes repeatedly in front of the reader. Tales of seamy love appeared in *My*

Secret (August 1949), *Our Secret* (December, 1949), *My Secret Marriage* (May 1953), and *G.I. War Brides* (April 1954).

Superior also published other genres as well, including westerns such as *Lone Rider* (April 1951) and humor like *Super Funnies* (December 1953).

Superior Comics' horror comics died with their January 1955 issues, as the Comics Code took full effect, and their romance comics lasted only another year.

TIMOR PUBLISHING COMPANY (1953–1954)

Joseph A. Wolfert was sole owner of Timor Publishing Company, one of the smaller 1950s comic publishers.

Crime Detector #4, © 1954 Timor Publications

He tried two titles, *Algie* (December 1953), a teen comic, and *Animal Adventures* (December 1953), featuring "Soopermutt." Both lasted for four months before being replaced by two other titles, *Blazing Western* (January 1954) and *Crime Detector* (January 1954). These two titles lasted nine months.

After publishing a total of sixteen comic books, Timor Publishing folded.

TOBY PRESS (1949–1955)

Elliot A. Caplin began Toby Press with a firm background in both comic strips and comic

Li'l Abner #92, © 1954 Toby Press, Inc.

Blazing Western #1, © 1954 Timor Publications

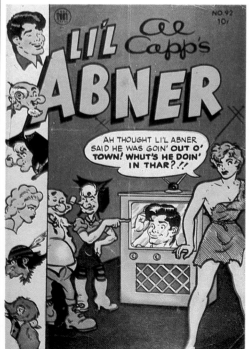

books. The brother of Al Capp (creator of Li'l Abner), Caplin himself wrote comic strips for most of his life. He specialized in soap opera/adventure strips such as "Abbie an' Slatts," "Dr. Kildare," and "The Heart of Juliet Jones."

Caplin entered the comic-book business as editor of *True Comics* for the Parents Magazine Institute. A few years later, he began the comic-book line for Toby Press.

Not surprisingly, the first comic book Caplin published was his brother's *Li'l Abner Comics* (1949). He followed that up with *John Wayne Comics* (Winter 1949), a western comic that was his most successful and longest-running title.

Felix the Cat #55, © 1954 King Features Syndicate, Inc.

Toby Press published other western comics as well, such as *Billy the Kid* (October 1950) and *Return of the Outlaw* (February 1953). Its other offerings were typical for an early 1950s comic publisher and included romance, horror, war, and humor titles like *Great Lover Romances* (March 1951), *Tales of Horror* (June 1952), *With the Marines* (1953), and *Super Brat* (January 1954).

For a time Toby Press also had the rights to publish both *Felix the Cat* (1951) and *Buck Rogers* (January 1951) in comic-book format.

Although Toby Press folded by late 1955, Caplin continued to be active in the field, writing the "Little Orphan Annie" newspaper strip from 1968 to 1973.

TOWER COMICS (1965–1970)

Tower Comics was started in late 1965 by Harry Shorten, a former MLJ/Archie editor, and Sam Schwartz, a former Archie artist. The men began the company in an attempt to cash in on the rapidly growing superhero business of the mid-1960s.

Although the company put out only eighty-one issues of eight titles, it employed some of the top comic-book artists in the field—including Wally Wood, Gil Kane, Steve Ditko, Al Williamson, and Reed Crandall.

Tower Comics' flagship title was *T.H.U.N.-D.E.R. Agents* (November 1965), a sixty-eight-page comic that featured an organization of such superheroes as Dynamo, Noman, and Menthor. *T.H.U.N.D.E.R. Agents* lasted twenty issues and spun off two other titles, *Dynamo* (August 1966) and *Noman* (November 1966).

Besides superhero titles, Tower published two war titles: *Undersea Agent* (January 1966) and *Fight the Enemy* (August 1966). Its three teenage titles included its longest running comic, *Tippy Teen* (November 1965), plus *Tippy's Friends Go-Go & Animal* (July 1966), and *Tippy Teen Teen-In* (Summer 1968).

UNITED FEATURES SYNDICATE (1936–1955)

United Features Syndicate, part of the Scripps-Howard publishing group, became the first newspaper syndicate to publish its own comic books.

Tip Top Comics (April 1936) was edited by

IRON MAIDEN: "I realize now that you are the only fit man for me . . . the only one worthy of my love! Team up with me and we could rule the Earth."

DYNAMO: "Sorry, I'd rather not rule the Earth. I just want to marry the girl next door and live in the suburbs."
—*T.H.U.N.D.E.R. Agents #3*

T.H.U.N.D.E.R. Agents #7, © *1966 Tower Comics, Inc.*

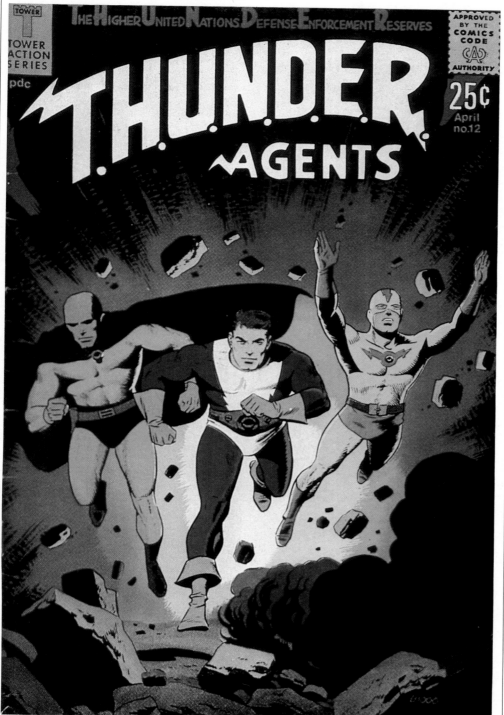

"Another injustice averted and another justice wrought, the Spark Man is swallowed by the shadows from which he emerges in his fight against evil!"
—*Sparkler Comics #6*
(January 1942)

Lev Gleason, a youngster who began his lengthy comic career at Eastern Color with *Famous Funnies* and who eventually launched his own publishing company three years later.

Tip Top featured newspaper-strip reprints of the United Features characters, such as Tarzan, Li'l Abner, Fritzi Ritz, Ella Cinders, and the Captain and the Kids. These characters dominated all of the United Features comic books for the next nineteen years. Except for occasional new material, United Features concentrated almost exclusively on newspaper-reprint comics.

Captain and the Kids #19, © 1950 United Features Syndicate

The syndicate did give a nod to the superhero boom of 1940–1941 by introducing original characters like Mirror Man and the Triple Terror to *Tip Top Comics*, and Spark Man to *Sparkler Comics* (July 1941).

Besides *Tip Top* and *Sparkler*, United Features' other major titles were *Comics on Parade* (April 1938), *United Comics* (August 1940), and *Single Series Comics* (1938), the last a series of comic books devoted to a single United Features character. All of these titles depended heavily on reprints of United Features' daily and Sunday strips.

In the late 1940s, United Features expanded its comic-book line by adding titles devoted exclusively to its most popular characters, such as *Captain and the Kids* (Summer 1947), *Ella Cinders* (March 1948), *Abbie an' Slatts* (March 1948), *Fritzi Ritz* (Fall 1948), and *Nancy and Sluggo* (1949). It also added two other reprint anthologies, *Sparkle Comics* (October 1948) and *Tip Topper* (1949).

United Features held onto most of its titles throughout the early 1950s. But, by the beginning of 1955, United had sold its three top titles (*Tip Top*, *Fritzi Ritz*, and *Nancy and Sluggo*) to St. John Publishing and, in Febru-

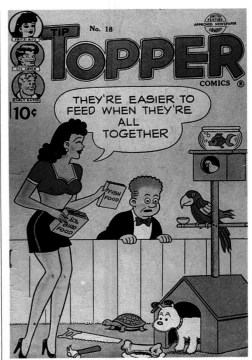

Topper Comics #18, © 1952 United Features Syndicate

ary 1955 ceased publication of its remaining titles.

WARREN PUBLISHING COMPANY (1964–1983)

James Warren published *Famous Monsters of Filmland*, a "monster" magazine consisting mostly of scary movie stills with pun-filled captions. His second magazine, *Monster World*, featured black-and-white monster comic strips, giving Warren the idea to publish a black-and-white magazine devoted entirely to monster-comic stories.

In 1964 Warren entered the comics busi-

Vampirella #1, © 1969 Warren Publishing Co.

Creepy #1, © 1964 Warren Publishing Co.

> "Writing in comics should be a little like good background music in movies. It makes a contribution that works toward the success of the overall piece, but you shouldn't specifically notice it. . . . What the reader should be thinking is, 'Wow, this is a great story,' and not be conscious of the writing for writing's sake."
> —ARCHIE GOODWIN,
> former writer and editor,
> Warren Publishing

ness with *Creepy Magazine*, an anthology of "comics designed to give you the creeps!"

Creepy featured work by such ex-EC artists as Al Williamson, Joe Orlando, and Frank Frazetta. Written by Archie Goodwin, the graphic horror stories were able to avoid emasculation by the Comics Code Authority because *Creepy* was distributed as a magazine and not as a comic book.

Eerie (September 1965) began as *Creepy*'s "graveside" companion. It too featured horror stories reminiscent of EC Comics. The next month brought the birth of *Blazing Combat* (October 1965), a homage to the EC war comics that lasted only four issues.

Vampirella (September 1969) enjoyed a fourteen-year run by starring a female vampire from outer space who evidently came from a planet where few clothes were worn.

Warren Publishing had other titles in its black-and-white comic magazine line-up, in-cluding *The Spirit* (April 1974) and an adventure title called *Rook* (November 1979).

With its February 1983 issues of *Creepy*, *Eerie*, and *Vampirella* Warren ceased regular publication.

ZIFF-DAVIS PUBLICATIONS (1947–1957)

Ziff-Davis Publications produced a variety of magazines in the 1940s. Among them were *Amazing Stories*, the first science-fiction magazine, and *Fantastic*, a companion fantasy magazine. Publisher William B. Ziff hired Jerry Siegel, co-creator of Superman, to edit his new comic-book line.

In 1947 Ziff-Davis test marketed a comic book by offering its science-fiction-magazine subscribers a copy of *Science Comics* by mail. Evidently the premium offer of a science-fiction comic book did not go over too well, and Ziff-Davis waited three years before trying it again. This time it offered its *Amazing Stories* subscribers a comic book called *Amazing Adventures* (1950) as a premium. The response must have been better, as the publisher launched a newsstand version of the comic book.

Ziff-Davis continued to rely heavily upon science-fiction and fantasy titles, following *Amazing Adventures* with *Weird Thrillers* (1951) and *Nightmare* (Summer 1952). The science-fiction comics, as well as most of the other books, usually were put out with beautiful painted covers that distinguished them from other comic books on the newsstands.

In addition to science fiction, Ziff-Davis issued titles in other genres, like the western comic *The Hawk* (Winter 1951) and the romance comic *Romantic Marriage* (1950). Another interesting title was *Famous Stars* (November 1950), which featured photo covers and cartoon biographies of movie stars.

G. I. Joe #11, © *1952 Ziff-Davis Publishing Co.*

Amazing Adventures #4, © *1951 Ziff-Davis Publishing Co.*

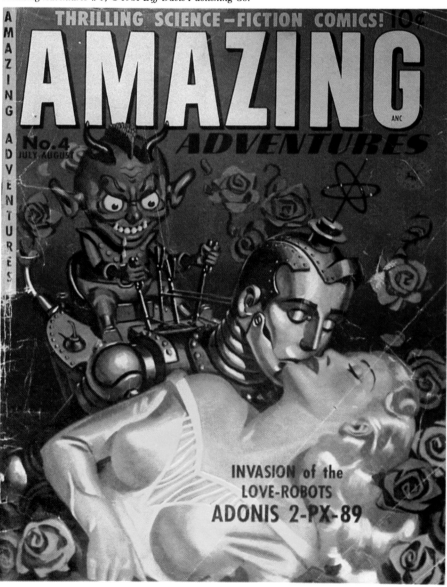

Ziff-Davis's most successful comic book, however, was the war comic *G.I. Joe* (1950), which lasted for seven years and fifty-one issues. With its gung-ho action and the chipper camaraderie among Joe and his sidekicks, the Yardbirds, young readers discovered just how much "good clean fun" war can be.

In 1953 Ziff-Davis sold many of its titles to St. John Publishing and by 1954 was publishing *G.I. Joe* as its only comic book. In June 1957 G.I. Joe finally made peace with America's enemies and was no more.

Football Thrills #1, © *1951 Ziff-Davis Publishing Co.*

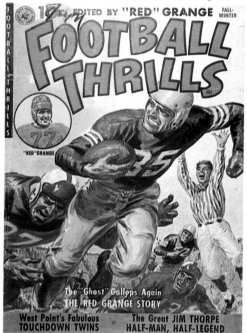

THE
COMIC BOOK
GENRES

From westerns to romance to horror to humor, comic books have been published in every category and genre. Like movies and novels, there are distinct types of comic books, and a survey of these genres provides an excellent cross-section of comic-book history.

In the beginning, there was only one type of comic book: the anthology, or collection of newspaper-strip reprints, best exemplified by *Famous Funnies*. The first comic books featured a variety of humor, adventure, and character strips, in order to appeal to the widest audience. These early titles read almost like a generic comic book, with at least one story to please each member of the family.

Eventually comic-book publishers decided to package comic books for specific reading audiences, like the pulp magazine publishers did with their lines of western, mystery, and adventure titles. The first comic book devoted to a single genre or theme was *Detective Picture Stories* (December 1936). Soon other early comic books specialized in all-western or all-detective stories, such as *Western Picture Stories*, *Detective Comics*, and *Cowboy Comics*.

Westerns and detective comics, then, were the first two comic-book genres. The birth of the comic-book superhero in 1938 created another genre, one that was unique to the comic-book field. Superhero comics quickly became the most popular type of comic book throughout the early 1940s.

As the 1940s got underway, publishers rushed other types of comic books onto the stands, such as the funny-animal and war comics. By the mid-1940s, they discovered teenage comics. In the late 1940s romance, jungle, and crime comics appeared on the scene. By the early 1950s horror comics became the popular genre of the day.

Publishers often tried to balance their lines of comics between the various categories or genres. DC Comics, for example, maintained a line of superheroes; a set of funny-animal titles; a few westerns, romances, mystery comics, movie adaptations, and teenage titles; and a couple of crime comics. Even a small publisher with only six titles would offer a couple of westerns, a romance, a crime, a horror, and a funny-animal comic.

The reason for so many different types of comic books, especially from 1945 to 1955, is that there were so many different audiences that read comics. The youngest readers read the funny-animal or cartoon-character comics. Young girls read teenage comics, and teenage girls read the romance titles. Young boys liked the superhero comics, while their older brothers read horror comics. Even adults often read western, crime, or romance comics.

As the general newsstand comic-book readership decreased in the 1970s and 1980s, publishers relied more and more upon the superhero comics because of the devoted following they commanded among comic-book readers. Such devotion was necessary, because comic books became increasingly difficult to locate due to distribution problems. As comic books lost their general newsstand positions and audiences, such genres as western, war, romance, teenage, and funny-animal comics dwindled and disappeared.

Of course, the popularity of each comic-book genre has risen or fallen over the years, according to readers' tastes and current dictates. Perhaps the most interesting example of a genre that experienced a remarkable revival is the superhero comic.

Credited with establishing the comic-book industry as we know it, the superhero comic book enjoyed unparalleled popularity from 1940 to 1944. By the end of World War II, however, superheroes were losing favor. By the early 1950s, superhero comics had been almost entirely supplanted by romance, western, and horror titles. In the early 1960s, however, superheroes enjoyed a tremendous resurgence of popularity, eventually coming to dominate the comic-book industry again.

Comic-book genres come and go for a number of reasons. Western comics were helped immensely by the Saturday morning movie stars like Gene Autry and Roy Rogers. War comics enjoyed their biggest success during the Korean War. Horror comics were killed by a strict industry code, and romance comics faded away because of a decline in female comic readership—perhaps supplanted by romance paperbacks and TV soap operas.

A sudden rise in popularity of one comic-book genre often caused other publishers to rush out similar titles, thus causing a "boom" in a genre and then a "bust" as the market becomes saturated. For example, the success of one publisher's single romance comic book in 1947 prompted nine other publishers to issue ninety-nine romance titles over the next two years. In the early 1970s, during the superhero slump, there was a revival of horror comics and interest in new genres like sword and sorcery, barbarians, and kung-fu fighters.

With all the thousands of different comic books that have been published, it is possible to categorize them ad infinitum according to genres, subgenres, and cross-genres. Collectors have concentrated on such minor themes and subgenres as pirate comics, comics about atomic energy, comics with Christmas covers, baseball comics, and comic books containing pin-up dolls!

For reasons of sanity, only the most significant and major comic-book genres have been selected for study here. A few minor genres, such as educational comics and satire comics, are included primarily to hint at the dozens of other types of comics that have appeared over the last sixty years.

CRIME COMICS

Crime and horror comics have been the most maligned of the comic-book genres. Crime comic books in particular were singled out as a possible cause for juvenile delinquency in

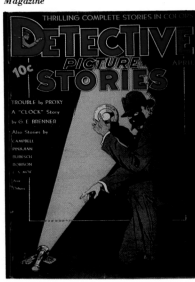

Detective Picture Stories, © 1937 Comics Magazine

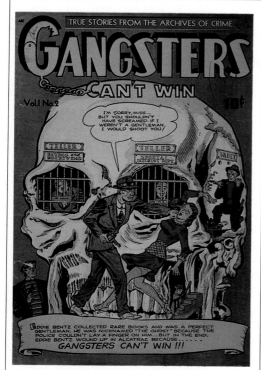

Gangsters Can't Win #2, © 1948 D.S. Publishing Company, Inc.

1950 and were subjected to a congressional investigation. Despite the accusations which portrayed crime comics as little more than "how to" manuals for murder and mayhem, no clear connection ever was established between reading crime comics and committing deviant social behavior. In fact, juvenile delinquency rates dropped from 1947 to 1949, the very years that the crime comics were peaking in circulation!

According to a congressional report on "Comic Books and Juvenile Delinquency" (March 1955), two striking changes took place in the comic-book industry between 1945 and 1954: "The first was the great increase in the number of comic books and the number of firms engaged in their publication. The second was the increased number of comic books dealing with crime and horror and featuring sexually suggestive and sadistic illustrations."

Crime comics, as the name implied, featured stories about criminals and crimes, true and fictionalized. They often suggested the "film noir" detective and mystery movies of the 1940s. Although every lawbreaker eventually was brought to justice, the graphically violent action and glorified criminal anti-hero of the crime comics probably overshadowed any underlying message of "crime does not pay."

The first crime comic book was named exactly that. *Crime Does Not Pay* (#22, June 1942) was introduced in 1942. In its first year the book produced barely more than a 200,000 monthly circulation. The next year's circulation was 300,000, then 500,000 in 1945, and by 1946 it had achieved an 800,000-plus monthly circulation. Only in 1946 did the second crime comic book appear. By the end of 1947, there were still only three crime comic books on the newsstands,

for about one and a half percent of the total industry titles.

A year later, however, there were suddenly thirty-eight crime comics, or fifteen percent of all comic book titles. The next year, the number of titles dropped to 33, and declined even more rapidly in 1950 to ten titles.

According to a DC Comic spokesperson in 1955, the reason for the waning popularity of crime comics from 1949 to 1950 was the increased interest in teenage and romance comics. Whatever the reason, 1948 was definitely "the year of the crime comic" with Lev Gleason's popular titles, *Crime Does Not Pay* and *Crime and Punishment*, selling over one and a half million copies per month.

Who was reading all those crime comics? Interestingly enough, a survey taken by Gleason in the late 1940s discovered that fifty-seven percent of *Crime Does Not Pay* readers were over twenty-one years old. Evidently a lot of crime-comic readers were the same young men who were picking up the mystery paperbacks and true-detective magazines off the newsstands as well. For awhile, *Crime Does Not Pay* carried the caveat on its covers, "Not Intended For Children."

Thrilling Crime Cases #49, © 1952 Star Publications, Inc.

Probably it is just as well that the majority of the crime-comic readers were of legal age. A story from *True Crime Comics #2* (May 1947), entitled "Murder, Morphine, and Me," contains pictures of drug injections, machine gunning, burning bodies, and a hypodermic needle poised to penetrate a victim's eyeball—and that's in just the first two pages of the fourteen-page story. The same comic book also shows criminals dragging people behind a car and over rocky roads in order to "erase their faces."

From 1947 to 1951, crime comics were published by almost every comic-book publisher at one time or the other. In addition to Gleason's second crime comic, *Crime and*

> "I had no idea how one would go about stealing from a locker in Grand Central, but I have comic books which describe that in minute detail and I could go out now and do it."
> —DR. FREDERIC WERTHAM,
> author of *Seduction of the Innocent*

> "It may be said that no acceptable evidence has been produced by Wertham or anyone else for the conclusion that the reading of comic magazines has, or has not, a significant relation to delinquent behavior."
> —PROFESSOR FREDERIC M. THRASHER,
> "The Comics and Delinquency: Cause or Scapegoat"

1st Issue Special #4, © 1975 DC Comics, Inc.

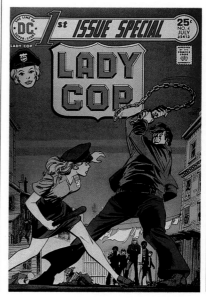

> **"In 1933 came the comic book, and while it swamped the nation with sensationalism, it became gradually clear that here was one of the most remarkable educational potentials yet discovered in man's history."**
> **—COULTON WAUGH,**
> author of *The Comics*

Punishment (July 1948), there were dozens of other titles like *Real Clue Crime* (June 1947), *Crimes Incorporated* (June 1950), *Men Against Crime* (February 1951), *Crime Can't Win* (September 1950), *Crime Must Lose* (October 1950), *Crime and Justice* (March 1951), and *Lawbreakers* (March 1951).

After the application of the Comics Code in 1954, most of the remaining crime comics faded away. Marvel Comics's *Justice* (Fall 1947) responded to the Code by becoming a tamer *Tales of Justice* (May 1955) and lasted for another two years. Marvel's *Caught* (August 1956) was another cleaned-up, post-Code crime comic. DC's so-called "crime" comics, *Big Town* (January 1951), *Mr. District Attorney* (January 1948), and *Gang Busters* (December 1947), were so restrained even before the Code that they handily survived it and lasted until the end of 1958—the last vestiges of the crime-comic explosion of the previous decade.

The 1960s and 1970s featured occasional police comics, such as Atlas's *Police Action* (February 1975) and DC's *Lady Cop* (July 1975). But by that time crime, indeed, did not pay.

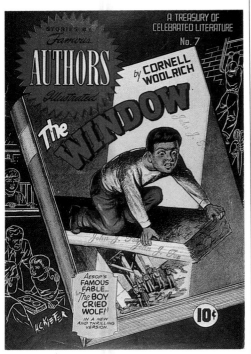

Famous Authors, © *1950 Famous Authors, Inc.*

entertaining and easily understandable format. The sequential use of words and pictures in a comic-book story is also handy for communicating information and explaining concepts in a step-by-step manner.

The early educational comic books, such as *True Comics* (April 1941), *Real Life Comics* (September 1941), and *Real Fact Comics* (March 1946), were anthologies of comic stories about famous people in history, literary figures, and historical events. These and other educational comics of the 1940s were produced by comic-book publishers in addition

Crime Comic Panel Cited by Dr. Wertham in **Seduction of the Innocent.**

Picture Stories from the Bible, © *1945 DC Comics, Inc.*

EDUCATIONAL COMICS

Comic books have long been used to educate and instruct as well as entertain. Comic books have appeared on such topics as atomic energy, bicycle safety, water conservation, and international economics. They have been used to educate children about such concerns as seatbelt safety, preventing AIDS, and the dangers of drug abuse.

Comic books have successfully educated millions of children because they communicate both visual and verbal information in an

Farming for our Future, © *1987 Custom Comic Services*

to their regular entertainment comic books and were sold on the newsstands.

By the early 1950s, however, the number of newsstand educational comic books was declining. Only the *Classics Illustrated* comics, with their adaptations of literary works, could successfully compete for newsstand space and sales. *Treasure Chest Comics* (March 1946), with their stories of Catholic saints and historical events, were still enjoying great success, but they were distributed almost entirely by teachers through classrooms.

Throughout the 1950s and 1960s, educational comic books were produced chiefly by advertising agencies, art studios, and public relations agencies for distribution by national associations, public utilities companies, and other businesses which wanted to educate children about the businesses' particular concerns.

Most of this type of educational comics were sixteen pages long with a paper cover and were never sold on the newsstands. Instead, they were given away free by the various sponsoring associations through schools, churches, and youth organizations. For example, the Soil Conservation Society of America produced a series of comic books for teachers to use in the classroom to explain to their students the value of soil and water conservation.

Produced and distributed through nontraditional channels, hundreds of educational comic books appeared from 1950 to 1970. Organizations such as the Red Cross, General Electric, the U.S. Army, and the New York Federal Reserve distributed educational comics on an amazing variety of subjects, such as *Adventures in Electricity, Bowhunting in Af-*

Sparky's Second Chance Year, © *1988 National Fire Protection Assoc.*

rica, Story of Consumer Credit, History of Natural Gas, Salute to the Boy Scouts, and *The Story of Rubber Heels.*

One member of the Democratic National Committee noted that the number of votes that Truman won the 1948 presidential election by was almost equal to the number of educational comic books that the Committee had distributed on *The Story of Harry S. Truman!*

In the 1980s educational comic books underwent a renaissance of new growth and uses. They often address social issues such as teenage pregnancy and drug abuse. With declining reading and literacy rates, educational comic books now are being used to reach both children and adults with information on such topics as child-abuse prevention, fire safety, citizenship, agriculture, and economics. In Japan, educational comics have long been touted as a reason for that country's amazing literacy rate.

The enormous potential of comic books for educational and instructional purposes has only now begun to be realized.

Super Rabbit #1, © *1943 Marvel Entertainment Group, Inc.*

FUNNY ANIMALS

"Funny animals"—talking ducks, stuttering pigs, and scheming cats—have starred in more comics than any group of characters except superheroes. While the use of talking animals for satire has been popular since Aesop's fables, the first comic-strip funny animals were George Herriman's Krazy Kat, Officer Pup, and Ignatz Mouse. The funny-animal comic books, however, are probably more indebted to the animated cartoons of the 1930s and 1940s than to the newspaper comic strips.

By the late 1930s the Disney characters had proven themselves to be eminently mar-

"We have met the enemy and he is us."
—POGO POSSUM

Pogo Possum #13, © 1953 Walt Kelly

"Laughter can ease, but it does not solve our problems. That takes wisdom and patience, and the time to learn both. The laugh is easier, for comedy can always be found in our aberrations. The laugh signifies the delight of recognition; we know we have discovered the enchanted islands, the lands where we learn to not take ourselves too seriously."
—WALT KELLY,
creator of *Pogo*

ketable. There had already been a regular monthly *Mickey Mouse Magazine* (Summer 1935). Dell Publishing decided the time was right for the first Disney comic book, *Walt Disney's Comics and Stories* (October 1940). The book, which reprinted the Disney newspaper comics, was an immediate success—setting the standard for all funny-animal comics to come. It lasted for more than forty years and probably achieved the highest overall circulation of any comic book in history.

Since the Disney characters were wrapped up, Dell Publishing obtained the Warner Bros. cartoon characters for *Looney Tunes and Merrie Melodies* (October 1941). Once Bugs Bunny and company were going strong, Dell next secured the comic-book rights to the 1930s cartoon characters of Walter Lantz and MGM Studios for two more new books, *New Funnies* (July 1942) and *Our Gang Comics* (September 1942). The Dell cartoon characters proved to be so popular that, by the 1950s, many of them rated their own comic books like *Andy Panda* (November 1952), *Daffy Duck* (March 1953), *Porky Pig* (November 1952), *Woody Woodpecker* (December 1952), *Mickey Mouse* (December 1952), and even *Pluto* (October 1952).

With the major animated characters appearing in Dell Comics, other comic-book publishers went for the minor studios. Marvel Comics negotiated with Paul Terry for the rights to publish his Terrytoon characters and Mighty Mouse in *Terry-Toons* (October 1942) and *Mighty Mouse Comics* (Fall 1946). DC Comics went to the even smaller Columbia Pictures cartoon shop and bought the rights to the Fox and Crow characters for *Real Screen Comics* (Spring 1945) and *Fox and Crow* (December 1951). The Paramount cartoon characters, including Herman and Katnip, Casper the Friendly Ghost, and Little Audrey, were initially published by St. John, and later by

Mickey Mouse #49, © 1956 Walt Disney Productions

Mighty Mouse #5, © 1948 Metro-Goldwyn-Mayer

Harvey Comics.

With hardly enough licensed cartoon characters to go around, many comic-book publishers created their own funny animals.

Marvel Comics became the second publisher to enter the funny-animal field with *Krazy Komics* (July 1942). It featured the first *original* funny-animal comic-book characters, Ziggy Pig and Silly Seal.

Coo Coo Comics (October 1942) from Better Publications introduced another original funny animal, Super Mouse. He became the "hero" of the seventh funny-animal comic book to ever be published. Better later added *Goofy* (June 1943) and *Happy* (August 1943) to its funny-animal lineup.

Fawcett's Funny Animals (December 1942) featured Hoppy the Marvel Bunny, who bore a close resemblance to Fawcett's own Captain Marvel!

Although the American Comics Group did not have any animated cartoon characters, it used the talents of cartoon animators to create dozens of original funny animals for *Giggle* (October 1943) and *Ha-Ha Comics* (October 1943).

Some funny animals, such as *Felix the Cat* (1943), came to the comic books from the newspaper strips. Others, like *Pogo* (April 1946), traveled the opposite direction, from comic books to comic strips.

An interesting variation on the funny-animal genre is the funny-animal superhero comics, like *Super Rabbit* (Fall 1943), *Super Duck* (Fall 1944), *Supermouse* (December 1948), *Super Pup* (March 1954), and *Super Goof* (October 1965). There were also atomic-powered animals like *Atomic Mouse* (March 1953), *Atomic Rabbit* (August 1955), *Atom the Cat* (October 1957), *Atom Ant* (January 1966), and, of course, the greatest super-animal hero of them all, *Mighty Mouse* (Fall 1946).

Many talented animators, newspaper cartoonists, and comic-book artists worked on funny-animal comics at one time or the other. The two acknowledged masters of the genre, however, are Walt Kelly, the creator of Pogo in *Animal Comics* (December 1941), and Carl Barks, the premier Donald Duck artist and storyteller.

Before his world-famous "Pogo" newspaper comic strip, Kelly wrote and drew a number of animal stories and books for Dell Publishing, including *Fairy Tale Parade* (June 1942), *Our Gang* (September 1942), and *Raggedy Ann and Andy* (June 1946).

Carl Barks, a former Disney studio employee, did his first comic-book work on *Donald Duck #9* (August 1942). He then proceeded to write and draw hundreds of Donald Duck stories for *Walt Disney's Comics and Stories* (#31, April 1943), *Uncle Scrooge* (March 1952), and *Donald Duck* until 1967. His stories are so outstanding, they have remained continually in print both in the United States and in countries all over the world (where they seem to enjoy an even greater popularity). The twenty-five-year output of Carl Barks has made him perhaps the most published and widely read comic-book artist of the past or present.

Barks, Kelly, and dozens of other funny-animal artists and writers created a genre that was at once accessible to the youngest reader, while also entertaining enough to appeal to the parent who, after all, would have to read the book out loud to that child.

The funny-animal genre was consistently strong all through the 1940s and 1950s, seemingly immune to the ups and downs of the superhero, western, romance, and other genres. By the mid to late 1950s, however, Dell Publishing had pretty much wrapped up

the funny-animal comic-book market. Gold Key continued its line of successful animated-cartoon-character titles all through the 1960s and 1970s.

The exit of Gold Key/Whitman Publishing from the comic-book business in 1984, however, signalled a dearth of funny-animal comics. Marvel Comics issued some titles through its Star line of comics, like *Top Dog* (April 1985), and DC reprinted some of its 1940s and 1950s material in *Funny Stuff Stocking Stuffer* (March 1985).

It was not until the entry into the field of Gladstone Publishing in 1986 that funny-animal comics gained new life. Gladstone revived the Disney comic-book line, and proceeded to publish both old and new stories of Donald Duck, Mickey Mouse, and all the Disney gang.

Carl Barks' Uncle Scrooge, © *Walt Disney Productions*

> "I was just a duck man—strictly a duck man."
> —CARL BARKS,
> artist and writer of
> *Donald Duck* and *Uncle Scrooge*

Bullwinkle and Rocky #1, © *1987 Marvel Entertainment Group, Inc.*

Spook Comics #1, © *1946 Baily Publications*

HORROR COMICS

Horror comics of the 1950s, with their graphic scenes of gore, dismemberment, cannibalism, torture, and bloodletting, offered plenty of damning evidence for the emerging critics of comic books. Along with the crime comics, the horror comic books of the 1950s provided all the impetus that was needed to establish the 1954 Comic Code Authority, an industry review board that effectively regulated horror comics out of existence by 1955.

Horror comics were extremely popular from 1951 to 1954. In 1952 they reached a peak publication of approximately one hundred and fifty titles—nearly thirty percent of all the comic books published that year.

Interestingly enough, horror comic books were much more popular among the small comic-book publishers than among the larger

The Thing #5, © 1952 Charlton Comics, Inc.

> **"In a horror story, it didn't matter if the story stank and artwork was rotten as long as it showed a lot of guts hanging out and bloodsucking and other perversions."**
> **—HOWARD NOSTRAND,**
> horror-comic artist in the 1950s

houses. Except for a few mystery titles, DC Comics published no horror comics. Fawcett and Quality Comics had only two or three titles apiece, and Dell Publishing would not let a hint of horror invade its line of Disney and kiddie comics.

Marvel Comics led the pack with twenty-five titles devoted to horror and fantasy, such as *Adventures into Terror* (November 1950), *Adventures into Weird Worlds* (January 1952), and *Uncanny Tales* (June 1952). Marvel (or Atlas, as it was known then) packed its horror comics with five or six stories per issue and probably published more horror comic stories than anyone else. It did not, however, publish the first horror comic book.

Uncanny Tales #18, © 1953 Marvel Entertainment Group, Inc.

As early as 1946, there were comics devoted entirely to horror themes, such as the obscure *Spook Comics* from Baily Publications. In 1947 Avon Comics came out with one issue of what is usually considered the first horror comic book, *Eerie* (January 1947). However, it would not publish another issue until four years later.

In the meantime, American Comics Group (ACG) began publishing the first continuous and longest running horror comic, *Adventures into the Unknown* (Fall 1948). ACG added other horror titles to its lineup, including *Forbidden Worlds* (July 1951), *Out of the Night* (February 1952), and *Skeleton Hand* (September 1952). These comics relied heavily upon formula stories of vampires, werewolves, and zombies.

Another early publisher of horror comics was EC Comics, which came out with *Vault of Horror* (April 1950), *Haunt of Fear* (May 1950), and *Crypt of Terror* (April 1950)—later renamed *Tales from the Crypt*. EC's comics set the standard for all horror books to come.

Haunt of Fear #20, © 1953 William M. Gaines

Moody captions, twist endings, and adult themes of love and revenge elevated EC's horror comics above the simple shock slop that often appeared in other horror comics.

Lest they be perceived as too literary, however, EC's comics featured a horror host each issue—like the Old Witch, the Vault Keeper, or the Crypt Keeper—who would invite readers to "strap on their drool cups" and to "read another revolting regurgitation from my library of lecherous literature, this choice chunk of chilling charnel chatter."

While EC Comics's "charnel chatter" occasionally brushed against the boundaries of good taste, some 1950 horror comics charged beyond the hinterlands of human decency. One horror comic, *Mysterious Adventures #15* (August 1953), featured a decapitation, several strangulations, one carving-up of a face, two incidences of acid being thrown in someone's face, and a front cover that shows a ghoul using a human head as a bowling ball. The comic modestly promised "Thrilling Tales of Suspense" to any youngster brave enough to take it home.

After several hundred other examples of such excess, the Comics Code in 1954 effectively eliminated horror comics in part by prohibiting the use of vampires and werewolves in comic books or even the words "horror" or "terror" in a comic-book title.

Thus the horror comics that remained after 1954 were transformed into much tamer science-fiction, mystery, or fantastic-suspense comic books. Interestingly enough, the best horror comics published after 1954 came from Dell, a company which never submitted its comics to the Comic Code Authority for review because it maintained its titles were always beyond reproach. Dell's *Ghost Stories* (September 1962) and *Tales from the Tomb* (October 1962) featured well written stories. Their comic-book adaptations of Edgar Allan Poe tales and Universal horror films, such as

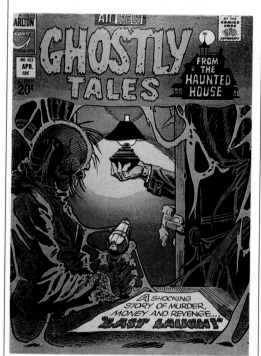

Ghostly Tales #103, © 1973 Charlton Press, Inc.

Dracula (October 1962), also qualify as post-1954 horror comics.

Another publisher that avoided the Comics Code was James Warren. Warren's *Creepy* (1964) and *Eerie* (September 1965) were black-and-white magazines with stories and artwork reminiscent of the EC horror comics, featuring shock endings and "horror hosts."

Although the genre essentially lasted for only about four years, the dark images and bloody excesses of the horror comic books left an indelible impression upon the comic-book landscape.

JUNGLE COMICS

From Tarzan to Sheena to Ka-Zar to Rulah, every jungle comic had its king or queen. The jungle heroes were always physically magnificent white men or women who watched over a world populated by animals and natives—friendly and otherwise.

Jungle Comics (January 1940) was the first *original* jungle comic book, inspired by the success of the Tarzan newspaper-strip reprints in other comic books. This was soon followed by *Sheena* (Spring 1942) and then *Nyoka, the Jungle Girl* (Winter 1945).

In 1947 Victor Fox published over a half-dozen jungle titles, most of them featuring jungle goddesses with unlikely names (Zegra, Tegra) starring in comics with unlikely titles (*Zoot* and *Zago*).

In the early 1950s Marvel and other publishers contributed such books as *Jungle Action* (October 1954), *Jungle Tales (September 1954)*, *Jann of the Jungle* (November 1955), *Jungle Thrills* (February 1952), *Jungle Jim* (January 1949), and *Ramar of the Jungle* (1954).

A resurgence in jungle comics occurred in the 1960s and early 1970s, with Dell's *Toka Jungle King* (August 1964), Skywald's *Jungle Adventures* (April 1971), DC's *Rima the Jungle Girl* (April 1974) and Marvel's *Ka-Zar* (January 1974).

Almost all of the jungle comics followed the same formula. The world of the jungle king or queen is suddenly disturbed by vicious animals, crazed natives, poaching hunters, Nazi war criminals, or soulless white men. The jungle god or goddess fights the invaders but is usually captured after a fierce struggle. Friendly jungle animals or natives help free the bound jungle hero, who then dispatches

Sheena #14, © 1951 Fiction House, Inc.

Tarzan #122, © 1961 Edgar Rice Burroughs, Inc.

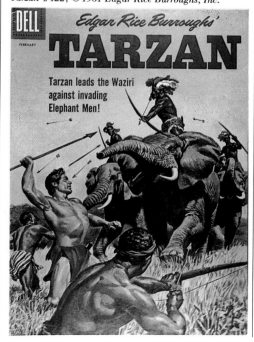

"The jungle heroines were really the only ones who managed to assert themselves properly and to establish a specific genre. Girls exposed to jungle life simply had to wear brief leopard-skin bikinis, just as Tarzan wears a G-string. Thus the female copies of Tarzan provided a pleasant feast for the eyes. They were the white goddesses before whom the superstitious black 'wild men' retreated in awe and fear."
—REINHOLD REITBERGER and WOLFGANG FUCHS,
authors of
Comics: Anatomy of a Mass Medium

evil and restores harmony to the peaceful jungle domain.

The appeal of jungle comics stems from the popularity of the original King of the Apes, Tarzan. Edgar Rice Burroughs's character had been featured in a number of comic books since 1936, all reprints from the newspaper strips until Dell Comics published *Tarzan* (September 1947) in a series of original adventures that lasted for almost twenty-five years. The Dell version of Tarzan was particularly well realized by the artwork of Jesse Marsh, whose African natives, wildlife, and locales looked natural and just right for the book.

Tarzan later was published by Gold Key and drawn by Russ Manning, who also drew both the excellent newspaper strip and a spin-off comic-book title, *Korak, Son of Tarzan* (January 1964). Tarzan next was passed over to DC Comics, in 1972, and then to Marvel Comics in 1977. After a five-year hiatus, in 1984 Marvel brought Tarzan back briefly to capture the honor of being the last newsstand jungle comic book.

KID COMICS

Kids have been a favorite subject for the comics ever since the 1897 debut of Rudolph Dirks's Katzenjammer Kids as a newspaper comic strip. The Katzenjammer Kids were a pair of original mischief makers who tirelessly tormented the Captain and the Inspector, the authority figures in their world. They embodied the enormous energy and imagination of childhood, unbridled by adult rules and limitations.

The Katzenjammer Kids appeared in a series of comic books and collections from 1903 to 1954. They became the model for many of the "little kid" comic strips and comic books.

Perhaps the most famous and well-liked little-kid comic was *Little Lulu* (June 1945). Based upon Marjorie Buell's *Saturday Evening Post* cartoon character, the *Little Lulu* comic book was initially drawn and written by John Stanley. For eighteen years Stanley wrote almost every *Little Lulu* story. He created a memorable cast of characters, including one who gained his own book, *Tubby* (August 1952).

Many of the *Little Lulu* stories played upon the typical prepubescent boy-girl rivalry. Lulu Moppet might be fooled by Tubby and the boys once, but she always triumphed in the end due to her own ingenuity and cleverness. Stanley's stories captured both the warmth and absurdity of growing up, and his rich characterization never slipped or faltered.

Like Little Lulu and her friends, Dell's *Our Gang Comics* (September 1942) also focused upon a group of kids who played off each other in a series of comic misadventures. Drawn by Walt Kelly of "Pogo" fame, the *Our Gang* comic stories were a humorous look at the dynamics of kids playing and growing up together.

Little Lulu #75, © 1954 Western Publishing Co.

Dell also produced several other popular kid comics, many of them based upon successful newspaper strips, such as *Henry* (October 1946), *Little Iodine* (April 1949), and *Nancy* (1957).

Harvey Comics experienced big success with its "little" comics, including *Little Audrey* (April 1949), the Paramount cartoon starlet; *Little Dot* (September 1953), who had an unhealthy obsession with dots; and *Little Lotta* (November 1955), a big girl with a gargantuan appetite. Harvey's kid star, however, became *Richie Rich* (November 1960), the "poor little rich boy" who had his own butler and an allowance larger than the gross national product of most countries.

Little Audrey #21, © 1952 Paramount Pictures Corp.

Katzenjammer Kids #19, © 1952 King Features Syndicate, Inc.

The most widely recognized little-kid comic in the world appeared first in a March 12, 1951, newspaper cartoon from the pen of Hank Ketcham. Two years later, the blonde-haired terror received his own comic book, *Dennis the Menace* (August 1953). Drawn by Al Wiseman and other Ketcham "ghosts," and written by Fred Toole, the *Dennis the Menace* comic book was published for nearly thirty years by a string of publishers, including Standard/Pines, Fawcett, and Marvel Comics. Dennis always managed to get away with creating incredible havoc without even being spanked!

The fantasy of punishment-free mayhem appealed to young readers, so other comic-book publishers soon created their own versions of The Menace. Archie Comics came up with *Pat the Brat* (June 1953) and *Li'l Jinx* (November 1956). Charlton's *Li'l Genius* (1954) was a red-haired version of Dennis, and Marvel unleashed a trio of terror tots like *Willie the Wise Guy* (September 1957), *Dexter the Demon* (September 1957), and *Melvin the Monster* (July 1956).

DC Comics only had one kid comic, but it was a classic: *Sugar and Spike* (April 1956) featured a boy and a girl too young to talk, but intelligent enough to get into misadventures. Written and drawn by comic-book veteran Sheldon Mayer, *Sugar and Spike* was a charming fantasy of how two imaginative two-year-olds might view the adult world.

Another type of kid comic was spin-off titles from other comics, such as *Little Archie*

"Dennis The Menace was a freewheeling throwback to the era of mischievous kids—the flavor and characters of the Katzenjammers in Eisenhower suburban settings."
—RICHARD MARSCHALL, comic historian

Dennis the Menace #41, © *1960 Halldem Pubs.*

Sugar and Spike #95, © *1971 DC Comics, Inc.*

Little Archie #7, © *1958 Archie Comic Publications, Inc.*

> "I went to more screenings than the movie critics in New York . . . every damn movie that came out we went to see."
> —L.B. COLE,
> editor at Dell Comics, 1961-1964

(1956) from the Archie line of comics. Chronicling the preteenage adventures of Archie, Betty, Veronica, and Jughead, *Little Archie* comics already had a built-in readership.

Harvey Comics followed the same line of reasoning when it issued *Little Sad Sack* (October 1964), a comic that gave fresh meaning to the term "army brats."

Even the Three Stooges produced offspring, of a sort, with the comic book *Little Stooges* (September 1972) drawn by Norman Maurer, son-in-law of Stooge Moe Howard. Marvel Comics also issued several kid comics under its Star imprint line in 1988, including *The Flintstone Kids* and *The Muppet Babies*.

The little-kid comics were popular because they created a fantasy world, where children tested their limits of creation and destruction and where adults were either absent or controlled. In the pages of a kid comic book, young readers could transcend the limitations of childhood and triumph over parents, teachers, and adult society—not a bad deal at all for ten cents!

MOVIE AND TV COMICS

Movies, television, and comic books have always enjoyed an incestuous relationship. Although there have been movies and television shows based upon comic-book characters, such as Batman, Wonder Woman, and Superman, the comic books have generally borrowed more heavily from cinema and television than vice versa.

Movie Comics (August 1939) from DC was the first comic book to be based upon the popular movies of the day, such as *Son of Frankenstein*, *Stagecoach*, and *Gunga Din*. Fiction House's *Movie Comics* (December 1946) had

Captain Video #6, © 1951 Fawcett Publications, Inc.

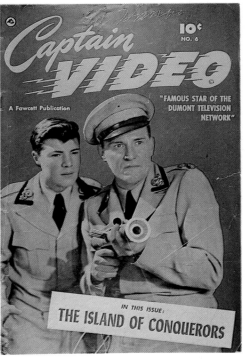

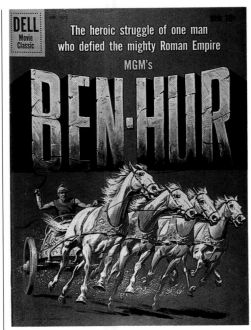

Ben-Hur #1052, © 1959 Loew's Incorporated

the same name and about the same amount of success as its predecessor, lasting less than a year.

Fawcett's luck was a little bit better. Both *Fawcett Movie Comics* (1949) and *Motion Picture Comics* (1950) lasted almost two years, thanks to featuring current hit movies such as *When Worlds Collide* and *The Red Badge of Courage*. Fawcett also concentrated heavily upon western movies in both comic-book titles, since western comics were selling well at the time.

DC Comics' *Feature Films* (March 1950) offered photo covers of movie stars like Bing Crosby and Bob Hope, but lasted only four issues. Magazine Enterprises had less luck with its *Movie Thrillers*, which evidently thrilled few since it lasted but one issue.

The most successful series of comic-book movie adaptations came from Dell and Gold Key. From 1953 to 1969 Dell published sixty-seven movie comic books which featured a variety of movies, from *Bambi* to *Ben-Hur* to *Dracula*.

In a ten-year period from 1962 to 1972 Gold Key Comics came out with seventy movie comics, relying heavily upon Disney, family, and animated movies such as the *Yellow Submarine*, *Mary Poppins*, and *How The West Was Won*. Almost all of the Dell and Gold Key movie comics were one-issue specials, not part of a series. The last Gold Key movie adaptation was based upon the 1980 film, *Flash Gordon*.

Perhaps the most successful series of comic books taken from the movies was *Star Wars* (July 1977), which lasted for nearly ten years by expanding the basic storyline of the original movie.

In the 1980s Marvel enjoyed success by adapting *Raiders of the Lost Ark* (September 1981), *For Your Eyes Only* (October 1981), and *Who Framed Roger Rabbit* (1988). DC

Comics' contribution to the 1980s movie adaptations was the *Star Trek Movie Special* (June 1984).

Movie adaptations have been consistently popular because they attract a larger readership than the typical comic-book audience. In many cases, the comic book publisher will work with the movie studio in advance of the movie's release, in order to have the comic book ready at the same time the movie appears. This means that the comic book often is based on a movie script or stills, so it may be slightly different from the actual movie after directors make last-minute changes.

Although television is sometimes blamed for the declining comic-book readership of the 1950s, comic-book publishers also were quick to capitalize on the medium's new popularity.

I Love Lucy #5, © 1955 Lucille Ball & Desi Arnaz

The first comic book to be based upon a television show was Dell Comic's *Howdy Doody* (January 1950). One of the next early television comic books was *Uncle Milty* (December 1950), which featured Milton Berle, "America's greatest TV comic." Fawcett's *Captain Video* (February 1951) was the first comic book based upon an adventure television show.

Throughout the 1950s other comics were adapted from popular television shows, such as *I Love Lucy* (February 1954), *My Little Margie* (July 1954), *Gunsmoke* (February 1956), *Jackie Gleason* (June 1956), *Sgt. Bilko* (May 1957), *Leave It to Beaver* (June 1958), *Sea Hunt* (August 1958), and *Dobie Gillis* (May 1960).

It was not until the 1960s, however, that Dell and Gold Key Comics began to produce the great flood of television comic adaptations. Almost every popular television show that could possibly appeal to a comic-book audience was optioned for adaptation.

Television's situation comedies provided such comic books as *Beverly Hillbillies* (April

Beverly Hillbillies #16, © 1967 Filmways TV Productions

1963), *McHale's Navy* (May 1963), *The Munsters* (January 1965), *Bewitched* (April 1965), *Get Smart* (June 1966), *F-Troop* (August 1966), and *Flying Nun* (February 1968). Even such eminently forgettable and short-lived television comedies like *Run Buddy Run* (June 1967) and *Captain Nice* (November 1967) appeared briefly in comic-book format.

Television adventure series also were natural fodder for comic-book adaptations. The 1960s produced comics like *Bonanza* (June 1960), *Twilight Zone* (March 1961), *Ben Casey* (June 1962), *Outer Limits* (January 1964), *Man From U.N.C.L.E.* (February 1965), *I Spy* (August 1966), and *Mission Impossible* (May 1967).

Man From Uncle #12, © 1967 Metro-Goldwyn-Mayer

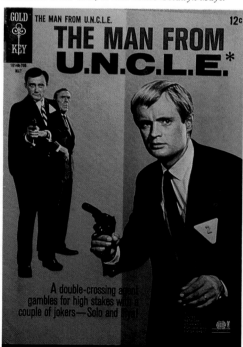

Dr. Who #5, © 1985 Marvel Entertainment Group, Inc.

"Now you see it! You see the killer backed against the wall—You see the low gun muzzle rammed against his throat—You see the police pack actually run the murder-mad man into his hole— You'll see it all because the whole detective story is told in *pictures*."

—Advertisement for the first issue of *Detective Picture Stories* (December 1936)

The record for the longest running television-show comic book was set by *Star Trek* (July 1967), which was published for twenty years by three different publishers: Gold Key, Marvel Comics, and DC Comics.

The 1970s produced adaptations such as *The Partridge Family* (March 1971), *Space: 1999* (November 1975), *The Six Million Dollar Man* (June 1976), *The Bionic Woman* (October 1977), and *Happy Days* (March 1979).

In the 1980s Marvel Comics brought the BBC's *Dr. Who* (October 1984) to American audiences and also has enjoyed tremendous success with its adaptation of the television show *Alf* (March 1988). DC Comics has adapted both *Star Trek: The Next Generation* (February 1988) and *The Prisoner* (1988) for comic-book readers.

Keen Detective Funnies #1, © 1940 Centaur Publications

MYSTERY AND DETECTIVE COMICS

During the late 1930s mystery novels, detective stories, and private-eye movies were extremely popular. The first comic book to be devoted to this theme was Comic Magazine's *Detective Picture Stories* (December 1936). A few months later, DC Comics issued *Detective Comics* (March 1937), which later featured one of the most famous costumed detectives, the Batman. Centaur continued the 1930s anthology mystery-comic titles by publishing *Keen Detective Funnies* (July 1938).

As Superman and his imitators began to dominate the comics after 1938, the comic-book private eye gave way to the superhero. Action, not cerebral detection, was what the comic-book medium demanded, and colorful costumed crime fighters supplanted their private-eye counterparts in the comic books.

Interestingly enough, it was the newspaper strips which gave the comic detectives a wel-

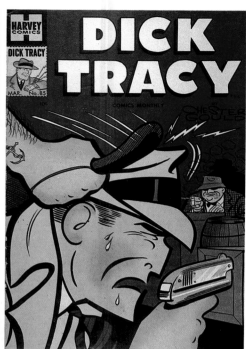

Dick Tracy #85, © 1955 Chicago Tribune

come home. Reprints of the "Dick Tracy" newspaper strip had been appearing in comic books since 1936, but it was not until the late 1940s that Dell Comics gave him his own regular comic-book series, *Dick Tracy* (January 1948).

Other newspaper-strip detectives who made it into their own comic books were *The Saint* (August 1947) and *Kerry Drake* (1948). Fictional detectives who made the transition to the comic-book format included *Charlie Chan* (June 1948), *Ellery Queen* (May 1949), *Sherlock Holmes* (October 1955), and *Perry Mason* (June 1964).

Some private eyes were created especially for comic books, such as *Sam Hill Private Eye* (1950), *Ken Shannon* (October 1951), and *Mike Shayne* (November 1961).

The detective and mystery comics, unlike the crime comics, relied more upon characterization and plotting than on violence and bloodshed to attract and hold their readers. Generally appealing to an older audience than other comics, the detective and private-eye comic books faded in the 1960s and 1970s as superheroes pushed them aside.

NEWSPAPER-COMIC CHARACTERS

The first comic books were collections of popular newspaper comic strips, like "Joe Palooka," "Mutt & Jeff," "Katzenjammer Kids," "Tarzan," "Popeye," and "The Phantom." The major comic-strip reprint titles, such as *Famous Funnies* (July 1934), *Popular* (February 1936), *King* (April 1936), *Tip Top Comics* (April 1936), *Ace* (April 1937), *Super Comics* (May 1938), and *Magic* (August 1939), were the top-selling comic books until the superhero explosion of 1940.

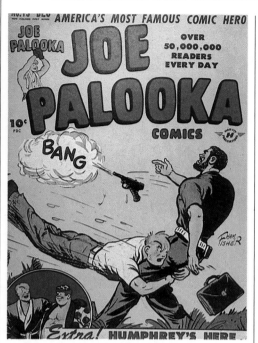

Joe Palooka #15, © 1947 Harvey Features Syndicate

The first newspaper-strip comic books consisted of ten or more different strips that were reprinted in comic-book form. The anthology format allowed publishers to appeal to the widest readership by balancing humor and adventure strips each issue.

In some of the newspaper-strip anthologies, the most popular character would gradually take over the entire book. Thus, *Comics on Parade* (April 1938), which originally reprinted a half-dozen or more newspaper strips each issue like "Tarzan," "Li'l Abner," or "Ella Cinders," switched over to featuring only one character per issue.

It was soon apparent that comic books devoted to the most popular newspaper characters would also enjoy the best sales. At the same time, there were only so many news-

Peanuts, © 1962 United Features Syndicate, Inc.

paper strips available to fill up a monthly comic book. The syndicates, which licensed the newspaper characters to the comic-book publishers, then began to turn out new material for comic books based upon their most popular newspaper-strip characters.

These new comic stories, created especially for the comic books, usually were drawn by syndicate "ghosts" or the strip artist's assistants. *Dagwood Comics* (September 1950), for example, still bore the signature of newspaper-strip creator Chic Young, but the comic-book stories often were drawn by Paul Fung.

A list of all the comic books based on newspaper-strip characters would almost be a rundown of all the popular comic strips of the past sixty years. A few of the more popular and well known include *Prince Valiant*, *Joe Palooka*, *Phantom*, *Beetle Bailey*, *Li'l Abner*, *Peanuts*, and *Barney Google and Snuffy Smith*, among many others.

More recently, popular newspaper strips of the 1970s and 1980s have been collected into paperback books, instead of in the comic-book format. These comic-strip reprint books have appeared often on best seller lists all through the 1980s, indicating that the public's long-standing love affair with the newspaper-strip comic characters is still going strong.

ROMANCE COMICS

With over three hundred titles and more than five thousand comic books devoted to true love, romance comics are the third most popular genre of comic books, outnumbered only by the superhero and western titles.

Romance comics have traditionally been purchased almost exclusively by girls and young women—nearly ninety-nine percent, according to most publishers' surveys. The readership for romance comics has also generally been older than for other comics.

In 1950, the year that more romance comics appeared on the newsstands than any other comic-book genre, the average romance comic-book reader was a fifteen-and-a-half-year-old girl, as compared to the typical twelve-and-a-half-year-old male comic-book reader of that day. Nearly half of the readers of romance comics in the early 1950s were women over eighteen years of age.

Small wonder, then, that the very first romance comic book, *Young Romance* (September 1947), proudly proclaimed on its cover that it was "For the more ADULT readers of comics!" The first issue sold out its print run of half a million copies, and quickly jumped to a circulation of one million.

Created by Joe Simon and Jack Kirby, the dynamic team that was responsible for Captain America and dozens of other popular 1940s comic-book characters, *Young Romance* set the style for the thousands of romance comics yet to come.

Each romance comic typically had three or four stories, six to eight pages long. Unlike

> "The comic strip may functionally be defined as a serially published, episodic, open-ended dramatic narrative or series of linked anecdotes about recurrent, identified characters, told in successive drawings regularly enclosing ballooned dialogue or its equivalent and minimized narrative text."
> —BILL BLACKBEARD and MARTIN WILLIAMS,
> editors of *The Smithsonian Collection of Newspaper Comics*

My Date #1, © 1947 Hillman Publications

"I didn't even want him to kiss me, but I let him when I thought he was rich! I feel cheap and soiled! I'm just a. . . ."
—*Heart Throbs*
(April 1950)

superhero or western comics, there were no continuing characters, and the plots were comfortably predictable.

Catering to young girls' wishes to be "beautiful" and loved, a typical romance story featured a beautiful heroine who must choose between two eligible men. One man is flashy, aggressive, reckless and perhaps rich. The other suitor is kind, sensitive, but somehow unable to express his feelings of true love. After discovering the superficiality and crassness of the flashy suitor, the woman gratefully sinks into the arms of the nice guy whose qualities she finally recognizes.

As an added plot twist, the woman in the romance comic story sometimes must overcome an obstacle, such as seeing her true love through a rough time or enduring his infatuation with an "undeserving" woman.

Typically, the heroine must also learn an important lesson, usually through emotional

Radiant Love #3, © 1954 Gilmore Magazines, Inc.

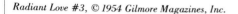

THE RETURN OF CLIFF MASTERS · TRAIL TO ROMANCE
A STRANGER AND HIS DOG · VENGEANCE AT MESA RIDGE

Cowboy Love #10, © 1950 Fawcett Publications, Inc.

suffering and turmoil. Through her mistakes and pain, the heroine learns to see through her own fickleness or to change her wild and spoiled behavior. Pain, suffering, misunderstanding, despair, and loneliness always precede the obligatory happy ending on the last page.

The romance comic originated in the teenage comics of the mid-1940s. Other publishers were quick to notice the Archie Comic success formula of stories built upon teen flirtations and eternal love triangles.

The early romance comics went a step beyond the innocent teenage malt-shop humor of the teen titles. Early titles like *Romantic Picture Novelettes* (1946) and *My Date* (July 1947), while not truly romance comics, took a step in that direction. To attract an older readership during the 1950s, the romance comics used a sensationalistic confession-magazine format. Instead of using comic-book art for their covers, romance comics often featured photo covers in an attempt to emulate the popular newsstand confession magazines.

Even the stories in the romance comics were titled similar to the confession magazines, such as "I Joined A Teen-Age Sex Club," "My Mother, My Rival!", and "I Was A Pickup!"

The romance comic books played upon such common themes that their titles often sounded the same. Consider that Superior Comics alone published *My Secret*, *Our Secret*, *My Secret Marriage*, and *My Own Romance*.

Fox Comics produced twenty-five romance comics, and most seemed to begin with "My," such as *My Great Love*, *My Intimate Affair*, *My Love Story*, *My Love Secret*, *My Love Life*, *My Love Affair*, *My Love Memories*, *My Past*, *My Private Life*, *My Secret Life*, and *My Secret Story*.

There was also *Love and Romance, Love*

and Marriage, *Love at First Sight*, *Love Diary*, *Love Confessions*, *Love Experiences*, *Love Lessons*, *Love Letters*, *Love Life*, *Love Problems*, *Love Romances*, *Love Secrets*, *Love Stories*, *Love Adventures*, and *Love Tales*.

Teenagers, the biggest audience for romance comics, were certainly not forgotten, with titles like *Teen-Age Brides*, *Teen-Age Love*, *Teen-Age Romances*, *Teen-Age Temptations*, *Teen Confessions*, and *Teen Secret Diary*.

Romance comics, more so than other types of comics, also were often wedded with other genres to produce interesting crossbreeds, like western romances, war romances, and supernatural romances.

Since westerns were the other hot genre of the early 1950s, publishers figured they couldn't lose with such hybrid titles as *Cowboy Love*, *Western Love*, *Real West Romances*, *Cowgirl Romances*, and *Saddle Romances*.

When the Korean War broke out, publishers rushed out such titles as *Wartime Romances*, *G.I. Sweethearts*, *G.I. War Brides*, and *True War Romances*.

Haunted Love #1, © 1973 Charlton Press, Inc.

With the interest in gothic novels peaking in the early 1970s, DC and Charlton spruced up their romance lines with *Dark Mansion of Forbidden Love*, *Sinister House of Secret Love*, and *Haunted Love*.

Other interesting inbreeding in the romance genre produced such titles as *Love Mystery*, *Negro Romance*, *Movie Love*, *Hollywood Romances*, and *Career Girl Romances*.

Although many of the comic-book artists of the 1950s produced work for the romance comics, only a few are closely identified with the genre.

Joe Simon and Jack Kirby's work for Prize Comics (*Young Romance*, *Young Love*) cer-

tainly put their imprint on the new genre. Matt Baker, an artist who drew pinup queens for Fiction House and the Phantom Lady for Fox Features, rendered glamorous romantic heroines and dashingly attractive males for St. John Publishing. Bob Powell, a prolific comic-art genius who worked for almost every company and in every genre, drew the best "clinch kiss" in comics for both Harvey Comics and Fawcett Publications. Bill Ward drew steamy, lonely lasses for the Quality Comics romance line, while Alex Toth distinguished Standard's romance books.

Although 1952 was the peak year for romance comics, there were always at least thirty romance titles on the stands until the early 1960s. The genre saw an immediate growth spurt after the institution of the 1954 Comics Code as publishers converted their more objectionable crime and horror comics to the tamer love books.

Still, the taming down of the passion and "sexiness" of the romance comics by the Comics Code eventually took its toll. The older romance readers gradually gravitated toward the steamier confession-story pulp magazines, and by the 1970s romance comics were more likely to be read by pre-teen girls than by their older sisters or mothers.

The last of the minor comic-book publishers folded in 1963, leaving only DC, Marvel, and Charlton publishing romance comics. Still, the genre was popular enough that, as late as 1973, there were still seventeen romance titles on the newsstands.

However, as newsstand distribution of comics became increasingly spotty during the late 1970s and early 1980s, female readership of the comics declined. The romance comic faded away thirty-five years after its birth.

True Love #2, © 1986 Brent Anderson

Young Romance Vol 3, #5, © 1950 Joe Simon and Jack Kirby

"I'm constantly running into people who tell me their whole life was changed by the early *Mad*."
—HARVEY KURTZMAN,
creator, *Mad Comics*

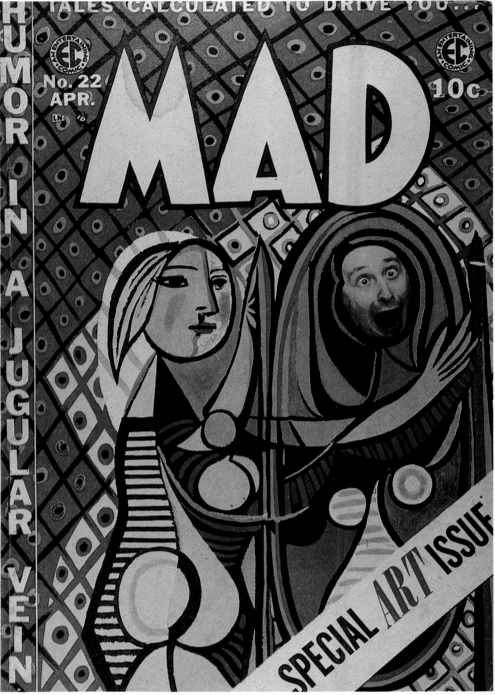

MAD #22, © 1955 William M. Gaines

SATIRE COMICS

Although humor comics were extremely popular through the 1940s, there had never been a comic book quite like *Mad* (October 1952). No cutesy funny animals; no wholesome teenage-dating humor nor slapstick antics, would ever be found in the pages of *Mad*.

Instead, *Mad* served up hilarious parodies on popular movies, television shows, advertising, literature, and even the comic books themselves. *Mad* was self-consciously a comic book satire: It poked fun at itself, at its readers, and at its competition. In the world of *Mad* Superduperman uses his X-ray vision to peer into women's restrooms, and the Lone Stranger is left to burn at the stake by his not-so-trusted Indian companion, Pronto.

The creator and first editor of *Mad*, Harvey Kurtzman, used the talents of such EC artists as Bill Elder, Wally Wood, and Jack Davis to create stories that were packed with visual sight gags and exaggerated caricatures. By its fourth issue, *Mad* was a fantastic success—spawning dozens of imitations and a companion EC title, *Panic* (February 1954).

Although *Panic* used some of the same artists as *Mad*, *Panic* lasted only twelve issues. Its editor, Al Feldstein, soon assumed the editorship of *Mad* upon Kurtzman's departure.

To increase its distribution, *Mad* was transformed into a black-and-white newsstand magazine with the July 1955 issue. Since then, nearly three hundred issues have been published with an average circulation of around a million copies.

Panic #4, © 1954 William M. Gaines

(Will Elder, Jack Davis, Wally Wood), but failed to find a strong readership after eleven issues. Almost two years later Kurtzman tried again with *Help!* (August 1960), a magazine aimed at college students who had graduated from reading *Mad*. *Help!* featured the work of several early underground cartoonists and was considered rather avant garde for its time.

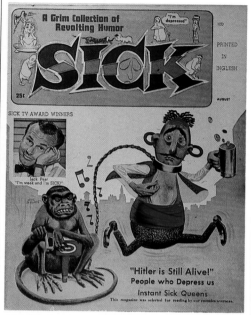

Sick #1, © 1960 Feature Publications

On the other hand, many of the *Mad* imitations in the mid-1950s lasted for only five to ten issues. Marvel, Charlton, St. John, Star, and other publishers all came out with their versions of *Mad* under such titles as *Whack* (October 1953), *Crazy* (December 1953), *Wild* (February 1954), *Madhouse* (March 1954), *Riot* (April 1954), *Unsane* (June 1954), and *From Here to Insanity* (February 1955).

After leaving *Mad* in 1956, Kurtzman was hired by Hugh Hefner of *Playboy* to edit a slick adult satire magazine called *Trump* (January 1957). *Trump* lasted only two issues, and Kurtzman returned to a more comic-book-type format with his next satire publication, *Humbug* (August 1957). Like *Trump*, *Humbug* used some of the same original *Mad* artists

Other satire magazines (*Wacko*, *Trash*, *Nuts*, *Blast*), appeared throughout the 1950s and 1960s, but only *Cracked Magazine* (February 1958) and *Sick Magazine* (August 1960) gave *Mad* serious competition. Both magazines relied on Jack Davis, a former *Mad* artist, to give their magazines a *Mad* style. Although *Cracked* and *Sick* never quite achieved the freshness or quality of *Mad*, both nevertheless managed to attract a respectable spillover readership.

Throughout the rest of the 1960s, satire comics were limited to short-lived titles like Archie Comics's *Tales Calculated to Drive You Bats* (November 1961) and Marvel's *Not Brand Echh* (August 1967), a parody of the 1960s comics scene.

In the 1970s DC used the talents of Basil Wolverton, another *Mad* alumnus, to draw the covers for *Plop* (October 1973), its new satire comic book. Marvel tried the field again with *Arrgh!* (December 1974).

By the late 1980s, however, the only satire comic magazines remaining on the newsstand were *Mad* and *Cracked*.

Help #22, © 1965 Help Publishing Co.

Cracked #40, © 1964 Major Magazines

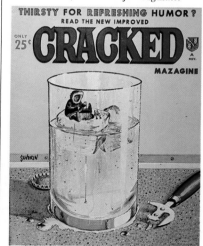

SCIENCE-FICTION COMICS

Since science fiction and comic books are the two genres most often associated with imaginative literature, it's not surprising that they share common origins, publishers, creators, and themes.

The first science-fiction comic strips were Dick Calkin's "Buck Rogers" (1929) and Alex

Raymond's "Flash Gordon" (1934).

The "Buck Rogers" newspaper strip's first appearance in a comic book occurred in *Famous Funnies #3* (1934), where it continued for the next twenty-two years. Buck Rogers also appeared in a series of comic books from Toby Press in 1951 and again in Gold Key books in 1964 and 1979.

Flash Gordon made his comic-book debut in McKay's *Feature Book #25* (1941). His face continued to grace the pages of newsstand comics for the next forty years—under the auspices of Dell Comics (1940s), Harvey Comics (1950s), King Comics (1960s), Charlton Comics (1970s), and Gold Key Comics (1980s).

Pulp science fiction was very popular in the 1930s and 1940s. It often emphasized spaceships, space men, alien worlds, space queens, and bug-eyed monsters. Some writers, editors, and publishers of these science-fiction pulps soon migrated to the comic-book field.

In fact, the first science-fiction comic book, *Planet Comics* (January 1940), was a spin-off from Fiction House's *Planet Science Fiction* pulp magazine. *Planet Comics* featured such

Planet Comics #27, © 1943 Fiction House, Inc.

Superworld Comics #3, © 1940 Kosmos Publications

strips as Auro Lord of Jupiter, Star Pirates, Mysta of The Moon, and Star Rangers. Beautiful women and slobbering aliens were de rigueur for every issue of *Planet Comics*, which emphasized more adventure and action than any real science.

Outside of the Buck Rogers and Flash Gordon reprints, *Planet Comics* was the only continuous science-fiction comic-book title published during the 1940s.

In 1950, however, two things happened to spark a tremendous interest and growth in science-fiction comic books. First, unprecedented media attention and public interest in flying-saucer sightings prompted such titles as *Vic Tory and His Flying Saucer* (1950) and Avon's *Flying Saucers* (1950). Second, EC

Vic Torry and His Flying Saucer #1, © 1950 Fawcett Publications, Inc.

Weird Science #22, © 1953 William M. Gaines

Comics published two new books called *Weird Science* (May 1950) and *Weird Fantasy* (May 1950).

The EC science-fiction titles often "borrowed" plots and concepts from top science-fiction writers of the day, most notably Ray Bradbury, and gave their readers beautifully drawn stories with messages more powerful than ever before found in the comic-book medium.

As a result of EC Comics and the interest in flying saucers, a number of other publishers brought out science-fiction comics.

DC Comics responded with *Strange Adventures* (August 1950) and *Mystery in Space* (April 1951), two titles edited by long-time science-fiction fan and agent, Julius Schwartz.

Mystery in Space #39, © 1957 DC Comics, Inc.

Weird Science-Fantasy, © 1953 William M. Gaines

Schwartz often used writers from science-fiction magazines to write his comic-book stories, and the stories were as carefully crafted, if more pedestrian, than the EC titles.

Ziff-Davis, publisher of the world's oldest (since 1926) science-fiction magazine, *Amazing Stories*, tried to enter the comic-book field as early as 1947 when the company mailed its

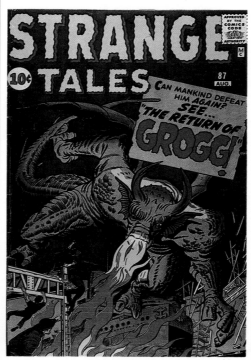

Strange Tales #87, © 1961 Marvel Entertainment Group, Inc.

magazine subscribers an eight-page promotional comic book called *Science Comics* (May 1947). Evidently reader response was not overwhelming, and nothing was done until another test mailing was done in 1950 with a title called *Amazing Adventures*. The timing was right this time, and Ziff-Davis published several science-fiction comics, among them *Weird Thrillers* (September 1951) and *Space Busters* (Spring 1952).

Like Ziff-Davis, Avon Publishing also was an active publisher of paperback and magazine science fiction. Avon's entries in the comic-book field included *Flying Saucers* (1950), *Strange Worlds* (November 1950), *Earthman on Venus* (1951), and *Space Detective* (July 1951).

Outer Space #25, © 1959 Charlton Comics Group

Charlton Comics tested the waters with *Space Adventures* (July 1952) and then converted its *Cowboy Western Comics* to *Space Western* (October 1952), an unlikely hybrid that featured cowboys fighting Nazis on the moon! Charlton tried for another cross-genre title seven years later with *Space War* (October 1959).

The 1950s produced dozens of other science-fiction titles, like *Weird Tales of the Future* (March 1952), *Captain Science* (November 1950), and *John Carter of Mars* (February 1952). The last memorable 1950s science-fiction title was EC's short-lived *Incredible Science Fiction* (August 1955).

Science fiction continued to appear in comic books all through the late 1950s, in various series from DC, Charlton, and Marvel Comics. *Outer Space* (May 1958), *Mysteries of Unexplored Worlds* (August 1956), and *Tales to Astonish* (January 1959) all featured aliens, spacemen, and adventures on faraway planets.

In the 1960s, Dell Comics issued *Space Man* (January 1962), *Flying Saucers* (April 1967), and a title inspired by television, *Outer Limits* (January 1964).

Television and the movies also provided the impetus for other science-fiction comics like *Star Trek* (July 1967), *Lost in Space* (October 1973), and *Space: 1999* (November 1975). One of the more popular science-fiction comic books of recent years was Marvel's adaptation of *Star Wars* (July 1977), which enjoyed an almost ten-year run.

SUPERHEROES

No other genre has been so closely associated with comic books as the costumed superhero. Since the debut of Superman, there have been over a thousand major and minor comic-book superheroes in a fifty-year period.

From 1939 to 1946, superhero comics powered the incredible growth of the new comic-book industry. In the early 1960s superheroes again played hero by pulling the fading comic-book industry out of the doldrums. Since the early 1960s, superhero comics have accounted for well over half of all comic-book sales!

Superheroes have dominated comic books for a number of reasons. First, they are dramatic and powerful characters particularly well-suited for the colorful comic-book page. Second, they appeal to young readers' fantasies of personal power and total freedom. Finally, the comic-book superhero provides adolescents with a larger-than-life heroic model as they outgrow their other childhood heroes and fantasy figures.

The origins of the comic-book superhero have been traced back in part to Egyptian, Norse, Babylonian, and Greek mythological beings who helped in the affairs of mortals. Heroic figures have always existed in legend and literature, from Homer's Odysseus to Sir Walter Scott's Lancelot. The more recent origins of the American comic-book superhero,

Smash Comics #14, © 1940 Everett M. Arnold

however, can be found in the popular pulp-fiction magazines of the early 1930s.

Characters like the Shadow, Doc Savage, and the Spider were all popular pulp-magazine characters with secret identities, costumes, and super physical powers. Since many comic-book creators also were writers of the pulp adventure stories, and many comic-book publishers originally published pulp hero magazines, the similarities are not coincidences.

Perhaps the most distinguishing trait of the comic-book superhero is the costume. Since comic books are a full-color medium, comic-book creators borrowed the colorful costumes of circus performers and acrobats to dress their heroes. The colorful costume also served another important purpose, as well. It allowed comic-book readers to easily identify the superhero from all the other characters in a book. This was an important consideration, since early comic books often were so poorly drawn and printed that a costume sometimes was the only way to clearly distinguish one character from another!

Besides a distinctive costume or mask, the comic-book superhero always possessed some type of super power, either physical, magical, or attributable to a weapon or device. Along with special powers and costume, the superhero usually had a normal identity or alter ego for reasons of protection and privacy. Finally, the superhero generally is motivated to do good deeds because of high moral values and a desire to work for the common good.

How does one become a superhero? Usually a normal person suddenly becomes endowed with super powers through accident or cosmic design. Superman was given his powers through an accident of birth—he is an alien being whose powers stem from living on earth. Wonder Woman and Captain Marvel gain their powers through a mythological or

Silver Streak Comics #6, © 1940 Lev Gleason Publications

cosmological process of initiation. The Flash becomes the fastest man alive by an electrical-chemical accident. Green Lantern is granted a magical power ring by the Guardians of the Universe. The Fantastic Four mutate into super-beings after exposure to atomic radiation, and Peter Parker is transformed into Spider-Man by the bite of a radioactive spider.

The super powers that comic-book heroes can possess comprise a lengthy list. It includes super strength, invisibility, ability to fly, supersight, superhearing, enormous ability to stretch, control over the elements and temperature, the ability to shrink or enlarge, transformation, materialization, time travel and whatever else the human mind can imagine.

On the other side of the coin, superheroes often have a vulnerability or limitation that can render their powers impotent. Kryptonite and magic harm Superman; Green Lantern's power

Flash Comics #102, © 1948 DC Comics, Inc.

The Funnies #54, © 1941 Dell Publishing Co., Inc.

ring is powerless against yellow objects; and Billy Batson can only become Captain Marvel when he can utter the word "SHAZAM!"

Once they have super powers, superheroes next devise a costume, create a name or secret identity, and set out to right wrongs. Usually superheroes have jobs and alter egos that make it convenient for them to fight crime, such as a newspaper or radio reporter, a detective, or even an idle socialite.

Another popular element of the superhero mythos is the presence of a younger sidekick, such as Robin the Boy Wonder in *Batman* comics. Soon after Robin's first appearance, other superheroes got their own sidekicks, in order to increase young readers' identification. All through the 1940s to 1960s spinoffs or junior versions of adult superheroes, like Wonder Girl, Captain Marvel Jr., and Kid Flash, expanded popular offerings to this market.

DC Comics's Legion of Superheroes series

in *Adventure Comics* (April 1958) introduced the idea of a team of teenage superheroes, which struck a strong responsive chord in young readers. Marvel Comics expanded upon the teenage superhero with such characters as the Human Torch, Spider-Man, and the X-Men—heroes with super powers but teenage problems. In *Teen Titans* (January 1966), DC Comics's juvenile heroes Kid Flash, Wonder Girl, Speedy, and Robin the Boy Wonder came into their own as teenage superheroes, freed from their adult counterparts.

While the first comic-book superheroes all were male, DC Comics's *Wonder Woman* (Summer 1942) broke the sex barrier. Marvel Comics quickly followed with *Miss Fury* (Winter

Target Comics #6, © 1945 Novelty Press

"I believe in the brotherhood of man and peace on Earth. If I could do it with a wave of my hand I'd stop all this war and this silly nonsense of killing people. So I used the super heroes' powers to accomplish what I couldn't do as a person. The super heroes were my wish-fulfillment figures for benefiting the world."
—GARDNER FOX, comic writer and creator of such characters as Flash, Hawkman, Atom, Justice Society of America, and Justice League of America

"I can make you invisible! You shall fly through space within seconds! Nothing physical will harm you! All you need to do is rub the birthmark on your wrist . . . Whenever you rub it, I will enter your body and you will become *Captain Triumph*!"
—*Crack Comics #27*

The Avenger #3, © 1955 Magazine Enterprises

1942). Fawcett Comics added *Mary Marvel* (December 1945), a superheroine counterpart to Captain Marvel.

Later in the 1940s other female heroes entered the arena, like Harvey's *Black Cat* (June 1946) and Doll Girl in Quality Comics *Doll Man* (December 1951). Supergirl, the cousin of Superman, debuted in *Action Comics* (May 1959) and had her own book. Marvel Comics complemented its heroes with *Spider-Woman* (April 1978), *Ms. Marvel* (January 1977), and *She-Hulk* (February 1980). All in all, however, the superhero field has been about ninety percent male, which seems to be about the same demographics as the readership of most superhero comics.

Despite the fact that superhero comics have dominated the market ever since the mid-1960s, almost all of the original superhero concepts were developed between 1938 and 1943 (with the exception of the early '60s Marvel characters like the Hulk, Spider-Man, and the Fantastic Four, whose super powers resulted from radiation exposure). Of the seven most significant comic-book superheroes, only one was created after 1943. Indeed, most of the 1960s superheroes were revivals or revisions of the original 1940s heroes. And, during the 1970s and 1980s, most superheroes have been either revivals or continuations of the 1960s heroes or even secondary reprisals of 1940s heroes.

The superhero comics ran in definite cycles, with the first period being from 1938 to 1943. During this five-year period, the first superhero (Superman) appeared and, within three years, superhero titles formed the majority of all comic books. Almost every major superhero character was created in this five-year span. Out of the forty-five comic-book publishers in business during this period, thirty-six published superhero titles!

From 1941 to 1942 the annual circulation of *Captain Marvel*, the watermark of all superhero titles, rose from 2,631,934 to 6,447,715. By 1944 the comic had more than doubled its circulation again, to 14,067,800. Clearly, the war years were some of the very best times for the superhero comics.

Following the end of World War II, the superhero comics lost two things: their audience of servicemen and their Nazi/Japanese villains. Very few new superheroes were introduced after 1944 and, by 1945, the annual circulation of Captain Marvel was on the way down. By 1949 Captain Marvel had lost nearly half its readership of five years earlier. Many superhero titles were canceled or transformed into romance, western, or crime comics.

By the mid 1950s only DC's Superman, Batman, and Wonder Woman survived. Fawcett's Captain Marvel ceased publication by late 1953, and Quality's Plastic Man lingered only until 1956. For most of the 1950s the superheroes were in suspended animation. Marvel did bring back Captain America, Sub-Mariner, and the Human Torch for a brief period in 1954, but retired them again for a seven-to-nine-year hiatus.

Some interesting experimental attempts at revival were made in the 1950s. Sterling Comics' *Captain Flash* (November 1954) was a truly original effort and perhaps the forerunner of the Second Heroic Age of Comics, as the 1960s superhero revival is sometimes called. Charlton Comics brought out *Nature Boy* (March 1956) at the very depths of the superhero depression and also reprinted some issues of the *Blue Beetle* (February 1955).

The second great cycle of superheroes began quietly in the mid-to-late 1950s with DC Comics' *Showcase #4* (October 1956). The comic featured a revival of the 1940s super-

Strange Suspense Stories #75, © 1965 Charlton Comics Group

Captain Flash #4, © 1955 Sterling Comics, Inc.

Daredevil #10, © 1965 Marvel Entertainment Group, Inc.

hero, the Flash. He got his own book, *Flash #105* (February 1959), and DC then revitalized such other 1940s superheroes as *Green Lantern* (July 1960), *Atom* (June 1962), and *Hawkman* (April 1964).

Marvel Comics brought back the Human Torch as a reincarnated character in the *Fantastic Four* (November 1961), and also revived the Sub-Mariner and Captain America. Both DC and Marvel also created new superheroes for the 1960s, like Spider-Man, Iron Man, Thor, the Metal Men, and Adam Strange.

By the mid-1960s, superheroes had rejuvenated the comic-book industry. Moreover, in 1966 the new "Batman" television show gave

Doctor Solar #10, © 1965 K. K. Publishing

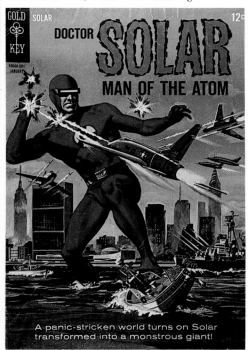

a hardly needed shot of adrenalin to the already hyped-up superhero field. From 1965 to 1967 over one hundred superheroes were created or revived by comic-book companies, both old (Harvey, Archie, Dell, and Gold Key) and new (Tower, MF Enterprises, and Milson).

In 1965 the monthly circulation of *Batman* led the industry with 898,470 copies. By the following year, the circulation had dropped by one hundred thousand—signaling the beginning of the end of the 1960s superhero boom.

By the late 1960s only Marvel and DC were publishing superhero comics with any great success. During the 1970s the companies experimented with other genres as well, including horror, sword and sorcery, and straight adventure. By the 1980s superheroes were undergoing personality changes and character transformations.

No longer super human, the comic-book su-

Dynamo #4, © 1966 Tower Comics, Inc.

perheroes began to have problems with drugs, alcohol, and even sex. A hint of amorality started to surround some of the superheroes as they worked more and more on the borderlines of the law. Retribution and revenge even became acceptable motives for becoming a superhero, like Marvel Comics' *The Punisher* (July 1987) who seems to be a walking arsenal waiting for bad news to happen.

For the most part, however, the superheroes of the 1980s are extensions and updated versions of their 1960s and 1940s counterparts. From 1986 to 1988 DC Comics did a revamp of all its major characters: Superman, Batman, Wonder Woman, Flash, and Green Lantern. Marvel Comics's best selling superhero titles have been its *Spider-Man* books and *X-Men* titles.

Tales to Astonish #100, © 1968 Marvel Entertainment Group, Inc.

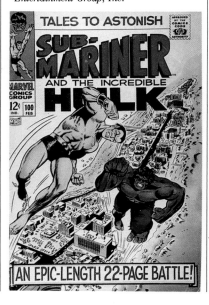

Action Comics #285, © 1962 DC Comics, Inc.

The Significant Seven

Out of the hundreds of superhero characters, seven stand out as most historically important: Superman, Batman, Wonder Woman, Spider-Man, Captain America, Captain Marvel, and Plastic Man.

Superman (Summer 1939) was the first sig-

Batman #52, © 1949 DC Comics, Inc.

nificant comic-book superhero. Created by Jerry Siegel and Joe Shuster for *Action Comics* (June 1938), Superman was appearing in six different comic books by 1941 and had his own radio show, newspaper strip, and animated cartoon series. Superman was drawn by a number of artists after Joe Shuster, notably Wayne Boring in the 1940s and 1950s, and Curt Swan in the 1960s. Part of Superman's success can also be attributed to the brilliant editing by Mort Weisinger, who perhaps had more influence over the character than any other individual. Weisinger helped develop many of the concepts that Superman is famous for: kryptonite, the Phantom Zone, the planet Krypton, and even Supergirl herself. After Weisinger left the Superman titles in 1970, circulation began declining until the Man of Steel was selling almost at a break-even point by the 1980s. DC revised and updated the character, and began a new series in the late 1980s with *Superman* (January 1987).

Batman (Spring 1940) was the first non-super superhero. His only powers came from his self-developed physique and trained detective mind. He supplemented his natural abilities with gadgets from his utility belt like smoke bombs, collapsible trapezes, and bat boomerangs called "batarangs." He also was the first superhero to have his own elaborate base of operations, the Bat Cave, as well as an entire line of conveyances like the Batmobile, the Batplane, and even a Batmarine.

Bob Kane, the artist, and Bill Finger, the writer, are credited with creating Batman in the May 1939 issue of *Detective Comics*. Since then Batman has been drawn by a variety of artists, among them Jerry Robinson, Dick Sprang, Carmine Infantino, Marshall Rogers, and Frank Miller.

Wonder Woman (Summer 1942) was expressly created by a psychologist, Dr. William

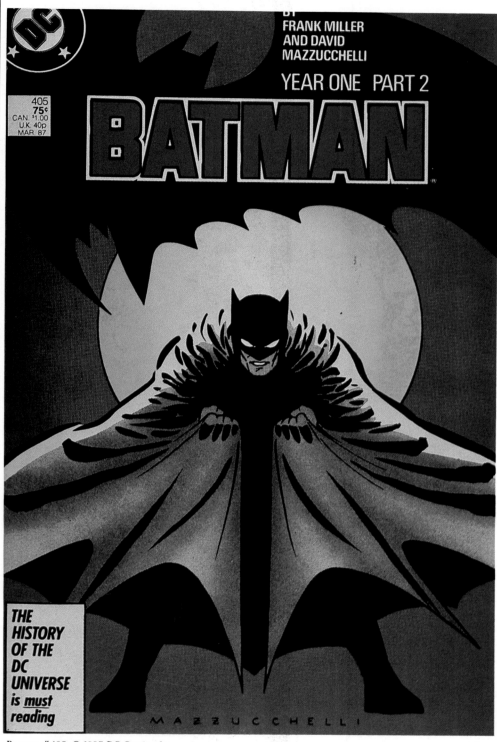

THE HISTORY OF THE DC UNIVERSE is _must_ reading

Batman #405, © 1987 DC Comics, Inc.

Wonder Woman #37, © 1949 DC Comics, Inc.

Moulton Marston, to appeal to young girls. Illustrated by H. G. Peter, Wonder Woman was the first and most successful of the superheroines.

Wonder Woman was a princess and the daughter of Amazon Queen Hippolyte. She lived on Paradise Island, where no man may set foot, and she came to America to help fight World War II. Her star-spangled costume of red, white, blue, and yellow, along with her golden lasso, were distinctive trademarks. She later gained an invisible robot plane and an ineffectual boy friend named Steve Trevor. Continually published for more than forty-five years (discounting a short 1986–87 break),

Wonder Woman is the most successful female superhero of all time. She was given a "new" origin by DC in 1987.

Spider-Man (March 1963) was created by Stan Lee and artists Jack Kirby and Steve Ditko. Spider-Man first appeared in the August 1962 issue of *Amazing Fantasy* and soon received his own book, which was drawn by Steve Ditko for the first thirty-eight issues. A shy high-school science student, Peter Parker, is bitten by a radioactive spider and discovers he can climb walls and leap about. He develops a web-shooting device and devises a costume.

Spider-Man is perhaps the most truly origi-

Amazing Spider-Man #12, © 1964 Marvel Entertainment Group, Inc.

"Can they be *right*? Am I *really* some sort of crack-pot, wasting my time seeking fame and glory? Am I·more interested in the adventure of being *Spider-Man* than I am in helping people?? Why do I do it? Why don't I give the whole thing up? And yet, I *can't*! I must have been given this great power for a *reason*! No matter how difficult it is, I *must* remain *Spider-Man*! And I pray that some day the world will understand!"
—SPIDER-MAN
The Amazing Spider-Man #4
(September 1963)

nal superhero of the 1960s. His litany of personal problems—love, financial, and family—made him unique among superheroes and set the tone for dozens of Marvel superheroes to come.

Captain America (March 1941) is the most famous creation of the Joe Simon-Jack Kirby comic-book team. Although not the first patriotic superhero, Captain America became the most popular, best remembered, and longest-lived. He epitomized American values during World War II, and his comic book lasted until the waning days of the 1940s superheroes.

Revived by Marvel for its superhero team, the *Avengers* (*#4*, March 1964), Captain America starred with Iron Man in *Tales of Suspense #58* (October 1964), and eventually got his own book, *Captain America* (April 1968). Written and drawn by over one hundred different people, the definitive Captain America was the one drawn by Jack Kirby in both the 1940s and again in the 1960s.

Captain Marvel (January 1941), created by artist C. C. Beck and writer Bill Parker, originally appeared in *Whiz Comics* (February 1940). The simplicity of Beck's artwork, coupled with the straightforward storytelling, made Captain Marvel the best selling superhero comic of all time. His success spun off other titles, like *Captain Marvel Jr.*, *Mary Marvel*, and the *Marvel Family*. Captain Mar-

Captain America #111, © 1969 Marvel Entertainment Group, Inc.

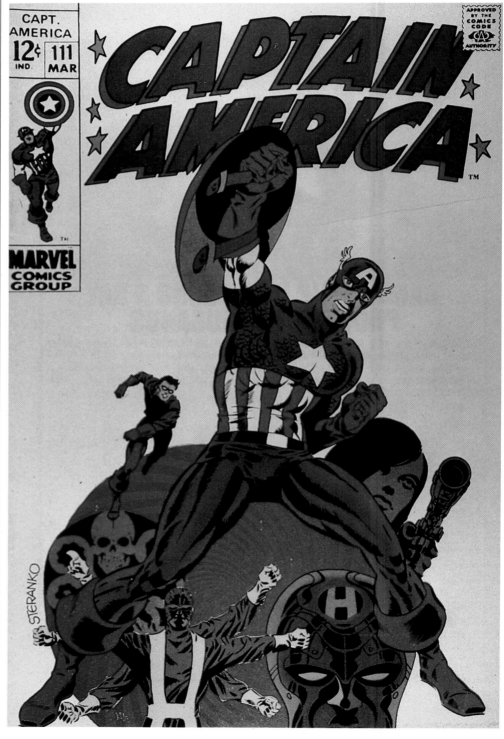

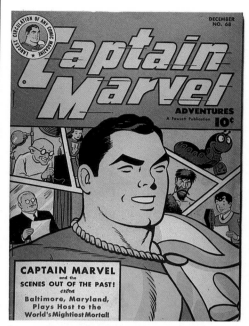

Captain Marvel #68, © 1946 Fawcett Publications, Inc.

-vel has been described as the classic example of American naivete, cheerfulness, and undying optimism.

Faced with declining circulation figures and a lawsuit by DC Comics over copyright infringement of their Superman character, Fawcett Comics dropped the Captain Marvel character and the publisher's entire line of comics by the end of 1953. The character was revived in name only by M.F. Enterprises in 1966 and quickly expired.

In 1968 Marvel Comics introduced a Captain Marvel character and gave him his own book, *Captain Marvel* (May 1968), although he bore no relation to the original Fawcett character. DC Comics, now the owner of the original Captain Marvel, brought the character back briefly in *Shazam!* (February 1973), and gave him a supporting role in their *Justice League International* (May 1987).

Plastic Man (Summer 1943) was created by humor artist Jack Cole for *Police Comics* (August 1941). The first parody of the superhero comics, Plastic Man kept his tongue always in cheek as he stretched and slithered after criminals. Plastic Man was played strictly for laughs, and his adventures were refreshingly different from the deadly serious crimefighters of the day.

Plastic Man was so popular that he was the only other superhero, besides Superman, Batman, and Wonder Woman, to survive the Comics Code. He was published until almost the end of 1956. Since then, DC Comics has revived the character three times, in 1966, in 1976, and again in 1988.

Although comic-book superheroes have been optioned for other media, including radio, television, and movies, they seem to have found their most comfortable niche in the pages of the comic books. Only within the sanctity of the comic book can superheroes with names like Insect Queen and Elastic Lad cavort about in skin-tight color costumes and not appear ridiculous. And, if nothing else, the comic-book superheroes have provided us with a pantheon and mythology that may rival any previous culture.

TEEN COMICS

Teenagers did not really exist as a separate social group until the 1930s, when movies, swing music, and slang language made America aware of their existence. In the late 1930s a radio show featuring the teenage antics of Henry Aldrich was so popular that a series of movies were made about the fictional teenager. His success provided the inspiration for America's most famous comic book teenager, Archie Andrews.

Archie and his friends first appeared in *Pep Comics #22* (December 1941). They soon received their own line of comic books beginning with *Archie* (Winter 1942), *Archie's Pal Jughead* (1949), and *Archie's Girls Betty and Veronica* (1950).

Plastic Man #45, © 1954 Comic Magazines

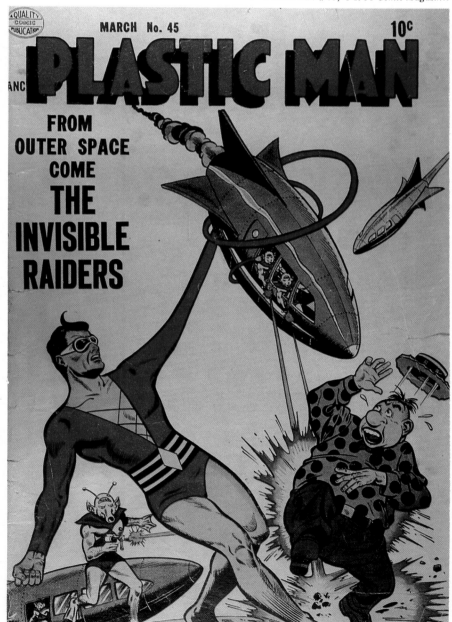

"Jughead was the original hippie."
—RICHARD GOLDWATER,
publisher of Archie Comics

All through the 1950s and 1960s, Archie comics enjoyed tremendous popularity. Every year or so a new Archie title was added, such as *Archie's Joke Book* (1953), *Archie's Mechanics* (September 1954), *Life with Archie* (September 1958), *Archie and Me* (October 1964), and *Archie at Riverdale High* (August 1972). During one period over a dozen different Archie comic books appeared each month.

The strong appeal of Archie and other teen-age comics comes from the attractive fantasy they offer their pre-teen and young-teen readers. In the world of Archie, teenagers are free from adolescent problems of acne, acceptance, and self-identity. In a teen comic book all the tensions of dating, of popularity, and of young love are winked at and laughed away.

More importantly, teen comics give their young readers a chance to explore and test their feelings about their own impending male-female relationships. Month after month, comic book after comic book, Archie and Betty and Veronica survived the disasters of teenage courtship with friendships still intact. Small

Pep Comics #70, © 1948 Archie Comic Publications, Inc.

Andy #21, © 1948 Current Books, Inc.

wonder that pre-teen readers found the characters in Archie and similar comics to be attractive, if unrealistic, role models.

In fact, it is the characters in the simply drawn and written teen comics that have made the genre so popular. Without exception, every teenage comic book has its "gang." Within the gang, there is usually an attractive boy (Archie), his side-kick friend (Jughead), and his rival in love (Reggie). There are also usually two attractive girls (Betty and Veronica) who happen to be friends, rivals, or both. Also in the teenage gang is the big dumb football player, the school brain, and a spoiled rich kid. With this panoply of stereotypical characters, the teen comic book could reflect and magnify almost any real or imagined situation that could happen to a teenager.

Although Archie Comics led the teen comic field, other publishers quickly joined in. DC Comics's response to *Archie* was *Buzzy* (Winter 1944) and *Binky* (February 1948). ACG Comics, a leader in the humor-comic field, produced its teen title called *Cookie* (April 1946). Quality Comics had *Candy* (Summer 1947), a teenager endowed well beyond her years.

Single-name teen titles became the rage in the late 1940s, and Ace Publishing rushed out such titles as *Andy* (June 1948), *Dotty* (July 1948), *Ernie* (September 1948), and *Vicky* (October 1948). Standard Comics offered *Dudley* (November 1949) and *Kathy* (September 1949), while Archie struck back with *Suzie* (Spring 1945), *Wilbur* (Summer 1944), and *Ginger* (1951).

Dell Comics finally landed the rights to the teenager who started it all and published *Henry Aldrich* (August 1950). Dell followed him up with another media teenager, *Andy Hardy* (April 1952).

Henry Aldrich #5, © 1951 Clifford Goldsmith

chie artists to create a decent imitation with *Tippy Teen* (November 1965) and *Tippy's Friends Go-Go and Animal* (July 1966). Even the fly-by-night MF Enterprises had a teen comic called *Henry Brewster* (February 1966).

New teen comics became scarce through the 1970s, although the first black teenage comic, *Fast Willie Jackson* (October 1976), was published that decade. By the 1980s only the redoubtable Archie Comics were still prospering in the teenage comic market.

Although the teen-comic genre may have withered with the advent of teen movies and television situation comedies, the teen-fantasy world of malt shops, jalopies, and innocent dates still calls forth a time when adolescence was indeed bliss.

An interesting relative of the teenage comic was the fashion-model comic. Comics like *Millie the Model* (1945) and *Patsy Walker* (1945) still included plenty of dating, flirtation, and innocent misunderstanding, but they offered something else, too: clothes! Marvel's other teen titles included *Patsy and Heddy* (February 1952), *My Girl Pearl* (April 1955), and *Modeling with Millie* (February 1963), often featuring fashion models to appeal to the fantasies of their girl readers.

Archie's own clothes horse, *Katy Keene* (1949), inspired several other titles—among them *Katy Keene Fashion* (1955) and *Katy Keene Pinup Parade* (1955). Readers would often send in their own dress designs for the comic characters to wear. *My Little Margie's Fashions* (February 1959) was the third of Charlton Comics's trilogy of teen titles, along with *My Little Margie* (July 1954) and *My Little Margie's Boyfriends* (August 1955).

The 1960s brought a resurgence in teen comics with Dell's *Thirteen Going on Eighteen* (November 1961), an extremely well-done comic written by John Stanley of *Little Lulu* fame. Stanley also created a pair of likable teenage Lotharios for Dell called *Dunc and Loo* (October 1961).

Archie Comics developed a title starring three teenage girls called *Josie* (February 1963), who later starred in a television cartoon series called "Josie and the Pussycats." DC Comics's teen entries for the 1960s were *Swing with Scooter* (June 1966), an attempt to capitalize on British rock-music popularity, and *A Date with Debbi* (January 1969).

Harvey Comics had its teen title, called *Bunny* (December 1966), a comic book that tried to be "psychedelic-ious" and offered readers a chance to join the "Bunny Ball In Club."

Tower Comics used the talents of some Ar-

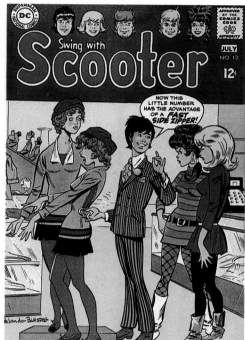

Scooter #13, © 1968 DC Comics, Inc.

UNDERGROUND "COMIX"

Underground comic books ("comix") emerged during the counterculture upheaval of the 1960s. Unlike regular comic books, underground comix originated entirely with the artist and were usually distributed through nontraditional channels and sold exclusively to an adult audience. Never before had the art form of the comic book been used for such liberal self-expression or dealt with personal and social issues previously untouched by comics and many other art forms.

Comix originally were labeled "underground" because of their association with the underground press and newspapers of the mid-1960s that first published new cartoonists, such as Robert Crumb, Jay Lynch, and Gilbert Shelton. The subject matter of the new comic books—drugs, political revolution, and sex—was also tied to the underground and counterculture youth movement of the 1960s.

Although such underground cartoonists as

"Well, Tippy, you'll have to decide whether you're willing to toss aside Tommy's years of loyal devotion just for a date with a good looking guy."
"You're right . . . I'll call Tommy and tell him I'm sick!"
—*Tippy Teen #21* (November 1968)

> "Obscene, anarchistic, sophomoric, subversive, apocalyptic, the underground cartoonists and their creations attack all that middle America holds dear."
> —JACOB BRACKMAN,
> "The International Comix Conspiracy," *Playboy* (December 1970)

Frank Stack (*Adventures of Jesus*, 1962), Vaughn Bode (*Das Kampf*, 1963) and Jack Jackson (*God Nose*, 1964) produced early independent comic books which were underground in spirit, it was not until R. Crumb's *Zap Comics* (February 1967) appeared on the scene that the underground comic book came into its own.

Zap was the breeding ground for many underground cartoonists (all strongly influenced by the early *Mad*), such as S. Clay Wilson, Robert Williams, Gilbert Shelton, and Spain Rodriguez. The underground artists delineated drug-induced enlightenment, sexual revolution, and the political paranoia of the Sixties with an explicitness never seen before in comic books.

Most of the early underground comics originally were published by loose collectives of artists, counterculture businesspeople, and comic-book fans. Because the print runs of most underground comics was low (usually two thousand to ten thousand copies) and because distribution was spotty at very best, many of the underground comic-book pub-

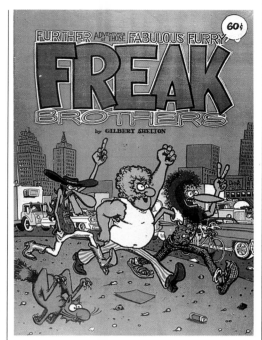

Fabulous Furry Freak Brothers, © 1972 Gilbert Shelton

lishers maintained marginal operations and erratic publishing schedules.

Even so, underground comix prospered mightily all through the late 1960s and early 1970s. Such comics as *Bijou Funnies* (1968), *Yellow Dog* (1968), *Slow Death Funnies* (1970), *Mr. Natural* (1970), *The Fabulous Furry Freak Brothers* (1971), and *Wimmen's Comix* (1972) were among the more popular titles. There were also literally hundreds more minor underground comics, some distributed only locally. From *Acne-Pimples Comics* to *Zodiac Mindwarp*, over twenty-three hundred underground comics were published in a ten-year period.

By the early 1980s, however, underground comics as a separate subspecies had van-

Young Lust #3, © 1972 Bill Griffith

Zap Comics, © 1967 R. Crumb

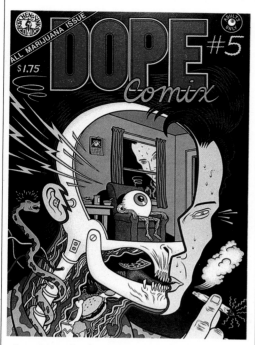

Dope Comix #5, © 1984 Kitchen Sink Press

ished. They had either been replaced by self-published "minicomics," which also allowed for the total expression of individual artistic vision, or they had been absorbed into the new independent comic-book marketplace which was now the home for alternative-press titles. The decline of the underground comic book can be attributed both to a change in the political and cultural climate of the 1980s, which meant less need for this type of work to go "underground," as well as to the collapse of the counterculture boutique stores ("head shops") which had been their main distribution outlets.

By the late 1980s some of the original underground artists of the 1960s appeared in alternative magazines like *Weirdo*, or in comics like *Hup Comics* (1987) still published sporadically by such long-time underground publishers as Rip Off Press and Last Gasp Comics.

Weirdo #14, © 1985 R. Crumb

WAR COMICS

War, with its life-and-death dramas and high visual impact, has always been a natural subject for comic books. The first comic book devoted entirely to war stories was Dell's *War Comics* (May 1940), which appeared a year before America's entry into World War II. Quality's *Military Comics* (August 1941) lasted throughout the war years, then changed its name to *Modern Comics* (November 1945).

Few other all-war comics appeared during the years of World War II. *War Heroes* (July 1942) focused on real-life war heroes and events but, except for a plethora of superheroes battling Nazis and "Japanazis" on nearly every comic-book cover during the war years, that was the extent of war comics during the 1940s.

Wars, however, beget war comics. With the beginning of the Korean War in the summer of 1950, war comics proliferated from every publisher. By the time the Korean War ended three years later, there would be over one

Frontline Combat #9, © 1952 William M. Gaines

"The grit and gore of the battlefield could be shown with some semblance of reality and it would still evoke glory and romance in the mind. War comics had taken their sweet time getting born, but now [in 1952] they were a full-fledged genre and here to stay."
—MICHAEL USLAN,
editor of *America at War: The Best of DC War Comics*

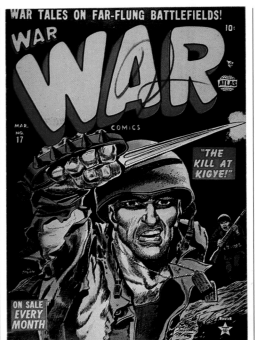

War Comics #17, © 1953 Marvel Entertainment Group, Inc.

hundred war-comic titles.

The 1950s war comics appealed to both the young American servicemen and would-be servicemen. Besides this new audience, the readers of crime and horror comics were also attracted to the realistic violence portrayed in war comic books.

The first and best war comic of the 1950s was Harvey Kurtzman's *Two-Fisted Tales* (November 1950) from EC Comics. Scrupulously accurate, the comic book originally featured war and adventure stories from all historical periods, but focused heavily upon Korean battles as the war progressed. EC's other war comic, *Frontline Combat* (July 1951), featured

Jet Fighters #7, © 1953 Standard Magazines, Inc.

special issues on the Civil War, Iwo Jima, and the Korean War. The stark portrayal of human suffering and destruction in the EC war comics almost made them anti-war comics.

Most of the early 1950s war comics, however, were unabashedly jingoistic in both their treatment of the Korean War and reprise of World War II.

Ziff-Davis's *G.I. Joe* (1950) usually featured Joe smiling in bloodlusty ecstasy as he rams a gun butt or tank turret down the throat of a subhuman enemy soldier.

Marvel's war comics of the 1950s were raw, dark, and tautly violent. Marvel's first war title, *War Comics* (December 1950), was followed by a string of over a dozen war and battle comics like *Battle* (March 1951), *Battle*

Our Fighting Forces #85, © 1964 DC Comics, Inc.

Action (February 1952), and *Battleground* (September 1954). Marvel created its own war heroes, too, with *Combat Kelly* (November 1951), *Battle Brady* (January 1953), and *Combat Casey* (January 1953). These war comics presented the Korean War as a hand-to-hand knife fight between American soldiers and dehumanized Communists.

Between 1951 and 1955 nearly every publisher had war comics on the stands. There was Harvey's *Warfront* (September 1951), Toby Press's *Fighting Leathernecks* (February 1952), Hillman's *Frogman Comics* (January 1952), Farrell's *War Stories* (September 1952), Ace's *War Heroes* (May 1952), and Fawcett's *Battle Stories* (January 1952).

Charlton Comics took no chances on slighting any branch of the service. It published *Fightin' Marines* (May 1955), *Fightin' Army* (January 1956), *Fightin' Navy* (January 1956), and *Fightin' Air Force* (February 1956).

Perhaps the most successful 1950s war

Sgt. Fury #76, © 1970 Marvel Entertainment Group, Inc.

Another war comic, however, Milson's *Super Green Beret* (April 1967), was less restrained in its portrayal of American servicemen subduing godless communists.

With the end of the Vietnam War, most war comics returned to fighting World War II again. It was a safer war, with an enemy that was more clearly defined. DC Comics and Charlton Comics together kept almost a dozen war titles on the stands all through the 1970s.

Marvel Comics returned to the war-comics business with its *G.I. Joe* (June 1982), a comic-book spin-off of a toy-and-cartoon show. Aimed at a younger audience than previous war comics, the book enjoyed tremendous popularity with the under-twelve set.

A more adult effort was Marvel's *The 'Nam* (December 1986), which presented a detailed if somewhat sanitized recounting of a soldier's life in Vietnam. Its next war title, *Semper Fi* (1988), featured stories of the U.S. Marines.

Super Green Beret #2, © 1967 Milson Publishing Co.

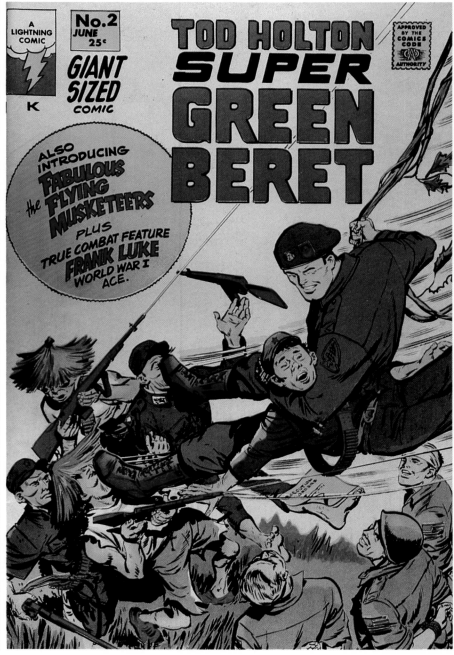

comics were those from DC Comics which lasted until the late 1980s. The first three war titles came out at the same time: *All American Men of War* (August 1952), *Our Army at War* (August 1952), and *Star Spangled War Stories* (August 1952). DC completed its series later by adding *Our Fighting Forces* (October 1954) and *GI Combat* (January 1957).

DC's success with its war comics can be attributed to three factors: the writing and editing by Robert Kanigher, the artwork of Joe Kubert and Russ Heath, and the cast of finely realized continuing characters, such as Sgt. Rock of Easy Company, Johnny Cloud the Navaho Air Ace, Jeb Stuart and The Haunted Tank, and a World War I German pilot called Enemy Ace.

Marvel's 1960s war comic was *Sgt. Fury and His Howling Commandos* (May 1963). Set in World War II, the comic book featured a group of ethnically diverse American commandoes led by the rough 'n' tough sarge who chomped cigars and kicked Nazi butts with equal aplomb. The book's good-natured team of wisecracking characters kept it going for eighteen years.

The Vietnam War was portrayed in war comics as early as 1962. Dell Comics's *Jungle War Stories* (July 1962) was exploring the jungle guerilla warfare in southeast Asia before many people had even heard of Vietnam. Some of Dell's other comics featured stories set in Vietnam, as well, such as *Air War Stories* (September 1964) and *Combat* (October 1961). It was not until late 1966, however, that a comic book called *Tales of the Green Beret* (January 1967) focused entirely upon American involvement with the war. Like the other Dell war comics, *Tales of the Green Beret* presented the war's events in a matter-of-fact way, neither criticizing nor endorsing the action.

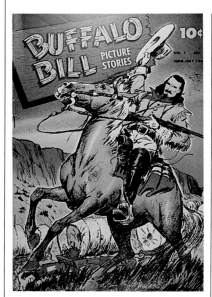

Buffalo Bill #1, © 1949 Street and Smith Publications, Inc.

"No understanding of the West, its implications, resonances and extensions as a living mythology, can be arrived at without knowledge and study of Western films and of Western comics."
—**MAURICE HORN,**
author of *Comics of the American West*

WESTERN COMICS

The American cowboy has been a major entertainment figure ever since nineteenth-century pulp magazines first dramatized the Old West. The first popular movie (*The Great Train Robbery*) and television's most successful dramatic show ("Gunsmoke") were both westerns. Western comic books are perhaps the most American of all literature, being the offspring of a truly American genre and a truly American art form.

The first comic books devoted entirely to the West were *Western Picture Stories* (February 1937) and *Star Ranger* (February 1937). During the rest of the 1930s, other anthologies of western cowboy strips appeared, including *Western Action Thrillers* (April 1937) and *Cowboy Comics* (July 1938). All of the 1930s western comics were shortlived, however, and faded before the end of the decade.

Star Ranger, © 1937 Ultem Publications

The first successful western comic book was *Red Ryder Comics* (September 1940), which originally consisted of reprinted episodes from the "Red Ryder" newspaper comic strip. That same month saw the publication of *Tom Mix Comics* (September 1940), which was offered as a premium to listeners of the Tom Mix radio show. These two comics established the pattern for western comics. For the next eight years, almost every western comic book was either reprints of newspaper comic strips or adaptations of stories about famous western stars from movies or radio.

The more successful western comic books of the early 1940s were *Gene Autry Comics* (December 1941), *Hopalong Cassidy* (February 1943), *Roy Rogers* (April 1944), and *Lone Ranger* (August 1945). All of these titles enjoyed fifteen-to-twenty-year publishing spans, no doubt helped by the continuing popularity of the cowboy characters they were based upon.

Lone Ranger #65, © 1953 Lone Ranger, Inc.

The real explosion in western comics, however, began in 1948. Fueled by the declining readership of superhero comics and by the rising popularity of the Saturday morning "B" western heroes, western comic books soon became the most popular comic-book genre on the newsstands.

Comic-book publishers tended to publish western comics in two categories: those that were based upon western movie, radio, and television stars and those that were original creations. Dell and Fawcett led in sheer volume of licensed characters, often using photo covers of the popular western stars to sell their comics. Fawcett Comics, in particular, had a lock on the "B" movie cowboys, producing such comics as *Tom Mix Western* (January 1948), *Rocky Lane Western* (May 1949), *Lash Larue Western* (Summer 1949), *Bill Boyd Western* (February 1950) and *Smiley Burnette Western* (March 1950).

Although the movie-cowboy comics sold well, there were only so many licensed western characters to go around, and they usually involved the expense of a licensing fee. Some comic-book publishers got around this problem by either creating their own cowboy stars or by reviving famous cowboys of the past.

Wild Bill Hickok (September 1949), *Jesse James* (August 1950), *Buffalo Bill* (June 1949) and *Annie Oakley* (Spring 1948) were reincarnated in several comic books from a variety of publishers over the years.

Marvel Comics created original cowboy heroes, with the three most popular characters being *Kid Colt Outlaw* (August 1948), *Two-Gun Kid* (March 1948), and the *Rawhide Kid* (March 1955). These three titles survived until the late 1970s, long past the peak era for western comics. Marvel was perhaps the most prolific publisher of western comics through the mid 1950s, with titles like *Arizona Kid* (March 1951), *Western Outlaws* (February

1954), *Wyatt Earp* (November 1955), and *Western Gunfighters* (June 1956).

DC Comics issued *Western Comics* (January 1948), *All American Western* (November 1948) and *All Star Western* (April 1951). The comics featured such continuing characters as Pow Wow Smith, an Indian detective; the Trigger Twins; the Wyoming Kid; and Johnny Thunder.

From 1948 to 1954 every publisher had a western comic book. The popularity of western comics spilled over into romance, crime, and science-fiction genres with hybrid titles like *Cowgirl Romances* (January 1950), *Western Crime Busters* (September 1950), and *Space Western* (October 1952). There were also many Indian comics among the "cowboy and injun" titles, including *Indian Braves* (March 1951), *Indian Warriors* (June 1951) and *Indian Chief* (July 1951).

After the demise of many western comics and comic-book publishers from 1955 to 1956, Charlton Comics purchased several defunct western titles from the out-of-business publishers and also added its own titles. Charlton's *Cheyenne Kid* (July 1957), *Kid Montana* (November 1957) and *Texas Rangers in Action* (July 1956) enjoyed an almost twenty-year run in various incarnations. Charlton continued to produce western comics all through the late 1950s and into the 1980s, and by the 1970s had become the largest publisher of comic-book westerns.

Dell Comics, already happily publishing *Lone Ranger*, *Gene Autry*, and *Roy Rogers*, decided to wrap up the new television cowboys as well. Among its television western series were *Gunsmoke* (February 1956), *Maverick* (April 1958), *Bat Masterson* (August 1959), and *Rawhide* (September 1959).

By the mid-1960s only Marvel and Charlton were publishing western comics on a regular basis. It was the height of the superhero revival, and cowboys would not be a viable alternative until the costumed character comics took a downturn in the late 1960s.

DC Comics's *Bat Lash* (October 1968) was an interesting, light-hearted anti-hero cowboy comic. Although it lasted only a year, the comic book broke the ice for DC's revival of *All Star Western* (August 1970). DC's next venture into the western realm was a cross-breed western comic, *Weird Western Tales* (June 1972). This comic book introduced a disfigured and amoral western hero who later earned his own title, *Jonah Hex* (September 1979).

By 1985 DC Comics had stopped publishing *Jonah Hex*. The next year Charlton Comics, the only remaining publisher of western comics, went out of business.

Rawhide Kid #15, © 1957 Marvel Entertainment Group, Inc.

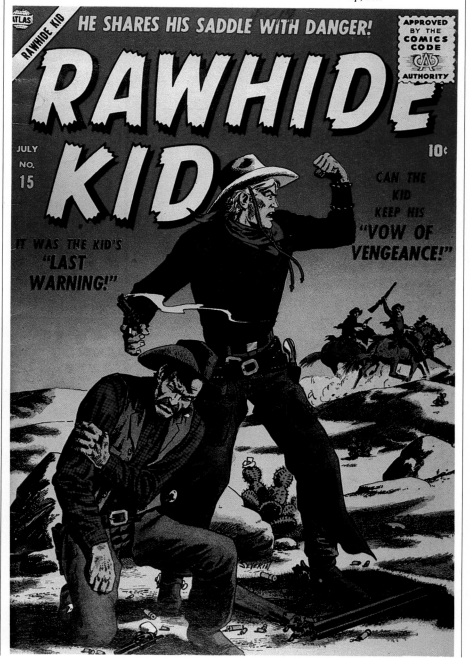

Rawhide #1097, © 1960 Columbia Broadcasting System

REFERENCES

Aldridge, Alan and George Perry. *The Penguin Book of Comics*. Baltimore: Penguin, 1971.

Bails, Jerry and Hames Ware, editors. *The Who's Who of American Comic Books* (4 volumes). Saint Clair Shores, Michigan: Jerry Bails, 1973–1976.

Barrier, Michael and Martin Williams, editors. *A Smithsonian Book of Comic-Book Comics*. New York: Smithsonian Abrams, 1981.

Benton, Mike. *Comic Book Collecting for Fun and Profit*. New York: Crown Publishers, 1985.

Daniels, Les. *Comix: A History of Comic Books in America*. New York: Crown Publishers, 1971.

Feiffer, Jules. *The Great Comic Book Heroes*. New York: Dial Press, 1965.

Fuchs, Wolfgang and Reinhold Reitberger. *Comics: Anatomy of a Mass Medium*. Translated by Nadia Fowler. Boston: Little, Brown, 1971.

Groth, Gary and Robert Fiore, editors. *The New Comics*. New York: Berkley Books, 1988.

Goulart, Ron. *The Great Comic Book Artists*. New York: St. Martins, 1986.

Goulart, Ron. *Ron Goulart's Great History of Comic Books*. Chicago: Contemporary, 1986.

Horn, Maurice. *Comics of the American West*. New York: Stoeger, 1977.

Horn, Maurice. *Sex in the Comics*. New York: Chelsea House, 1985.

Horn, Maurice, editor. *The World Encyclopedia of Comics*. New York: Avon, 1976.

Jacobs, Will and Gerald Jones. *The Comic Book Heroes from the Silver Age to the Present*. New York: Crown, 1985.

Lupoff, Dick and Don Thompson, editors. *All in Color for a Dime*. New Rochelle, N.Y.: Arlington House, 1970.

Lupoff, Dick and Don Thompson, editors. *The Comic-Book Book*. New Rochelle, N.Y.: Arlington House, 1973.

Overstreet, Robert M. *Official Overstreet Comic Book Price Guide*. New York: House of Collectibles, 1988.

Robbins, Trina and Catherine Yronwode. *Women and the Comics*. Gurneyville, California: Eclipse, 1985.

Rovin, Jeff. *The Encyclopedia of Superheroes*. New York: Facts On File, 1985.

Senate Committee on the Judiciary. *Comic Books and Juvenile Delinquency*. Washington, D.C.: Government Printing Office, 1955.

Special Committee to Investigate Organized Crime in Interstate Commerce. *Juvenile Delinquency*. Washington, D.C.: Government Printing Office, 1950.

Steranko, James. *The Steranko History of Comics* (2 volumes). Reading, Pennsylvania: Supergraphics, 1970 and 1972.

Waugh, Coulton. *The Comics*. New York: The Macmillan Company, 1947.

Wertham, Frederic. *Seduction of the Innocent*. New York: Rinehart and Co., 1954.

Wooley, Charles. *Wooley's History of the Comic Book: 1899–1936*. Lake Buena Vista, Florida: 1986.

INDEX

Action Comics #59, © 1941 DC Comics, Inc.

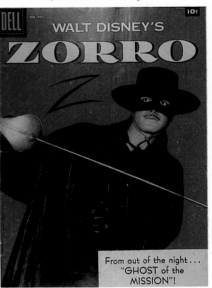

Zorro #920, © 1958 Walt Disney Productions